Academic Writing Programs

Edited by Ilona Leki

Case Studies in TESOL Practice Series

Jill Burton, Series Editor

Teachers of English to Speakers of Other Languages, Inc.

Typeset in Berkeley and Belwe
by Capitol Communication Systems, Inc., Crofton, Maryland USA
Printed by Kirby Lithographic Company, Inc., Arlington, Virginia USA
Indexed by Coughlin Indexing Services, Annapolis, Maryland USA

Teachers of English to Speakers of Other Languages, Inc.
700 South Washington Street, Suite 200
Alexandria, Virginia 22314 USA
Tel 703-836-0774 • Fax 703-836-6447 • E-mail tesol@tesol.org • http://www.tesol.org/

Director of Communications and Marketing: Helen Kornblum
Managing Editor: Marilyn Kupetz
Copy Editor: Marcia Annis
Cover Design: Ann Kammerer

ISBN 0-939791-89-7
Library of Congress Catalogue No. 00-136375

Dedication

To the real Kenny, with love.

Table of Contents

Acknowledgments

I would like to thank David Nunan for first involving me in this project and Jill Burton and Marilyn Kupetz for their help in bringing it to completion. I would also like to express my sincere gratitude to Sima Sengupta of Hong Kong Polytechnic University and Marcia Annis of TESOL, who in different ways but always with patience and kindness were invaluable to me in the preparation of this volume.

Series Editor's Preface

The Case Studies in TESOL Practice series offers innovative and effective examples of practice from the point of view of the practitioner. The series brings together from around the world communities of practitioners who have reflected and written on particular aspects of their teaching. Each volume in the series will cover one specialized teaching focus.

◈ CASE STUDIES

Why a TESOL series focusing on case studies of teaching practice?

Much has been written about case studies and where they fit in a mainstream research tradition (e.g., Nunan, 1992; Stake, 1995; Yin, 1994). Perhaps more importantly, case studies also constitute a public recognition of the value of teachers' reflection on their practice and constitute a new form of teacher research—or teacher valuing. Case studies support teachers in valuing the uniqueness of their classes, learning from them, and showing how their experience and knowledge can be made accessible to other practitioners in simple, but disciplined ways. They are particularly suited to practitioners who want to understand and solve teaching problems in their own contexts.

These case studies are written by practitioners who are able to portray real experience by providing detailed descriptions of teaching practice. These qualities invest the cases with teacher credibility, and make them convincing and professionally interesting. The cases also represent multiple views and offer immediate solutions, thus providing perspective on the issues and examples of useful approaches. Informative by nature, they can provide an initial database for further, sustained research. Accessible to wider audiences than many traditional research reports, however, case studies have democratic appeal.

◈ HOW THIS SERIES CAN BE USED

The case studies lend themselves to pre- and in-service teacher education. Because the context of each case is described in detail, it is easy for readers to compare the cases with and evaluate them against their own circumstances. To respond to the wide range of settings in which TESOL functions, cases have been selected from diverse EFL and ESL settings around the world.

The 12 or so case studies in each volume are easy to follow. Teacher writers describe their teaching context and analyze its distinctive features: the particular demands of their context, the issues they have encountered, how they have effectively addressed the issues, what they have learned. Each case study also offers readers practical suggestions—developed from teaching experience—to adapt and apply to their own teaching.

Already published or in preparation are volumes on

- action research
- assessment programs
- bilingual education
- community partnerships
- content-based language instruction
- distance learning
- EFL in primary schools
- English for specific purposes
- intensive English teaching
- interaction and language teaching
- international teaching assistants
- journal writing
- mainstreaming
- teacher education
- teaching English as a foreign language in primary schools
- technology in the classroom

◈ THIS VOLUME

The authors in this volume portray the international role of written English in the academic context, and clearly demonstrate how writing is integrated in all aspects of academic communication in English. Writing from all over the world, the authors address how English teachers of nonnative speakers can bring educational content and life experience into academic writing programs in English and, in turn, how TESOL can be included in mainstream academic programs.

Jill Burton
University of South Australia, Adelaide

INTRODUCTION

Accessing Communities and Disciplines Through L2 Writing Programs

Ilona Leki

In tertiary academic settings, writing is a privileged skill. It has received a great deal of research attention, probing the cognitive process of writing through protocol analyses, for example, and the conveniently stable product (or succession of products in drafts) through text analyses. Writing also has dramatically visible consequences for students' academic lives, particularly in English-medium institutions, where not only students' writing or language skills are evaluated but also, through essay exams, their disciplinary knowledge can be evaluated. Sometimes conclusions are even drawn (unfairly) about students' intellectual capacities based on the second language (L2) writing they produce. Writing samples open and close doors to academic advancement for students in ways no other language skill does. For these reasons, teaching L2 writing has taken on enormous significance.

This volume of the Case Studies in TESOL Practice series focuses on innovative courses and programs designed to teach L2 writing in a wide range of academic settings worldwide—ESL and EFL, elective and required, intensive and regular, in English-medium and non-English-medium institutions—and to a variety of student types—professionals and graduate students with extensive disciplinary knowledge and experience; young, inexperienced undergraduates; those with high and low levels of language proficiency; students in English-speaking countries on visas and as immigrants, some having little academic experience in any language. Each chapter begins by describing the historical, institutional, and, sometimes, community context of the L2 writing course, and then details the workings of the program and its distinguishing features. Not all the chapters included here describe radical innovations (though some do, and what is radical in one context may well be the norm in another), but each one represents a unique response to perceived L2 writing needs and local solutions to local problems confronting L2 writing teachers in many geographical locations, in different contexts, and at different levels of proficiency.

Most noteworthy about the courses and programs described in this volume, however, are not the differences but certain similarities of basic assumptions underlying the many local solutions to the question of how best to teach L2 writing. Many of these programs consciously position themselves as focused on what language needs they think students will face in their other academic courses or as participants in the social and political life of their communities. In each of the programs, learning to write in an L2 is not considered to be an end in itself but, rather, learning to use a tool with a special capacity to link and integrate other language skills; to probe and consolidate budding disciplinary knowledge; to unite the L2 writers with other individuals and communities; and to facilitate access to different social, political, and intellectual worlds.

Rather than teaching L2 writing in isolation, then, language skills such as reading, conversation, academic listening, and data gathering play significant roles in nearly all of the programs described here (e.g., in Flowerdew's integrated science and English courses and Hall's student-directed program in Australia). Linking and integrating these kinds of skills includes, in some programs, use of the first language (L1) as an appropriate and natural bridge to expressing real ideas and information in the L2 (e.g., in Hirose's course for English majors in Japan).

In these programs, L2 writing courses are designed to give L2 writing students easier, more profoundly enabling access to new worlds of disciplinary knowledge and community—a role that is arguably more important than integrating language skills. Note the number of L2 writing courses that are adjuncted or linked in some way to other disciplinary courses, for example, to a classics course (see, e.g., Smoke, Green, & Isenstead), to biology (e.g., Flowerdew), to various general education courses (e.g., Babbitt; Johns; and Weigle & Nelson), and to courses in students' own major areas (e.g., Cargill, Cadman, & McGowan; Hall; Vann & Myers; and Xiao). These courses clearly are more demanding of teachers than writing courses that remain isolated and self-referential.

In their contributions, Weigle and Nelson warn that creating the type of course that can make good use of intellectual content to aid in language and writing development requires content knowledge on the part of the L2 writing teacher. Some time ago, Spack (1988) warned against writing teachers teaching disciplinary writing because we do not know enough about all the subject areas our students might want or need to write in. She is right, but if we doggedly refuse to learn anything about any areas that could be useful to students in helping them learn language and writing, then we will remain peripheral to the lives of our institutions, teaching service courses with no content. This is the very situation that Hunter and Morgan resisted in developing their L2 writing courses, with their focus on the public sphere, on the local community, and on the world beyond the writing class.

Pennycook (1997) has suggested that we think of ourselves not as writing and language teachers but as cultural workers, as people who know something about the world we live in beyond how to teach writing and language, and that we use that knowledge in our classes. Such courses would not infantilize L2 students. (See Schenke, 1996, for a critique of more typical and insipid ESL/EFL courses that attempt to use socially provocative topics, such as feminism, and end up vitiating these courses of any real intellectual content.)

Thus, a strong theme running through a number of these innovative programs is the importance of intellectually stimulating content—that students learn something as well as how to do something with what they have learned. We do not find here courses with short, high-interest readings used to stimulate writing that requires students to express simplistic, binary, for-or-against opinions on topics like censorship without any in-depth information on subjects. Instead, these settings take students—and teachers—seriously and assume that important, not trivial, intellectual work can go on in L2 writing classrooms.

In programs described in the chapters by Cargill, Cadman, and McGowan, and by Vann and Myers, graduate students draw on their developing disciplinary knowledge. In the Hirose and Williams chapters, undergraduate students do not explore just what they already know about a setting, a limit that would work to stunt their L2 intellectual growth and keep them at the childish level of having opinions on things they know little about; instead, they are pushed to learn more about their world however they can, including by gathering information in their L1, if necessary, to ensure that the sophistication of the information matches the intellectual level of the students in these academic settings. The value of having appropriately mature knowledge to work with in a L2 far outweighs presumed benefits of insisting that students work only in their L2 because it is good practice, no matter how contrived.

Finally, a number of these programs specifically have on their agendas the goal of linking students to the larger world, either by linking L2 students with other L2 English students to form communities of learning (e.g., Babbitt; Hall; and Smoke, Green, & Isenstead), with native-English-speaking (NS) students (e.g., Vann & Myers), with colleagues in their major areas (e.g., Cargill, Cadman, & McGowan), and with members of communities in which the students live and work and whose sociopolitical sphere they cohabit (e.g., Hunter & Morgan).

This volume begins with an exploration of EFL settings. Xiao focuses on the importation into Hong Kong of a North American-style writing center and the adaptations that were necessary to make it useful in its new home. Flowerdew explains how English teachers at an English-medium university in Oman worked with science faculty to link the two courses of study, resulting in more L2 writing in the science courses and instruction in disciplinary vocabulary and language functions in the English writing course. Hirose's writing course for English majors in Japan employs process-oriented innovations to develop both fluency and accuracy.

The rest of the volume deals with teaching L2 writing in settings where English is the primary public language. The major innovations described in Part 2 seek to build a sense of local or disciplinary community. Babbitt's program develops community among L2 English undergraduates by block scheduling their courses in their first semester. Johns's program first carefully links writing courses and general education courses and then culminates in L2 writing students' collaboration with students in an area high school. Vann and Myers's program sets up writing classes that allow L2 undergraduates and graduates to share their own cultural expertise with NS students. Cargill, Cadman, and McGowan discuss a program in Australia that integrates new graduate students more fully into their disciplinary areas.

Part 3 focuses on writing courses in which students use academic writing as a tool to examine their social, intellectual, and political environment or as a means of learning academic course content. Hunter and Morgan describe an L2 writing course in Canada that challenges students to explore their social world and its interactions with government and the news media. Williams's students critically analyze such familiar features of their lives as product advertisements using academic language and carefully guided analytical procedures that are difficult and new to them. Weigle and Nelson describe an unusual writing program in an intensive English setting in which students learn both U.S. history as content and how to write essay exams covering that content. Similarly, Smoke, Green, and Isenstead's linked course in the Latin and Greek roots of English uses that academic course content as the basis for the L2 writing course for matriculated L2 students in the United States.

Finally, Hall describes the most radical structural innovation represented here—

an integrated reading, writing, and research course in L2 English in Australia in which the students themselves entirely decide on the course content, coming from their own disciplinary areas or from academic areas otherwise of interest to them.

We hope that this volume will contribute to a definition of academic writing by increasing our awareness both of the varying demands that academic writing places on L2 learners and teachers in different environments and of successful efforts to meet those demands. The purpose of these examinations of innovations in L2 academic writing is not to provide a template for programs or courses in other contexts but, rather, to inspire the generation of new ideas to meet local needs.

CONTRIBUTOR

Ilona Leki is professor of English and director of ESL at the University of Tennessee. She is the author of *Understanding ESL Writers: A Guide for Teachers* (Boynton/Cook, 1992), *Academic English* (Cambridge University Press, 1995), and *Reading in the Composition Classroom* (with Joan Carson, Heinle & Heinle, 1993). She coedits (with Tony Silva) the *Journal of Second Language Writing*. Her research interests center around the development of academic literacy, and she was the 1996 recipient of the TESOL/Newbury House Distinguished Research Award.

PART 1

Exploring L2 Writing Program Innovations in EFL Settings

CHAPTER 1

The Writing Assistance Programme: A Writing Center With Hong Kong Characteristics

Maida Kennedy Xiao

◈ INTRODUCTION

The Writing Assistance Programme (WAP) at the Hong Kong Polytechnic University is a second language (L2) writing program that has been developed along the lines of a first language (L1) writing center, but with characteristics that suit the EFL environment of Hong Kong. The WAP provides assistance to undergraduate EFL students in the form of one-to-one conferencing. Its aims are to help these students develop a critical awareness of their own writing and a richer understanding of writing processes and issues involved in constructing written academic text. The WAP offers an alternative to the product-oriented approach to writing that most Hong Kong students were taught in secondary school.

In this chapter, I describe the context that has influenced the development of the WAP. I examine the structure of WAP writing conferences and discuss approaches employed by WAP teachers to assist writers. I also discuss three features that distinguish the WAP from most North American L1 writing center models and suggest issues to consider when setting up similar L2 programs in different settings. In closing, I look at future developments planned for the WAP.

◈ CONTEXT

Hong Kong Polytechnic University is located in the heart of the Kowloon district of Hong Kong, a city of 6.5 million people. Hong Kong was a British colony until July 1, 1997, when it became a Special Administrative Region of the People's Republic of China (PRC) under China's One-Country-Two-Systems policy. Most of its Chinese inhabitants (98% of the population) speak Cantonese, although Putonghua (i.e., Mandarin), the official language of the PRC, is growing in popularity. There is a widespread belief within the Hong Kong community that English standards should be maintained, even enhanced, if the region is to keep its position as a service center of banking, finance, commerce, insurance, and shipping, and its status within Asia and the international community as a bridge linking East and West. This belief is being reinforced by the economic challenge Hong Kong has felt from Singapore and Shanghai since the 1997 handover. Indeed, an English-proficient workforce is key for Hong Kong to keep and attract multinational companies.

Written English, and to a lesser extent spoken English, is used to varying degrees within governmental, educational, industrial, and business sectors of the society. In recent years, however, there has been a growing debate within Hong Kong about the declining standards of English among secondary school graduates, although those countering charges of a fall in standards have argued that any perceived decline is due to greater numbers of students having access to higher levels of secondary and tertiary education than to any actual decline.

The Secondary School Experience

The majority of students entering the Hong Kong Polytechnic University have graduated from local Anglo-Chinese secondary schools that use English, in some cases only nominally, as the medium of instruction (a smaller portion of students come from Chinese-medium secondary schools). However, the amount and quality of secondary school English varies among students graduating from the more exclusive Band One schools, whose exit examination scores are better than those of the students graduating from the four less exclusive, higher band schools (Bands Two–Five). Indeed, it is rare for Band Five students to even reach the tertiary level. The government, recognizing the problems with the quality of English instruction and students' inadequate knowledge of English at the secondary school level, has reversed its previous promotion of English-medium instruction at the secondary school level in favor of a mother-tongue policy. However, the implementation of this policy, which affects only schools deemed incapable of teaching in English, has met with considerable resistance from various sectors of society. Parents, educators, and the media have expressed concerns that using Chinese as a medium of instruction in secondary education will disadvantage students attempting to matriculate into any of Hong Kong's primarily English-medium universities and may even make Chinese-medium students second class in comparison to their counterparts graduating from English-medium schools. Within the society as a whole there is also the belief that Hong Kong's special position as a bridge between the East and West will be weakened if English is downgraded.

Students graduating from Hong Kong's secondary schools are required to take the Hong Kong Certificate of Education Examination (HKCEE) at the end of their fifth year (the equivalent of 10th or 11th grade in the United States and other Western countries). If they receive passing marks on enough of the HKCEE's various subject areas, including English, they have the opportunity to continue studying for the last 2 years of secondary school. During Years 6 and 7 of secondary school, students prepare for the Hong Kong Advanced Level Examination (HKALE), the entrance exam for university-level study. The HKALE assesses students' abilities in English, Chinese, and several additional subject areas. The Hong Kong Examinations Authority, which designs, administers, and marks the HKALE, sets a wide range of scores (e.g., A, B, C, D, E, F, and U, Unclassified). With a few rare exceptions, most Hong Kong Polytechnic University students matriculating into bachelor-level programs must receive an overall score of E or above in the Use of English component of the HKALE.

Although bachelor's students are required to attain an overall score of E or above on the Use of English component of the HKALE, individual scores on the five subcomponents of this subject area (e.g., reading, writing, speaking, listening, and practical skills) may be as low as an F or U. In terms of the Test of English as a

Foreign Language (TOEFL), this rather low minimum means that students with the equivalent of a high 300 on the TOEFL can find themselves coping with an English-medium tertiary-level curriculum. Such scores are attained even though students may have studied English as a subject since kindergarten and may have studied in English since the start of secondary school (the equivalent of 6th or 7th grade in the United States). Understandably, many students are poorly motivated and lack the self-confidence they need to improve their English because they see their past efforts—more than 15 years, including preschool education—as having met with only limited success.

In addition to being poorly motivated, students often have a product-oriented view of writing. This orientation may be influenced, in part, by the memorization and practice required to master written Chinese characters. Commonly, characters are learned through rigidly following stroke patterns and reproducing characters hundreds of times. An additional influence is the amount of washback from the examinations required within the secondary school curriculum. Classroom teaching is often driven by the need to prepare students to perform well on these exams. (It should be noted that there is increasing pressure from educators to revise the secondary school system in order to decrease its exam-driven nature.)

In addition to the washback from examinations, the large class sizes common in Hong Kong secondary schools help shape the product-oriented approach to writing that most students experience. Many students entering university have only limited experience with prewriting, drafting, and revising strategies. Indeed, many view the writing process as careful, agonizing writing followed, if time permits, by quick proofreading. The teacher has two roles in this scenario. The first is to provide language and structural input before the writing begins or while it is taking place. (There is little attention given to the notion of writing with a particular reader in mind.) The second is to correct and grade the product, which entails marking the entire text, this supposedly allowing the student to see and learn from all the errors marked. It can be argued that this view is an understandable product of the realities of Hong Kong secondary classrooms, which put heavy demands on teachers to cover elaborate curricular requirements in order to prepare students for the public examinations in classroom environments where 30–40 students are the norm. These influences may account for the limited understanding of writing that many incoming university students demonstrate. In addition, the resulting teacher-directed learning that develops in this environment leads many students to expect and accept a large amount of direction and prescription from teachers.

The Hong Kong Polytechnic University Environment

The Hong Kong Polytechnic University, Hong Kong's largest tertiary institution, enrolls 19,449 students who study a wide range of undergraduate and graduate subjects. Its 29 academic departments are primarily professionally oriented, offering 16,229 full- and part-time undergraduate students diplomas, higher diplomas (the equivalent of associate's degrees) and 3-year bachelor's degrees in 120 programs, including such areas as occupational rehabilitation, social work, computer engineering, maritime studies, applied physics, design, and textile chemistry. Students matriculate into the university by entering into a department and a course of study. Although a credit-based system was introduced recently, it is still rare for students to change majors. Like most of the other six tertiary institutions in Hong Kong, the university uses English as the medium of instruction. With only very few exceptions, all course readings and writing assignments are in English, although outside the classroom students generally use Cantonese with each other and with their Cantonese-speaking teachers.

Regardless of their degree or subdegree programs, students are required to take a mandated English for academic purposes (EAP) class in their first semester. EAP courses are taught by the 60 full-time teaching staff members of the university's English Language Centre. The EAP syllabus requires students to study essay writing and seminar and oral presentation skills. Bachelor's degree students are required to take an additional class in their second year, English in the workplace (EIW), which teaches letter, memo, and report writing as well as interviewing skills. In EAP and EIW courses, there are assessed writing assignments, some of which are done as timed assessments in class and others of which are done out of class. In addition to these two courses, there are various other English language resources available to students, including a self-access center for independent learning, a speaking program, a small-group supplementary program for students needing additional help, an English Club, Web-based resources, and regularly scheduled workshops designed to help students with English.

In addition to the two mandated English courses, students are also required to take up to two mandatory Chinese courses and one general education class. With the exception of English, Chinese, and general education classes, students take almost all other courses from within their majors. The amount and quality of writing across the curriculum varies, with some majors offering intensive writing curricula and others requiring a minimal amount of written work. Regardless of what is required in individual courses within majors, most departments assign a standard final-year writing project that requires students to write a research report on some aspect of their field of study using primary and secondary data. For example, a building engineering student might do a report on a maintenance survey carried out on a local five-star hotel, and a textile student might do a report on research carried out on the durability of fabrics. These reports usually require students to write 20–40 pages and to follow the genre requirements of academic report writing within their disciplines.

Until the introduction of the WAP at the Hong Kong Polytechnic University, most students had little formal support for the out-of-class writing they were required to do and, with a few exceptions, only limited help with their final-year reports. The aim of the WAP was to provide undergraduates with one-to-one support for these writing assignments as well as to introduce and promote an alternative, less product-oriented understanding of writing.

◈ DESCRIPTION

The WAP began operating as a pilot program during the spring semester of 1998 and then on a permanent basis in the 1998–1999 academic year. Its stated aims are to provide students with a supportive and motivating environment where they can learn to evaluate their writing critically and to develop an appreciation for processes and issues involved in constructing written academic text. The WAP is administered by the English Language Centre and is staffed by 15 teachers who are scheduled up to 3 hours each week in lieu of an equivalent number of hours of other teaching. The

WAP offers one-to-one assistance in the form of writing conferences. Students bring any writing assignment they are working on or any questions related to writing. The WAP offers more than 70 half-hour appointments each week. (One-hour appointments are available on a limited basis.) Students find out about the WAP in various ways and attend on a voluntary basis as often as they like.

During the students' first conference, they receive a short introduction to the program. This introduction includes a discussion that aims to dispel any misconceptions the students may have about the program (e.g., that it is an editing service). Students are encouraged to come in as early in the process of writing as possible, to have realistic expectations about what they can accomplish in their half-hour conferences, and not to expect editing or polishing from WAP teachers. In addition to learning about the program's philosophy, students are given a tour of the facility, which includes a conferencing area and a waiting area with a photocopier, reference books, handouts on writing, and a computer station.

Students attending the WAP are required to complete some simple paperwork each time they attend. The paperwork indicates the type of writing or writing problem they have brought in and what kind of help they are seeking. Collecting this data is useful to WAP staff because it provides them with an understanding of the self-perceived needs of WAP students. At the same time, the paperwork also encourages students to reflect on their own needs before conferences begin. At the end of every conference, students also give written feedback on the conference.

The structure of most conferences is unpredictable, given their dynamic and fluid nature. Nevertheless, from the data collected on WAP conferences, it is fair to say that they generally have four components:

1. Prioritizing and limiting what can and should be done. This involves negotiating and setting realistic goals at the start of the conference.

2. Contextualizing the feedback. This involves focusing on specific aspects of the particular text (e.g., discussing ways to revise the introduction in a particular text or to improve the overall writing).

3. Globalizing from the text. This involves moving away from the text and focusing on larger issues, such as what information or insight can be learned and used in the future. The focus shifts from the writing itself to the development of the writer.

4. Summarizing what has been done and focusing on what remains to be done. At the end of the conference, the WAP teacher and student fill out a form with suggestions for what to do as a follow up to the conference.

The strategies and activities employed by WAP teachers in conferences vary. From the recordings and the documentation[1] made of sessions by teachers, it is clear that most involve a combination of two or more of the following: questioning, discussing, writing, reading, underlining, and teaching. The variation depends on the abilities of the students and the nature of their writing difficulties.

After each conference, teachers complete a Consultancy Record that documents the conference. The documentation often includes a description of what was done

---

[1] The recordings were audiotaped sessions, and Consultancy Records completed by teachers after each session were the documentation.

and what might be followed up on in subsequent sessions. The Consultancy Record is then placed into a file created for each student that contains the teacher's and the student's documentation of each conference as well as photocopies of the writing discussed.

Data from selected recorded and transcribed conference sessions as well as teacher feedback indicate that WAP conferences focus on a wide range of areas. Much of the variation appears, again, to depend on the ability and needs of the individual students. Common foci include discussing and clarifying

- assignment requirements
- genre requirements of the particular task
- organizational strategies
- content (e.g., amount, relevance, coherence)
- academic writing conventions (e.g., incorporating sources into a text, acknowledging sources)
- reader expectations of the text
- tone and register
- vocabulary
- syntax and grammar

The 800 student writers who attended one or more WAP conferences during the 1998–1999 academic year had higher order (e.g., organization, development, content) and lower order (e.g., grammar, vocabulary, syntax) writing needs. However, the data collected from student documentation indicate that students, especially when they started attending the WAP, describe their needs as stemming from lower order concerns (i.e., grammar and vocabulary) or from one particular higher order concern, organization. One possible explanation for this may be that students' past experiences have led them to view their writing problems as arising primarily from inadequate knowledge of grammar, vocabulary, and organization. It is hoped that the WAP will help these students to think and talk about their texts in new ways, that is, to help them develop a greater awareness of and ability to articulate a variety of writing needs.

⬧ DISTINGUISHING FEATURES

The WAP has adapted the North American L1 concept of a writing center to the L2 environment of Hong Kong. In developing a model that works, the WAP staff considered a number of issues carefully and flexibly. These issues involved the role of the teacher, effective approaches to conferencing, and the emphasis given to higher and lower order concerns. The manner in which these issues have been addressed points to features that distinguish the WAP from most of its L1 counterparts. In addition to these distinguishing features, the program was also designed to support and encourage action research into L2 writing center practice.

Staffing, Conferencing, and Concerns

In setting up the WAP program, the WAP staff consulted the voluminous literature on writing center practice. Although the existing literature does not directly address the issue or even define the notion of L2 writer centers, a number of researchers and practitioners discuss the special concerns of L2 writers with regard to conferencing and writing center practice. Harris and Silva (1993), Powers (1995), Goldstein and Conrad (1990), Thonus (1993), and Harris (1997) raise doubts about inflexibly adapting L1 assumptions and practices with L2 writers. These doubts also have surfaced with regard to several issues in the development of the WAP. The specific issues included who would staff the program, what approach to conferencing would be promoted, and what emphasis would be placed on higher versus lower order concerns within WAP conferences.

A Teacher-Student Model

The notion of peer response is widely promoted within L1 writing center literature. It is often discussed as being preferable to teacher-writer conferencing because it is thought to facilitate a less hierarchical, less threatening, more collaborative ethos between writer and tutor. However, within a Hong Kong context, the possibility of setting up a peer model proved problematic for two important reasons. First, there is a lack of qualified peer tutors. And second, cultural pressure discourages many people from displaying a higher standard of English than that of their peers (Fu, 1987). With this in mind, a model that incorporated teachers was proposed. Once a teacher-student model was decided on, concerns surfaced about whether the authority of the students would be diminished in such an environment. The potential for WAP teachers to unintentionally overpower writers with advice and to appropriate students' texts was, and continues to be, a very important issue in the program's development and operation. Dealing with these concerns became and remains a priority. Ongoing staff development initiatives offer teachers opportunities to become aware of ways they might unintentionally appropriate a text and allow themselves a chance to discuss and develop effective writing conference response strategies.

Before any teacher was asked to join the pilot program, each received basic information about what the work would entail. Only a handful of the English teachers at Hong Kong Polytechnic had any experience with writing centers, as most are from Hong Kong or England, where writing centers are not as common as they are on U.S. university campuses. All the teachers contacted expressed an interest in participating, and most mentioned that they saw their involvement as a way of developing professionally. This interest was important because a high level of commitment was expected from those participating in the pilot program. Teachers were given an extensive reading list and were offered initial and ongoing staff development workshops and meetings. The workshops and meetings involved discussion, and often debate, on effective response strategies, theoretical assumptions about the processes and issues involved in writing, composing strategies, ways of structuring conferences, and, most importantly, ways of avoiding appropriating a writer's text. In feedback collected on the program's pilot, all teachers reported that the workshops and, to a lesser extent, the readings had enhanced their ability to respond to WAP students.

A Flexible Approach to Conferencing

The notion that writers develop, even emerge, naturally in supportive, nondirective environments is another common theme in L1 writing center literature. The implication is that competencies are dormant, waiting to be coaxed out of writers. These assumptions promote a reliance on elicitation, or Socratic methods, as the primary strategy of talk within a conference, and, in extreme cases, the promotion of minimalist approaches to tutoring.

During initial and ongoing staff development discussions of particular approaches to conferencing, WAP teachers openly questioned the efficacy and the practicality of following rigid Socratic approaches with L2 writers or the idea of having a "preferred" WAP approach for responding to writers. Instead, most WAP teachers argued that rather than systematizing one approach, the WAP should promote its unique opportunity to meet individual needs in various ways. This willingness and desire to be flexible may be due to the teaching staff's confidence as experienced language teachers who feel comfortable responding to the needs of individual writers.

This amount of flexibility, however, requires that what goes on in conferences be documented and managed actively. In the WAP's case, this means that the program coordinator regularly reviews Consultancy Records and all other documentation in student files in order to address issues that arise with teachers on an individual basis or with all teachers through large group meetings, electronic discussion lists, or on the WAP electronic bulletin board. In addition, student and teacher feedback on the program is routinely solicited via questionnaires and interviews. The data from these sources not only help the program coordinator to assure the quality of what is taking place within conferences, they also indicate that WAP teachers use a variety of methods within conferences, ranging from minimalist, Socratic questioning to explicit teaching. Teachers indicate that the choice of approach depends on the needs of the student and the student's level of spoken English. Although most WAP teachers feel strongly that there is a place for explicit teaching in L2 writing conferences, the data indicate that explicit teaching rarely predominates in WAP conferences.

Acknowledgment of Higher and Lower Order Concerns

In addition to the emphasis given to peer response and Socratic approaches to conferencing, a third common theme within the L1 literature on writing center practice is that higher order concerns indicate underlying conceptual problems and, therefore, are more serious writing problems than lower order concerns. Lower order problems are viewed as careless errors and fixable if greater effort is paid to careful proofreading. The result is that L1 writers are often advised to read their texts slowly, silently or out loud, and to spot and correct errors. Sometimes L2 writers are advised to use checklists to detect and overcome their error patterns.

The WAP experience suggests that making a distinction between higher and lower order concerns can be unproductive in L2 writing conferences. Data from WAP Consultancy Records and more than 100 hours of audiotaped sessions suggest that higher and lower order concerns are often interrelated and blurred, as the following two examples from WAP conferences illustrate.

- Example 1: A student comes in with a written conclusion of an academic report that sounds awkward, at one level, due to the use of inappropriate vocabulary, which is typically viewed as a lower order concern. The writer's vocabulary difficulty has resulted in a number of bold, overreaching generalizations. Yet, the problem also involves a higher level, or conceptual, problem: The writer does not understand what is expected in the conclusion of an academic report, specifically, what degree of qualification, or hedging, is necessary.

- Example 2: A student wants feedback on the background section of an introduction. The student has case and article problems. At one level, the problem is merely grammatical. At another level, the student has not understood the importance of convincing the reader that the problems discussed in the background are generalizations. When the student understands that using plurals can convey this notion to the reader, the student can use this grammar as a tool to express an idea effectively.

In both examples, the student's concerns have lower and higher order dimensions. Making a distinction between what is higher and lower may actually discourage students and teachers from seeing important connections between different dimensions of a text, connections that may ultimately help students develop their writing. In acknowledging lower order concerns in conferences, the WAP experience is not suggesting that all concerns are equally important. What it does suggest is that L2 writing center practice must incorporate a broader range of foci and starting points within conferences, and that by doing so, it will address the multidimensional concerns of L2 writers.

Action Research Opportunities

A special feature of the WAP is that it has become a venue for reflective practice and action research on L2 writing center practice. Teachers are encouraged to audiotape sessions (approximately 100 have been recorded thus far) and to keep journals. As mentioned previously, teacher and student feedback for WAP staff is sought regularly through staff meetings, interviews, and questionnaires. In addition, a small collection of books and journals on writing center theory and practice was established within the WAP for teachers and researchers. To date, two action research projects have been funded. The first is a project related to writer and teacher development and the second is the development of an on-line support service.

◈ PRACTICAL IDEAS

There are a number of practical ideas that can be taken from the WAP experience. The following areas cover a broad range of program development issues.

Connect With Key People

Put together an advisory committee of key individuals within your unit or department, at the very least, in order to ensure that opinion makers are informed from the start and that they become stakeholders in the program. This was extremely important to the WAP's development.

Develop a Model

Spend time conceptualizing a model that will work in your own environment. Before deciding on a model, consult the literature on writing center practice. The *Writing Center Journal* and *The Writing Lab Newsletter* are useful resources. If possible, bring in outside consultants to share their experiences. The WAP was able to consult with various outside experts in its development. Most important, before establishing a model, do a needs analysis of your own environment in which you examine the needs of your students, your tutors, and the larger university community.

Examine Students' Writing Histories

Find out what types of writing experiences your students have had. The experiences of WAP students are generally homogeneous because most have graduated from secondary schools in Hong Kong. Find out what kinds of limitations and benefits these experiences may imply. The limitations for the WAP, as mentioned previously, were that prior experiences had been demotivating, had promoted a product-oriented mentality, and had given students the expectation of teacher direction and prescription. On the other hand, because our students have been through similar experiences, share the same L1, and have similar needs, we have had an easier time understanding their concerns and developing appropriate customized learning materials (e.g., handouts and informational sheets). Find out the strengths of the students and build on them. One strength that characterizes most Hong Kong Polytechnic University students is their openness and willingness to seek help.

Find out what kinds of writing assignments are required of students in your setting. The WAP used preexisting data to gain a general understanding of different departmental requirements. To collect more detailed information, the WAP presently is carrying out a further needs analysis to better understand the nature of the specific writing assignments typically required of students across the curriculum at Hong Kong Polytechnic University.

Consider Tutor and Faculty Attitudes Toward WAPs

Be considerate of the expectations and backgrounds of the tutors, whether they are peers or teachers. Be prepared to dispel misinformation that potential staff may have about writing centers and conferencing (e.g., that they provide editing services, that students who come to them are remedial). Offer initial and ongoing staff development and help fashion a teaching environment that is supportive and reflective. The WAP experience suggests that carrying out initial and ongoing teacher development workshops has been beneficial for staff. Teachers have reported that the supportive teaching environment of the WAP has created an enriching ethos. The WAP example points out that a writing assistance program, or L2 writing center, can be an agent of change for everyone involved, not just student writers.

Ensure Quality and Encourage Research

Develop documentation and feedback systems, in consultation with those who will use them, that allow for the smooth collection of useful data. In the WAP, this also means that all students are asked to give written consent, which allows their feedback, documentation, and taped session data to be used by the WAP. When asking students to sign consent forms, teachers are encouraged to explain to them that, given the alternative nature of the program, information collected from them will be used to assess the effectiveness of the program and to better develop it. Most students are very willing to give consent and the vast majority also agrees to be interviewed, at some future time, as well. (However, regardless of whether students agree to give consent, they are allowed to use the WAP.) Not only does the collected data help ensure the quality of the program, but they are also used to support funding requests. A caveat about documentation and feedback systems: Make sure that students and teachers do not become overburdened with filling out forms, and make all forms as concise and user-friendly as possible.

Include Clerical Support

Employ clerical staff to greet students and arrange conferences with teachers, collect and collate data, and keep systems operating. The WAP has been extremely fortunate to have friendly and competent clerical support.

Select an Appropriate Location and Support Materials

Create an inviting, user-friendly atmosphere for students to come to. Ours is located within an already popular subcenter of the English Language Centre, which is conveniently located across from a busy student canteen and lounge/study area. It is also worthwhile to invest time and money in the development of useful support materials. The WAP provides materials that students are allowed to keep.

Promote the WAP

Advertise your program or center throughout your campus among faculty and students. The WAP routinely sends flyers to university teaching staff as well as electronic notices to students and teaching staff. We also distribute flyers in the popular student meeting places, such as the student canteen.

◈ CONCLUSION

Program data have provided insights into perceptions of the program. The following insights are helping to direct the future development of the WAP.

Student, Faculty, and WAP Staff Perceptions

Response to the WAP has been overwhelmingly positive. Routinely, most of the available appointments are booked several days in advance. Over 99% of attending students indicate they would return and would recommend the program to classmates. Data also indicate that students see the program as a nonthreatening and practical way to develop their writing. The feedback comments from students also indicate that the program is having a positive effect. However, the amount and quality of this effect needs to be carefully studied before any firm conclusions regarding the WAP's impact are drawn.

Faculty members from many academic disciplines have been extremely positive about the program. Class teachers routinely request flyers to distribute in their classes, and, even more encouraging, some come to us directly to discuss the kinds of writing assignments they are giving or how they might incorporate writing into their courses.

Teachers working for the WAP also have reported that their WAP work is meaningful. Many teachers have indicated that their response to students within the WAP setting may have more impact than their classroom teaching because they are able to provide assistance early enough, and individually, on a face-to-face basis. Moreover, they have noted that they are able to address meaningful and authentic concerns, not simply the generic concerns of a class.

Teachers have also indicated that their experience with the WAP has been professionally enhancing to them. Specifically, they report that they are developing and refining response strategies and that this has influenced their teaching in other settings (e.g., the classroom). However, some WAP teachers are concerned that some students will rely too heavily on one-to-one help from the WAP and not develop the ability to work independently and to critique their own writing.

Future Developments

The previous feedback suggests that there are several areas of the WAP that can be developed.

Encouraging Self-Directed Evaluation and Revision

The first area of future development involves improving the critical abilities of WAP students. To accomplish this, the program is developing an on-line, Web-based extension of its service that will help Polytechnic University students to self-evaluate and revise their own writing in conjunction with seeking one-to-one assistance at the WAP.

Evaluating the Impact of the WAP

The second important area of future development involves action research into the earlier question regarding the nature and degree of the change that WAP students experience. The WAP wants to know whether and how well students who attend the WAP learn to evaluate and discuss their writing in new ways, and, if they do, whether they develop a deeper understanding of writing.

Contributing to the Development of L2 Writing Center Practice and Literature

The third area of development relates to the potential the WAP has to contribute toward a new body of L2 writing center practice and literature. The WAP's experience suggests that writing centers, a mainstay of L1 writing environments, can be adapted to L2 settings. The adaptation requires an understanding of the strengths and limitations of the particular environment. In addition, a successful adaptation may involve questioning L1 assumptions about writing center practice in order to meet the needs of one's own environment. As stated in this chapter, it is hoped that as this L1 practice is introduced into more L2 environments, a body of literature will develop that will address the issues and concerns of L2 writing center practice.

◈ CONTRIBUTOR

Maida Kennedy Xiao is the senior lecturer in charge of Special English Language Enhancement Programmes at the English Language Centre, Hong Kong Polytechnic University. She led the development of the Writing Assistance Programme and is now responsible for its administration. She has been an English language teacher at the tertiary level in the United States, China, and Hong Kong for the past 18 years.

CHAPTER 2

Toward Authentic, Specific-Purpose Writing at the Lower Levels of Proficiency

John Flowerdew

◈ INTRODUCTION

One of the dilemmas confronting designers of specific-purpose writing courses in some tertiary EFL settings is that, on the one hand, the level of English proficiency of learners is such that they are unable to tackle authentic academic writing tasks, such as essays, lab reports, and term papers; on the other hand, teachers of content subjects, aware of the students' limitations in English, do not require the students to perform such tasks but, instead, resort to one-word answer or multiple-choice-type formats for developing and evaluating students' knowledge and skills. Such a situation has important implications for the curricula of the content subject and of English.

For the content subject, one implication is that the curriculum is distorted because students are not required to perform the sort of tasks that would be expected of them in a native-speaker institution, either in their own first language (L1) or in an English-speaking environment. This has important long-term ramifications. Graduate scientists, engineers, and other professionals should clearly not only possess knowledge and skills in their fields, but they should also be able to communicate that knowledge and skill to others. Such a requirement is readily acknowledged by some tertiary institutions in English-speaking countries, for example, where communications studies are a required part of courses for native-English-speaking (NS) students of engineering and other specialities. This need to be able to communicate knowledge and skills through language becomes particularly apparent when graduates from English-medium institutions in non-English-speaking countries want to transfer to tertiary institutions in English-speaking countries, or, for instance, when they seek employment as graduate scientists or engineers, either at home or abroad, and their employers expect them to be able to communicate in writing.

With the English curriculum, two main problems arise. First, in situations such as the one above, it is difficult to motivate students to develop sophisticated writing skills when they know such skills are not required of them in their content-area studies. Second, it is difficult to devise authentic materials for writing courses without an appropriate model upon which to base a needs analysis.

This chapter reports on two aspects of an English for specific purposes (ESP) writing program developed at Sultan Qaboos University (SQU) in the Sultanate of Oman and how the program attempted to overcome the problem outlined above.

The first of these aspects involves the use in course design of a database of language used in science classes, the aim being to ensure authenticity of language learned and, therefore, optimum potential for appropriate use in science courses. The second aspect concerns the collaborative creation of writing tasks by language and content-area teachers, the purpose here being to ensure that writing tasks are authentic (i.e., they correspond to what scientists actually want) and appropriate (i.e., they require language that corresponds to what the students are actually capable of producing).

◈ CONTEXT

Formal education having only started in Oman in 1970, the SQU project was set up in the early 1980s, with a brief to plan the Sultanate's first university.[1] SQU, like most Arabian Gulf universities, was to be established as an English-medium (except for the humanities) institution. It received its first intake of students in 1986. From the inception of SQU, planners were aware of the need for intensive efforts to improve the students' level of English as they entered this largely English-medium institution (Adams-Smith, 1984; Bint, 1982; Holes, 1985). Various English tests of the target population had indicated that standards would be well below those normally expected by U.S. and British universities for overseas students. The first-year science foundation course (SFC) for students in all scientific disciplines required a heavy input of English teaching (12–15 contact hours per week) compared to a relatively light load of science (3 hours of lectures, 2 hours of lab work per week) and math (3 hours per week). The project also recognized the need for close collaboration between English and science staff in addressing the particular language needs and problems of students of science.

The SFC was structured in such a way that the three content-area subjects of biology, chemistry, and physics were taught in sequence, in blocks of 10 weeks each. The rationale for this is in large part linguistic to ensure that students have only one specialized register of English to deal with at any one time. After initial experimentation, the English course was broken down into three components:

1. listening/speaking
2. reading
3. writing

These components were taught in parallel throughout the year. Each English component drew on the content-area courses for its syllabus and materials.

◈ DESCRIPTION

For the writing component, the syllabus was organized around the main conceptual areas dealt with in biology, chemistry, and physics (e.g., structure, function, process), sequenced as far as possible to follow the content of the lecture course and lab

---

[1] I designed and coordinated the course described in this chapter over a number of years. I have since relocated to Hong Kong. However, subsequent reports on the course have indicated that the concordance-based and collaborative approach has continued to be used successfully. (See, e.g., Cobb & Horst, 2001, for a report of recent developments.)

practicals. Grammar and vocabulary objectives accompanied each conceptual area, based, where possible, upon the content-area courses. Writing topics and tasks were partly drawn from the content-area courses and partly from elsewhere. Where possible, linguistic examples in the teaching materials were selected directly from the content-area course material.

Aspect 1: Use of a Language Database From the Content-Area Course in Course Design

Rationale

In order to ensure that the language taught is of optimum value to students in their studies, the syllabus and materials used in the writing course were developed with the use of a language database from the science courses. Because it ensures authenticity and applicability of the language presented, this procedure is likely to be highly motivating for students.

Makeup of the Database

Examples in this section are taken from the content area of biology, although similar work was done in chemistry and physics.

As mentioned above, the biology course comprised the first 10 weeks of study in the SFC (followed by 10 weeks of chemistry and then 10 weeks of physics). Due in part to the students' low level of proficiency in reading, most of their exposure to English in their content-area courses is through the medium of lectures, where lecturers have the opportunity to create comprehensible input (Krashen, 1981, 1982; Long, 1983). The lecture course in biology consists of a maximum of 30 lectures of 50 minutes each. Using a variety of lecturers, one complete set of lectures was recorded and transcribed. This formed the main core of the database, which consists of 92,804 words.

Although the Biology Department started with a prescribed textbook (Roberts, 1986), it was soon realized that this book was beyond the level of most students, in terms of language and study skills. In collaboration with the language center, the book was replaced after the first year by a set of simplified readings designed to accompany the lecture course. As with the lectures, therefore, an attempt was made to create comprehensible input. The readings, together, consisted of 11,679 words. These words were also incorporated into the database, bringing the total number of words to 104,483. The database thus consists of words from the lectures and the reading materials and represents most of the English that students are exposed to in their study of biology.

Analysis of the Database and its Application to Course Design

The database was accessed by means of computer programs for word frequency and concordancing (Poulton, 1990). The most striking feature revealed by the analysis of the database is that, in their study of biology, students are confronted with a relatively light lexical load. The total number of items is only 4,232. Moreover, this number decreases rapidly if low-occurrence items are excluded. Table 1 shows, for example, that if words occurring only once are omitted, the total number of items immediately reduces to 2,815; if words occurring only once or twice are omitted, the total number reduces to 2,266.

TABLE 1. FREQUENCY OF ITEMS IN THE BIOLOGY DATABASE

Total Items	4,232
Items with less than 1 occurrence	2,815
2 or fewer occurrences	2,266
3 or fewer occurrences	1,912
4 or fewer occurrences	1,654
5 or fewer occurrences	1,470
10 or fewer occurrences	975
20 or fewer occurrences	602

What these data suggest is that by concentrating on a relatively small number of frequently occurring items, students will be able to handle a large percentage of the discourse they are exposed to in their studies. In other words, relatively few linguistic tokens are needed for communication in the field of biology in the SFC. As far as the English course is concerned, it follows that focus on these items should bring students up to a level where they are able to communicate within the context of their studies.

Many of the high-frequency items in the frequency list (just over half) are structural or grammatical, such as *the* or *of*, as opposed to lexical items, such as *cell*.

This high ratio of structural to lexical items is unremarkable, as it fits in with theories regarding the common core (Bloor & Bloor, 1986; Crystal & Davy, 1969; Quirk, Greenbaum, Leech, & Svartivik, 1985), which predict that all language varieties have as their most frequently occurring language forms the same common core of items. The significance of the data concerning these grammatical items, however, is not so much their overall frequency, which, as already suggested, is predictable without the need for empirical evidence from the database, but the way they are used.

Data on use was obtained by means of concordancing techniques. A concordancer is defined by Johns (1989) as "a computer program that is able to search rapidly through large quantities of text for a target item (morpheme, word or phrase) and print out all the examples it finds with the contexts in which they appear" (p. 9). Table 2 presents a sample printout of part of a concordance from the database for the word *made*.

Concordancing data has two applications in the present context. First, it allows the analyst or course designer to identify the various uses of particularly important items, for example, the use of the indefinite article with noncount singular nouns, or

TABLE 2. PART OF A CONCORDANCE FOR THE WORD MADE

or plasma membrane is seen to be	*made* of two dark layers
organelles in a cell are either	*made* of or surrounded by
and endoplasmic reticulum is	*made* of it. Mitochondria have two
are only about 5 mm thick and are	*made* of the protein actin

the use of *there is/there are* in a presentative function. Most of such information is available in standard reference and pedagogical grammar texts of English, so there is no real need for the database here. However, database analysis is very useful for identifying features that are especially important (because frequent) in the particular register of biological English. For example, concordancing of the word *or* revealed two important uses of this word in biology: to link a number of alternatives (e.g., when plants or animals or micro-organisms reproduce) and to introduce an alternative after a word just mentioned (e.g., a canal, or a channel; starch grains, or aminoplasts). Although these uses are explained in dictionaries and grammar texts, such reference sources also contain various other extraneous uses that do not occur in the database; in addition, the alternative-word use is given low priority in dictionaries and grammar texts, whereas it is very frequent in the database. To state another example, the database exhibits relatively frequent use of the definite article to refer to unique entities (e.g., the common earthworm, the nucleus, the heart), an instance of use that, again, is given low priority in dictionaries and grammar texts. Concordancing data on frequency of use thus provides criteria for selecting and grading grammatical items for the syllabus in terms of frequency of particular uses of a given item.

The second application of concordancing, and, indeed, its main value, is its ability to produce authentic contextualized examples for direct incorporation into the teaching material. Thus, for example, in teaching the stative verbs *be* and *have* (both problematic for Arabic-speaking learners of English), authentic examples already encountered by the students are presented from the biology content course (see Table 3).

Similarly, authentic examples are useful in differentiating uses of the same word or morpheme. Table 4 shows different uses, for example, of the *-ed* morpheme.

So far in the discussion, applications of frequency and concordancing data have taken language forms as their starting point. Formal items are selected for inclusion in the syllabus on the basis of frequency of occurrence in the corpus. In addition to this form-based approach, frequency and concordancing data can assist in the selecting and grading of items for the syllabus and in providing authentic examples from a notional perspective.

TABLE 3. AUTHENTIC EXAMPLES FROM THE DATABASE FOR STATIVE *BE* AND *HAVE*

be

The nucleus is the centre of the cell.

Movement is a characteristic of living things.

Animals are normally heterotrophs.

Animal cells are variable in shape and size.

have

The cell membrane has a "Fluid Mosaic" structure.

Paramecium has a number of important characteristics.

Mitochondria have two layers of unit membrane.

Grasses have fibrous root systems.

TABLE 4. PART OF A CONCORDANCE SHOWING DIFFERENT USES OF THE *-ED* MORPHEME

In event passive:

pectin. Cellulose is then	**secreted** by the cytoplasm of the cell
instructions (DNA) are	**stored** and used in a controlled way.
products. These must be	**removed** from the organism by excretion

In stative passive:

plant cells the nucleus is	**located** at the side, in the
cell sap. The cell is	**surrounded** by a tough and elastic
or ER. The cavities are	**connected** with each other, and the lining

As postmodifier:

his by means of a compound	**called** adenosine triphosphate (At
the middle of the vacuole	**attached** by strands of cytoplasm.
pectin wall of one cell	**fused** with the pectin wall of the

As premodifier:

is a diagram of a	**generalized** animal cell based on detailed
is necessary when old or	**damaged** cells have to be replaced by
carried out in a	**membrane-lined** vacuole into which several

In perfective aspect:

wall. After the cell has	**finished** growing, more layers of
these animals have	**developed** special respiratory surfaces
plants and animals that have	**died** and partly decomposed.

Inherent in the study of biology (and indeed the other sciences) is a need to understand and be able to express a number of fundamental concepts, or notions, such as shape, size, structure, process, and function. A general awareness of the need for such notions, refined by the detailed observation of the biology course and the study of the database, led to the writing component of the SFC, as mentioned above, taking a sequence of such notions as its overall syllabus framework.[2]

The notion-based use of the database took the following form. Once a notion had been selected, the frequency list was used to scan for lexical items used to express that notion. Concordancing of these lexical items again provided information on the grammatical structures associated with the items and authentic instances of the use of the items for incorporation into the materials. Thus, for example, Table 5 shows verbs from the frequency list that are used to describe function.

Tables 6, 7, and 8 show how this information is incorporated into a unit of course material dealing with describing function. An input section, which presents language to be focused on in the unit, is presented in the form of a true/false biology

---

[2] *Nucleus: English for Science and Technology* (Bates & Dudley-Evans, 1976) is a good example of a commercially available syllabus based on notional lines, and was influential in drawing up the syllabus for the SFC writing component.

TABLE 5. PARTIAL EXAMPLE OF VERBS IN THE DATABASE USED TO DESCRIBE FUNCTION

absorb	feed	prevent	remove
allow	get rid of	produce	show
bring	help	protect	stop

quiz (see Table 6). The quiz is composed of concordanced statements from the database, some of them judiciously edited to make them false. On the quiz, students are presented with a set of authentic statements from their biology course that incorporate some of the important verbs for describing function. In addition, the statements exhibit two different grammatical patterns used with these verbs: the formulaic (e.g., *the function of x is to y*) and the present simple tense (e.g., *x does y*). The rest of the unit develops these lexical and grammatical areas, focusing more overtly on the verbs for describing function (see Table 7) and the two grammatical patterns (see Table 8).

TABLE 6. SAMPLE MATERIALS FOCUSING ON DESCRIBING FUNCTION

Section 1: Input

Biology Quiz

These statements describe the functions of some of the components of plant and animal cells, but they are not all correct. Test your knowledge of this semester's biology by deciding whether each one is true or false.

1. The function of the chromosome is to carry hereditary material in the form of DNA.
2. One function of lysosomes is to transport oxygen around the body.
3. Another function of lysosomes is to destroy worn-out organelles within the cell.
4. Strands of plasmodesmata help material to move between cells.
5. Centrioles help the cell to form new cilia and flagella.
6. Chloroplasts absorb light energy and convert it to chemical energy by the process of photosynthesis.

(12 questions in all)

TABLE 7. VOCABULARY SECTION FOCUSING ON VERBS DESCRIBING FUNCTION

Section 2: Vocabulary

All the statements in the biology quiz in Section 1 describe the function of something. This is a list of some of the most common verbs in your biology course which you can use to describe functions.

Read the list. Which ones don't you know? Ask a friend or look in the dictionary. Can you write the Arabic meanings next to each one? After studying the list, try the self-test on page xx.

(See Table 5)

TABLE 8. GRAMMAR SECTION FOCUSING ON GRAMMATICAL PATTERNS FOR EXPRESSING FUNCTION

Look at some of the statements from exercise xx on page xx again:

1. The function of the chromosomes is to carry hereditary material in the form of DNA.
2. Another function of lysosomes is to destroy worn-out organelles within the cell.
3. Strands of plasmodesmata help material to move between cells.
4. Centrioles help the cell to form new cilia and flagella.
5. Chloroplasts absorb light energy and convert it to chemical energy by the process of photosynthesis.
6. The general function of rough ER is to transport the proteins which have been synthesized by the ribosomes.

All of these sentences describe the FUNCTION of something, but they use two different grammatical structures to do so. Look at the sentences carefully. Can you see the two structures?

Divide the six sentences into two groups according to their grammatical structure. Write the sentence numbers here:

FIRST GROUP _____

SECOND GROUP_____

All the sentences in one of your groups should contain a verb in the present simple tense.

All the sentences in the other group should contain the words:

"The function of .... is to ...."

These are two ways to describe the functions of things. We shall practise them one by one.

Aspect 2: Collaboration Between Language and Content-Area Teachers in the Creation of Writing Tasks

Introduction

If the use of the database in course design ensures authenticity of language taught and optimum potential relevance to the students in their science studies, there still remains the concern that appropriate use is made of the language learned in writing. Even though the language taught to science students may be authentic to their scientific studies, this learning will go to waste if science departments still require little or no written work from their students.

This section describes a set of practical writing tasks that were developed jointly by science (in this case chemistry) and English staff, with a view to exploiting the learning that was taking place in the writing course and to helping bridge the gap between the low level of writing proficiency of the first-year students and the intended writing requirements of science departments in later years.

Background

From the inception of the SFC, English staff observed the science lectures and lab sessions. The primary aim of this observation was to familiarize English teachers with the content-area material, much of which was also used in the English classes. As Johns and Dudley-Evans (1980) have pointed out, "The language teacher . . . needs to be able to grasp the conceptual structure of a subject his students are studying if he is to understand fully how language is used to represent that structure" (p. 8).

In addition, the lecture and lab observations helped familiarize the English staff with what the students experience in their science studies. In effect, each member of the participating English staff had the opportunity to do a very thorough, if informal, needs analysis.

As far as writing is concerned, the results of this needs analysis, at least initially, were rather negative. Anticipating the low level of writing ability of their students, science teachers required minimal writing as part of their courses. In lectures, little note-taking was expected because outline notes were often given, and no written assignments were given. In laboratory work, no reports were required; instead, students were given questionnaires requiring only single-word or phrase answers (although these were often not formally assessed, due largely to the difficulty in interpreting the students' English). Examinations and quizzes also necessitated minimal writing.

In spite of the fact that the science teachers accepted the low level of English proficiency of their first-year students, as attested by the minimal writing required in their courses, departmental heads still intended that students should do much more writing in their subsequent academic years.

Collaboration in Development and Administration of Tasks

Collaboration between the chemistry department and the language center focused on lab questionnaires because these offered the most scope for authentic writing, given the low proficiency level of the first-year students.

The purpose of the collaboration was to structure the lab questionnaires in such a way as to require, where possible, use of the language that was covered in the main English course. The aim was to provide an authentic communicative context for students to apply what they had learned or were learning in the English course, while at the same time making it more likely that the work produced would be understood more easily by the science teachers who had to evaluate it.

For example, questions asked in the first lab practical exploited work done in the English course, particularly on the use of conditionals, the passive or impersonal *you*, and modal verbs. Table 9 shows examples of the questions, target language, and model answers for this first chemistry lab practical (Experiments 1 and 2). (The actual question is all that the student sees of this material. The grammatical features in uppercase letters and the model answer in boldface italics are in the teacher's manual as an indication of what to look for in the student's answers.) Of course, if the student produced an appropriate answer to the question using alternative language, then this would be perfectly acceptable.

In terms of ongoing curriculum development, a two-way channel was developed between language and content. Not only were the form and scope of the chemistry questions influenced by the language proficiency of the students, but the main course syllabus was also adjusted to take into account the requirements of the writing tasks. Thus, for example, students soon realized that the impersonal *you* (e.g., as in "You should place a clean empty container on the balance.") was useful in many answers, whereas, as a means of de-emphasising the agent in a sentence, the course initially taught only the passive. The impersonal *you* was thus incorporated into the

TABLE 9. EXAMPLE QUESTIONS, TARGET LANGUAGE, AND MODEL ANSWERS FOR
LAB PRACTICAL 1

FOUNDATION SCIENCE COURSE: CHEMISTRY
LABORATORY MANUAL

Answer these questions on a separate sheet of ruled paper.

QUESTIONS ON EXPERIMENT 1

1. If you spill some strong acid on your skin, what should you do immediately?

    CONDITIONAL, MODAL VERBS, IMPERSONAL *YOU*, OR PASSIVE

    You should wash the acid off with plenty of cold water.

2. If some solid is spilled on the bench, should it be returned to the reagent bottle?
    Explain your answer.

    CONDITIONAL, MODAL, PASSIVE, *BECAUSE*, OR *OTHERWISE*

    *No, because it will be contaminated and it will contaminate the whole bottle if it is
    returned.*

3. What must you do when you have finished an experiment?

    MODAL VERB, IMPERSONAL *YOU*, OR PASSIVE

    *You must clean your apparatus and return items to the locker that belong there. You
    must leave your bench clean and tidy.*

QUESTIONS ON EXPERIMENT 2

1. Convert 0.358g to milligrams (mg).

    DISREGARD—NO LANGUAGE REQUIRED

2. Chemicals must never be weighed directly on the balance pan. What may happen if you
    weigh chemicals directly on the balance pan?

    CONDITIONAL, MODAL, IMPERSONAL *YOU*, OR PASSIVE

    *The chemicals will contaminate the balance and may damage the pan and the
    mechanism of the balance.*

3. Describe how you should weigh out accurately a small quantity (e.g., about 2g) of a
    chemical from a bottle containing 500g. What is this method of weighing called?

    MODAL VERB, IMPERSONAL *YOU*, OR PASSIVE

    *You should place a clean, empty container on the balance and set the balance to zero.
    You should then remove the container, put the chemical into it, return the container to
    the balance and record the mass. This is called "weighing by taring."*

4. Describe what you should do if you want to find how much salt is dissolved in
    seawater by evaporating a known volume to dryness in a beaker. What is this method
    called?

    MODAL VERB, IMPERSONAL *YOU*, OR PASSIVE

    *You should record the mass of the beaker, put seawater into it, and record the mass
    again. You can calculate the mass of the seawater. You should let the water evaporate
    and record the mass of the beaker with the dry salt on the same balance. You can
    calculate the mass of the salt, as it is the difference between this mass and the mass of
    the empty beaker. This is called "weighing by difference."*

main English course. Other examples of items that were introduced, given greater prominence, or resequenced, were

1. modals, such as

    You should write down the results.

    You must keep your books and papers away from water, chemicals, and flames.

2. cause and effect markers, such as

    The masses will probably be different, because all beakers are not exactly the same.

    You should write down the results. Otherwise, you will forget them.

3. use of future to mark cause and effect relations, such as

    If this is not done, the two solutions will not mix.

    It will contaminate the whole bottle if it is returned.

English and chemistry staff collaborated in the development and administration of the questionnaires. They adopted the following procedure for administering the questionnaires. First, the students were instructed to answer the questions in draft during or after the lab practical. They were then told to bring their drafts to the English class, where the questions were discussed in a plenary session, with the English teacher pointing out what language was likely to be required, although carefully avoiding providing answers regarding content (a sometimes difficult task, it must be admitted). The English teacher then checked students' drafts for language, but not content, problems. The students then rewrote a final draft for submission to the chemistry department for evaluation of content. Chemistry staff did not usually comment on language, although if a piece of work was still problematic, they might refer the student to the English teacher.

The collaboration in administering the questionnaires had advantages for the content-area and English staff. The content-area staff were assured of receiving answers written in reasonable English that were easier for them to grade for content. The English staff were provided with material for language review as well as for authentic application of language covered by their main core syllabus. An additional benefit, although not the focus of this chapter, was that teachers were given an opportunity to initiate students into the process of writing, with emphasis on the importance of redrafting, peer review, and neat and accurate presentation.

◈ DISTINGUISHING FEATURES

This chapter has reported on two aspects of an experimental approach to the teaching of tertiary-level ESP writing in an EFL environment, where English is the medium of instruction for other disciplinary courses. In allowing the syllabus and materials of the English course to focus on the finite set of linguistic items occurring in, for example, the biology course, the use of a database proved to be a powerful tool in ensuring authenticity of language taught and, therefore, optimum potential for authentic language use on the part of biology students. In the English course, the limited writing tasks represented by the lab questionnaires were an effective means of ensuring that students had an authentic purpose for the language they used in the labs. Students' awareness of the authenticity of language and the purpose for writing had important motivational as well as practical value for them. In addition, collaboration between English and science teachers in administering the questionnaires ensured that the science teachers received work written in English adequate enough to allow realistic grading for content. Furthermore, and perhaps most important in the long term, the questionnaires provided a realistic stepping stone in the direction of the more sophisticated writing that would later be demanded of students, such as full-blown lab reports, examination answers, and term papers.

Some readers may wonder why the language staff were not more proactive in attempting to bring about more radical change in the science curriculum. Why did they not request the science staff to incorporate more sophisticated writing tasks into their curriculum? Writers such as Benesch (1993) have been critical of ESP teachers for being too accommodating in their dealings with their peers in the disciplines they service. In retrospect, there is some justification in such a critique, but, at the time the SQU course was developed, it was felt that what was attempted was already quite radical. Further pressure on the content-area staff might have been counterproductive. At any rate, at no time did the language staff feel that they were subservient to the content-area staff. Indeed, as already indicated, on many occasions, the content-area staff sought the advice of language staff and acted upon their recommendations.

The approach described here was developed for a specific local setting. Nevertheless, especially because of its motivational appeal for students, such an approach could be adapted to many other similar EFL settings, particularly those in which students' L2 language proficiency does not yet equal disciplinary language demands or the students' own evolving disciplinary sophistication.

The two innovative aspects of the SFC described in this chapter contributed a level of authenticity to student writing. The use of the database of language from the science course ensured authenticity of language presented and learned, and, therefore, optimum potential for authentic use on the part of the learners. Cooperation between English and science teachers in the creation and administration of the questionnaires ensured authenticity of writing tasks and a correspondence between the language the students had been studying and what they were expected to produce.

◈ PRACTICAL IDEAS

To what extent might aspects of the SQU writing program be applied in other contexts? What problems should be signaled?

Consider Using Concordances to Select Authentic Disciplinary Instructional Vocabulary

At the time the SQU writing program was developed, concordancing programs were in their infancy and the approach adopted was quite revolutionary. Today, concordancing programs are widely available, so the application of the concordancing ideas should be relatively easy for anyone wishing to develop this aspect of the program. In addition, with today's sophisticated optical scanners, and because nearly all written material is available in electronic format, the creation of a database should be much easier.

Create Opportunities for Cooperation Between Disciplinary and English Faculty

One initial concern with regard to the collaboration between language and content-area staff was that cooperation might have been problematic. Experience proved the opposite. Language staff found that the content-area staff, many of whom had little idea of how to deal with nonnative-English-speaking students, were extremely receptive to any suggestions or initiatives coming from the language teachers. On the other hand, it is important that if the ideas presented here are to be employed on a large scale with more than a few committed teachers, time and effort should be directed toward staff development on the part of the language teachers. A program like the one described here requires motivated and committed teachers who can identify with its goals and who are willing to put in more time and effort than might be required of them in a more traditional English for academic purposes course.

❖ CONCLUSION

The SFC writing course was a step toward overcoming the problem outlined in the introduction of this chapter. The course addressed the inability of beginning science students to tackle the authentic writing tasks that customarily accompany the study of science and content-area teachers' consequent avoidance of setting such tasks—with its attendant ramification of long-term distortion to the content-area and the English curricula.

❖ ACKNOWLEDGMENTS

I would like to acknowledge the part played by James Scott in the development of the teaching materials for the course described here and the role of Richard Burnham, who collaborated in the writing of the chemistry questionnaires.

❖ CONTRIBUTOR

John Flowerdew has taught, designed curricula, and trained teachers in France, the United Kingdom, Venezuela, the Arab World, and Hong Kong. His research interests include discourse analysis, ESP/EAP, curriculum theory, and the use of English in Hong Kong. He is currently professor in the English Department at the City University of Hong Kong. He has published widely in applied linguistics, language teaching, and discourse analysis journals. He is the editor of *Academic Listening: Research Perspectives* (Cambridge University Press, 1994).

CHAPTER 3

Realizing a Giant First Step Toward Improved English Writing: A Case in a Japanese University

Keiko Hirose

◈ INTRODUCTION

English writing is not required for most Japanese university students. A large nationwide survey conducted to examine Japanese university English teachers' views on English language education at mainly first- and second-year undergraduate levels found that 20% of the respondents did not engage in writing instruction at all (Koike et al., 1983). Moreover, when writing was taught, the survey results showed that structures and expressions were most practiced (30.7%), followed by translation from Japanese to English (30.2%), free composition (17.0%), others (12.6%), and reproduction and précis writing (6.4%). English writing instruction therefore appears to be a service activity used to reinforce the teaching of grammatical structures or vocabulary.

How do Japanese students perceive writing in English? In fact, few of them conceive of the need or demand for writing in English, not to mention academic writing. Various questionnaire results have revealed Japanese university students' low level of motivation for writing English, especially when compared with their high level of motivation for speaking English. According to Koike et al. (1985), probably the largest survey to date to investigate Japanese university students' views on studying English, 61% of the students (N = 10,095) wanted speaking instruction, whereas only 3.1% wanted writing instruction. This is not at all surprising given that students in Japan scarcely perceive immediate goals in terms of written English.

Few Japanese students (e.g., 3.7% of the students in Koike et al.'s 1985 survey) view academic writing in English as a necessary goal. Those who do are probably undergraduates majoring in English literature, linguistics, or English language education—subjects that require students to write a graduation thesis in English. English writing courses are actually offered to these students. The writing program described in this chapter is a case in point.

In this chapter, I focus on my own writing course for first-year undergraduate students because this type of writing course can be considered important for several reasons in the Japanese context. First of all, this is one of the students' first exposures to English writing instruction. Although most Japanese students enter university with 6 years of highly controlled, formal English education,[1] they have never taken an English writing course per se before university. From my 20-year experience teaching English writing in the university, I know that what most students have experienced in terms of English writing before they enter university has not gone beyond translation. Second, this is the first writing course students take because first language (L1) writing instruction is not generally given. Third, the course includes content and methods that are considered innovative in the Japanese educational context, though not necessarily in other countries.

◈ CONTEXT

The context for this chapter is an English writing course that I taught at a small public university in Japan. The class makeup is basically homogeneous in terms of age, academic major, ethnicity, and previous educational background. The students are all majoring in British and American Studies in the Faculty of Foreign Studies, where they take courses in English-language skills as well as in a wide range of subjects, such as history, language, literature, economics, and politics in the United Kingdom and the United States.[2] English-medium instruction is mandated for the English courses, where native-English-speaking (NS) teachers as well as nonnative-English-speaking (NNS) Japanese teachers and students use only English as a medium of communication. Thus, my writing course is conducted exclusively in the second language (L2), and students are not allowed to speak Japanese in the classroom. The content courses across the curriculum often use books and articles written in English as teaching materials, but are conducted in Japanese, mostly by Japanese professors.

All students who are required to write a graduation thesis on their chosen subject in English during their fourth year are offered two semesters (12 weeks each) of English writing courses in their first year, and then a year-long (24-week) course in their second, third, and fourth years. The class size for first-year courses is approximately 20 students, which is relatively small in the Japanese context. Generally, the higher the year, the smaller the class size. Like other courses in Japanese universities, these writing classes commonly meet for 90 minutes once a week. The courses are taught by NS and NNS teachers. It is not unusual for Japanese teachers to teach English writing courses in Japan, where they outnumber NS teachers. The teachers are free to use any textbook and method they choose and do not have a set goal or curriculum to follow. Nevertheless, teachers and students alike perceive the ultimate goal for the courses as being sufficient mastery of academic writing to deal with the graduation thesis. Each graduation thesis is read and given a grade of A, B, C, or D (which is a failing grade) by individual supervisors from the students' chosen fields, who, with a few exceptions, are mostly Japanese professors.

---

[1] Some students have been partly educated in an English-speaking country, but such returnee students are the exception.

[2] The Department of British and American Studies has 19 faculty members, of which 3 are native speakers of English from England or the United States who mostly teach English-language courses. Ten are Japanese nonnative speakers of English (NNSs) who teach other subject-matter courses, such as literature and linguistics as well as English-language courses. I belong to this group. The remaining 6 NNS Japanese members teach subject-matter courses, such as politics and economics, in lectures and seminars.

English proficiency levels for first-year students majoring in English vary from low intermediate to advanced, the majority of these students belonging to the intermediate level. Their proficiency levels correspond to Comprehensive English Language Test for Learners of English (CELT) scores, which range from 182–269 (mean score = 204),[3] and also to Test of English as a Foreign Language (TOEFL) scores, which range from 460–573 (mean score = 487.4).[4] This illustrates the students' English proficiency level in one year, but proficiency levels of new students are similar every year. Their levels may be slightly higher than those of the average Japanese first-year university student because, as English majors, they have passed entrance examinations with the heaviest weight given to English.

◈ DESCRIPTION

In a 12-week course, I set a final goal of writing a research paper by the end of the semester. To this end, I start the course by introducing fluency-aimed writing, followed by preparation for writing the paper. Thus, there are journal and research paper-related writing assignments throughout the course.

Fluency-aimed writing is tangentially related to academic writing, and may not be a necessary component of an academic writing program. As pointed out earlier, however, Japanese students have not written English beyond the sentence level before they enter university. Thus, students appear to need not only formal paper writing but also fluency-aimed writing practice as preparation for academic writing, of which the latter can be regarded as warm-up for the former. I am not alone in proposing the combination or sequence of these two types of writing. For example, Mlynarczyk (1991) suggests that writing instruction with the ultimate aim of producing academic writing should start with personal writing, such as journal writing.

Fluency-Aimed Writing: Journal Writing

Journal writing is used for fluency-aimed writing. The primary goal of implementing journal writing is to let students get used to writing in English rather than to generating ideas, as originally proposed in L1 writing pedagogy, because the former seems to be the more immediate necessity for inexperienced Japanese writers of English. Japanese students are generally accustomed to writing about their personal experiences and feelings in their L1, so they can be expected to find little difficulty in adapting themselves to journal writing in an L2. The students in my class are told to write a diary entry at least 4 days a week outside the class throughout the course. In addition to instructions such as "Spend no fewer than 15 minutes when writing," "Try to write as much as you can about anything," and "Do not worry too much about spelling and grammar," they are told that only the amount of writing will be taken into consideration for grading this practice.

The subject of the journal writing is concerned with what students do in a day and what they think or feel about these experiences. Therefore, common topics are

---

[3] The CELT consists of structure, listening, and vocabulary sections, with a maximum possible score of 300 points (100 per section) (Harris & Palmer, 1986).

[4] The (paper-based) TOEFL consists of listening comprehension, structure/written expression, and reading comprehension sections, with a maximum possible score of 677.

mostly about university courses they take, including professors, classmates, tests, or assignments; part-time jobs they do after classes; and social activities they engage in outside of class (see Figure 1 for a sample student journal entry).

As depicted in the journal entry, many students complain that they cannot think of a topic because they follow a similar routine every day. I suggest possible topics at times, but some students explore their own ideas. In the end, they view journal writing as a good chance to think about themselves.

Fluency-aimed writing practice, such as journal writing or fast writing, has been implemented in Japanese university classrooms, not on a massive scale yet, but enough so that a few empirical studies have reported on its use. The effects on Japanese students have already been examined. First, because students are writing in a nonthreatening environment, they experience less anxiety about writing and become more comfortable with writing in English. Probably related to this effect, students have also gained writing fluency. Measuring fluency by the number of T-units and words, for example, Ross, Shortreed, and Robb (1988) found that students became more fluent in writing, especially in narrative writing. This increase in fluency may be caused by changes in students' writing processes, for example, from a word-for-word translation from Japanese to English, to direct writing in English. My students have also reported benefiting in at least one or the other of these areas.

Unlike academic writing, however, spontaneous writing, such as free or journal writing, does not require writers to do much planning beforehand. Furthermore, while writing, they do not have to, and are actually instructed not to, worry about coherence or organization either. Common sense dictates that coherent, well-organized writing does not come naturally from such fluent writing alone. In fact, although writing fluency has been an established effect, past studies have reported mixed results concerning the effects of journal writing on the quality of student writing (e.g., see Ross et al., 1988). This is where planned research paper writing comes into play.

Research Paper Writing

Consciousness-Raising Activities and Strategy Instruction

For their first L2 academic writing assignment, students do various consciousness-raising activities together before engaging in individual activities for completing a research paper on their chosen topics. Because students have not done much

---

Everybody (well not quite "Everybody" but nearly all of them) complained about writing journal, but even though she told us to continue writing. I do think writing a journal is a good way to improve our writing ability. We learn how we could express our feeling by writing in English everyday. Sometimes I find this interesting, especially when I have a topic I want to share with others. But apart from this, I feel tiring and bothersome to write a diary. Especially on the weekdays all I do is go to school and come back. I don't have anything to write in the journal. Even if I did, if that's my private thing I don't want anyone to read it. I don't see why my classmate has to read the journal. What's the point about that? I want to ask the teacher what?

FIGURE 1. Sample Student Journal Entry

academic writing in their L1, they do not know what is involved in L2 academic writing. Thus, I raise students' consciousness toward writing by eliciting their perceptions (see Prewriting, Consciousness-Raising Activities and Writing Processes).

Specific writing strategies found to be used by good writers are taught explicitly, such as planning content and organization, being aware of audience, and rereading and revising (Sasaki & Hirose, 1996), in the hope that the students' awareness of such strategies may have an effect on their own L2 writing. Unlike the case of fluency-aimed writing, therefore, the importance of planning and postwriting activities is emphasized for research paper writing. Such prewriting activities as free writing and outlining (e.g., making a list or drawing tree diagrams) are demonstrated before the students try them. More specifically, they have 10–15 minutes of hands-on experience with each of two types of prewriting activities (adapted from Unit 15 in Littlejohn, 1991). The students choose topics on their own for these activities, although several fallback topics are given for those who cannot think of topics on the spot. The intention is to enhance students' awareness of different approaches to getting started with writing and to let them discover which approach suits them best. After the activities, most students report they prefer outlining to free writing as an idea-generating activity for academic writing. With limited experience of journal writing, they appear as yet unable to translate the activity into an idea-generating prewriting activity. This may be attributable not only to their lack of writing experience, but also to individual preference.

In addition to generating ideas, the importance of organizing ideas is also emphasized by providing research papers from previous semesters as models. With such peer examples as a guide, students are instructed to include in their own research papers the three main sections (i.e., introduction, body, and conclusion), each of whose functions is explained explicitly. Students are also instructed to plan the main points and their sequence for the body of the paper. These prewriting activities do not necessarily connect with the work on the research paper. Students can wait to decide on a topic until after the consciousness-raising activities and strategy instruction. From the first class, however, students are informed that they have to work on a topic and examine whether it is feasible for the research paper. Thus, they are encouraged to think about how they will organize a paper on their chosen topics while they are receiving organizational instruction.

Writing a Research Paper

After the consciousness-raising activities and strategy instruction, the students announce their topics to the whole class and present brief outlines and the reasons for their choice orally in English. Students may work alone, but I also allow group projects. I am always impressed with the wide range and originality of topics students choose. For example, one group of students chose to investigate the size of packaged snacks in Japan. They wondered why large-sized snacks had become more popular in recent years. They called confectionery companies to investigate why they had started to manufacture large-sized snacks and also devised questionnaires for consumers (i.e., their university peers) to find out if, when, and why they buy big snacks. They collaborated to present the results of their investigation in a report entitled "Why Pochy [the name of a popular Japanese snack] has grown BIG!" Chosen topics cover serious subjects (e.g., the dismantling of Yugoslavia, the welfare system) and light ones (e.g., various effects of tea). They also reflect hot current issues. For example, the publication of a book featuring nude photos of a popular Japanese actress (about the students' age) motivated a group of students to select nudity as a topic. They based their questionnaire survey on what made people choose to pose nude. One of the most innovative aspects of this writing course derives from the topics students choose for their writing.

On the other hand, I also have found that students' ability to handle issues such as nudity and the dismantling of Yugoslavia in their first L2 research paper sometimes appears to surpass their English ability. Their experience in handling such issues is limited in their L1 academic writing as well. Maintaining their interest or intellectual level in L2 academic writing seems to be difficult for some students. For example, they may not have sufficient vocabulary for their topics. However, I never discourage them from selecting a topic of their own interest. Making reference to information in their L1, they can manage L2 prewriting research activities centered on their interests.

Inside and outside the classroom, students work on their own projects, starting with generating ideas and organizing them in the form of lists. Students do independent research activities, such as reading and conducting a survey, before writing their papers. After summarizing their findings based on their survey or reading, they begin writing their first drafts, mostly as homework assignments. In class, I give spoken and written feedback on the first drafts, whereas students give only written feedback to each other. Based on teacher and peer feedback, writers are encouraged to revise the drafts and then produce better papers for grading by the end of the semester.

Typing English on a word processor or personal computer, another skill related to academic writing, is required, too. For many Japanese first-year university students, this is their first serious attempt to type in English. Getting used to a computer makes their rewriting and revising easier. In addition, they know they will have to type their graduation theses.

In the last class, students make oral presentations on their projects in English and hand in their research papers. Students' papers are compiled in a typed class bulletin. I distribute a copy of the bulletin to each student with the hope that their first research paper writing experience will become a giant first step toward improving their English writing.

As described above, this is an integrated English course linked to producing academic writing, including learning how to do oral presentations, how to give peer feedback, and how to discuss in English. These multiskill activities may be one of the most distinguishing features of the program. In the next section, particular attention is given to four other features of the course that help distinguish it from traditional writing courses in Japan or elsewhere, which tend to focus on language structures and translation.

◈ DISTINGUISHING FEATURES

Prewriting, Consciousness-Raising Activities and Writing Processes

Prior student knowledge and experience of writing is elicited through questions such as "What do you think of writing?" (adapted from Unit 5 in Littlejohn, 1994). I pose questions used for consciousness-raising activities orally in the L2. Students seem to share the view that writing is not always easy, even in an L1, and they are especially anxious about formal writing. They describe L1 writing as "easier [than English]," "interesting," "troublesome," or "difficult." I also ask questions such as "What makes writing difficult?," "Do you have the same feelings about L2 writing?," and "What is good L1 and L2 writing?" Table 1 summarizes students' descriptions of L2 writing in 1996.

Through questioning, student perceptions of L1 and L2 writing are activated and then refined through discussions in the whole class. An innovative feature of this class discussion may be that different perceptions or ideas about writing emerge. For example, students consider good writing as being clear in the sense that the reader finds it easy to follow in the L1 and the L2. Many insist that good writing in English should be logical and direct, whereas good Japanese writing is not necessarily so. Students seem to be familiar with the dichotomy between direct organizational patterns in English and indirect counterparts in Japanese. Some students argue that they should quickly get to the point when writing in English. Others claim English is basically the same as Japanese. The former view tends to dominate. My own view on this controversial issue is that there is a perception by English readers that Japanese writing beats around the bush. I give students an illustration of such writing. However, I also add that Japanese writers can be logical in English as well as in Japanese, and that Japanese and English academic writing have much in common.

I also hold class discussion in the L2 of multidraft writing processes, from generating ideas to revising. More specifically, students draw a chart of their writing processes in a group (adapted from Unit 5 in Littlejohn, 1994), and then each group reporter presents the chart visually and orally to the whole class (see Figure 2 for an example of a finished chart).

The charts or diagrams the students complete in each group are not exactly the same. I elicit from students their own views of academic writing processes and then proceed to ask whether paper writing processes in English would be the same as those in Japanese. Student consciousness of L1 and L2 writing processes is raised because, at first, many students tend to regard the two processes as totally different. The focus, therefore, is on similarities in academic writing processes, for instance, prewriting research activities, such as outlining, and postwriting activities, such as revising.

TABLE 1. SUMMARY OF STUDENTS' DESCRIPTIONS OF L2 WRITING

Categories	positive	neutral	negative
	interesting (4)	needs a dictionary (4)	difficult (18)
	fun (3)	grammatical (2)	troublesome (3)
	enjoyable (2)	journal (1)	poor vocabulary (3)
	fashionable (1)	diary (1)	needs much (more) time (3)
	great (1)		hard (2)
	nice (1)		tired (2)
	sophisticated (1)		tiring (1)
	sounds wonderful (1)		anxious (1)
			boring (1)

N = 21

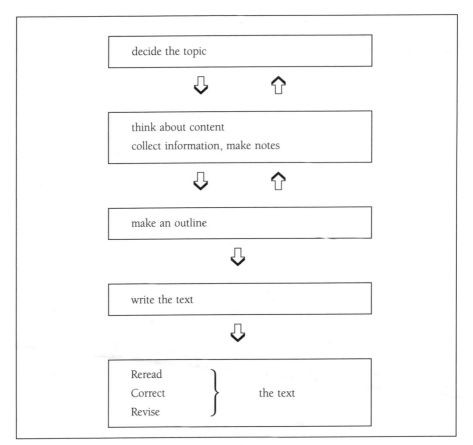

FIGURE 2. Sample Student-Generated Chart of the Writing Process

Written Peer Feedback in the L2

Peer feedback is an unfamiliar activity to Japanese university students because it is not usually part of their prior classroom experience. Without hands-on experience, Japanese student assessment of peer feedback might be negative at first. Two potential problems can be predicted concerning the introduction of peer feedback to Japanese students:

1. a student's inability to recognize and diagnose the problems of a peer's text

2. students' potential hesitation to point out the problems to each other[5]

When student readers identify a trouble spot or possible weakness in a peer's composition, they might think that it is their own fault not to have figured out what the writer wanted to say. In other words, when they do not understand a peer's English, they may not be completely certain that it is the writer's fault. Even when they are sure of errors and weaknesses in a classmate's L2 text, they may think it rude

---

[5] These problems are not necessarily unique to Japanese students. Any L2 learners can face them, especially when their L2 proficiency levels are low.

to point these out explicitly to the writer, especially when they do not know the writer well. This could also happen when they read a peer's L1 text.

Because spoken peer feedback in the L2 can be psychologically and linguistically difficult for them, I use written peer feedback in the L2 for both journal and paper writing. This not only creates another opportunity for students to practice writing in English, but also to write for a truly communicative purpose in particular. They are encouraged to ask questions, give comments, or express what they think about each other's work. I introduce peer feedback by preparing feedback prompts.

For fluency-aimed writing, students complete a journal checklist every week, indicating the number of lines for each entry for that week and the day they choose for a reader to read. The checklist also includes a blank column in which the reader writes questions or comments. The reader writes several English sentences in the column freely. Students spend approximately 10 minutes of the class time reading and giving written feedback to each other. This in-class activity is intended to ensure regular writing and raise students' awareness of audience when they do journal writing. The students generally enjoy sharing their journals with each other. For example, one pair of students handled peer feedback in the following way. One student wrote that he got home at 4 a.m. from a party, describing himself as *gozen-sama*, a Japanese slang expression for a person who plays around and gets home after midnight. Because he did not know its English counterpart, *night owl*, he translated the word literally into English as *Mr. Morning*.[6] He went on to write that he washed his car in the afternoon, which made him tired. His peer reader responded with the following comments:

> I REALLY enjoyed your journal!! I don't know if it is said "Gozen-Sama" "Mr. Morning" in English, either. But "Mr. Morning" seem so cute! I know your car, is it Honda's something, right? Take good care of your car and let him be your good partner! Anyway, I always like your sense of humor. P.S. But! you had better write much more lines in your journal.

For research paper writing, I give students the following instructions initially as prompts:

- Explain what you like best about the draft

- Give positive comments such as "a good point" or "I agree" when you are impressed with the writer's point or argument

- Underline the part that is unclear to you in terms of content or grammatical accuracy

- Put a question mark where you do not understand, where you cannot see the connection between clauses or sentences

- Give suggestions to improve the draft, such as, "Examples might help here" or "Elaborate this point"

- Confirm your understanding if you are not sure

---

[6] *Mr. Morning* is likely to be taken to mean the same as a *morning person*, the opposite of *night owl*, by a NS. Instead, *Mr. Late Night* is equivalent to *gozen-sama*. This example shows that the feedback, though well-intentioned, can also be misinformed.

My experience of using written peer feedback tells me that it works well with Japanese students. With successful experience, they can learn to give feedback and to be critical of each other's work. Peer feedback is a promising activity for English writing instruction in Japan, where a class size of more than 30 is not unusual and teacher-student conferences are often difficult, if not impossible, to arrange.

Use of L1 Strategies for Academic Writing

As is normally the case with any academic writing, student work necessitates research activities other than writing. To write an L2 report, the students research a topic by reading books, magazines, and newspapers, and by conducting surveys and interviews. Because students have not done much of this type of activity for L1 writing, these prewriting research activities provide a new experience for most of them. One of the characteristic aspects of such research activities is that students are most likely to do these in their L1. Information they want or need is more accessible and available in their L1. Surveys and interviews are conducted in the L1 because the participants are native speakers of Japanese. Furthermore, relevant reference materials are abundant in their L1 for almost any topic they choose. Although some students search for them in the L2, for example, on the Internet, it is more exceptional to resort to L2 information. Given limited time in which to research, it is faster for them to gather information in their L1; and even if they could access information quickly in the L2, they would be likely to find it difficult to digest and integrate into their L2 paper. Considering their English ability, the limited preparation time, and the wide availability of L1 references, we cannot dismiss L1 use from prewriting research activities. In fact, we should acknowledge the positive role of L1 use, especially in an early stage of L2 academic writing. Use of L1 information can be a good strategy to keep up students' intellectual and interest level in L2 writing (see Uzawa & Cumming, 1989).

When students use information originally produced in their L1 for their L2 writing, they have to translate it into the L2. I assume that many students resort to translation from Japanese to English while writing outlines or drafts. I do not encourage them to translate, but L1 use at the planning stage (e.g., taking notes, planning the content of the paper) may lead to such translation in writing. Thus, L1 use can activate L2 research paper writing. Kobayashi and Rinnert (1992) found positive effects of such L1 use on the quality of their students' L2 writing, especially among Japanese EFL students with lower proficiency levels.

NNS Teacher-Student Conferences

NNS teacher-student conferences are one of the most important characteristics of the course. Individual conferences are held at least four times in class using English to discuss the following: (a) the selection of topic, (b) the plan or the outline of a paper, (c) the first draft, and (d) the second draft. In the first conference, I give suggestions or advice, for example, on how to approach the chosen topic. In the second conference, I give feedback mainly on organization and content. Students are reminded of applying the three-part organization (introduction, body, conclusion) independently in their own writing. Finally, in the third and fourth conferences, I give feedback mainly on content, and point out major grammatical mistakes.

I hope the above descriptions of the conferences encourage NNS L2 writing teachers to employ teacher-student conferences more often. However, these conferences do not give students the kind of feedback they might get from a NS teacher, particularly in terms of feedback on language (e.g., word choice or style). In this respect, I am fully aware of my limitations, and feel that collaboration with a NS is desirable. If Japanese students receive comments on their writing only from Japanese readers, in the long run this may contribute to the creation of English that is acceptable only to Japanese readers. If possible, therefore, I make use of an external NS reader to read and check each student's English at a final stage.

◈ PRACTICAL IDEAS

I hope the writing program described in this chapter provides practical ideas and suggestions that can be applied or adapted by teachers in similar L2 contexts. The following may be particularly good candidates for such applications.

Combine Journal Writing and Research Paper Writing

The combination of journal and research paper writing is promising for L2 academic writing instruction, especially when students are novices in both types of writing. Research paper writing alone is not sufficient for these novice writers. Journal writing helps students to construct an identity that enables them to write English as a means of self-expression.

Have Students Write on Topics of Their Own Choice

For journal or research paper writing, students choose topics that motivate them to write. Given this autonomy, they can elaborate their individual personal interests in or through L2 writing. Although journal writing and research paper writing differ in terms of processes involved, both share this personal orientation.

Raise Consciousness and Teach Strategies

Various consciousness-raising questions are asked to help students reflect on writing and their prior knowledge about writing. Furthermore, prewriting activities (e.g., planning, organizing) are introduced when students are hunting for topics. Postwriting activities (e.g., rereading, revising) are also performed after students write their first drafts.

Permit Research and Information Gathering in the L1

Students usually resort to using L1 references, which are then used for L2 writing. This may be conspicuous because L2 use is emphasized throughout the course. However, use of L1 information is a reality of English academic writing in Japan. When students write graduation theses, many include references to L1 information, too.

Include Written Peer Feedback in the L2

A written form of peer feedback is employed, and prompts are prepared for students by the teacher to ensure or facilitate active exchange of feedback.

◈ CONCLUSION

This chapter has explained how a native-Japanese-speaking English teacher runs an English writing program using many procedures new to students in Japan. The course is considered an introduction to English academic writing, and its content is intended to be innovative to students. These new features should be incorporated more into English writing instruction in Japan. They can also be used extensively in a longer writing course with students of higher or lower levels of English proficiency in similar EFL environments. In Japan, students generally find it difficult to improve their English writing ability due to the paucity of writing practice in and out of the classroom. It is therefore necessary for teachers to give students opportunities to write. Given ample writing opportunities, my students find the coursework challenging and frustrating at times (recall the comments in Figure 1), but they seem to gain a sense of achievement by completing one or more journal notebooks and the typed paper in the course. As a result of the course, students appear to have become more accustomed to writing in English (i.e., it is no longer something out of the ordinary for them), and to have been motivated to further improve their L2 writing ability, although the instruction might not have led them to improve it immediately. This baby step can turn into a giant first step toward truly improved English writing, if they continue with journal and research paper writing on a regular basis. If students have a reason and an opportunity to communicate in English, for example, by e-mail, their motivation to write in English may be strengthened and may make such regular writing practice possible.

This study suggests several directions for future studies as well as implications for writing programs. First, fluency-aimed writing practice needs justification as preparation for academic writing. Although students do not seem to transfer journal writing directly to academic writing processes in a short course, such as the one described in this chapter, this aspect should be investigated over a period longer than a semester. Second, appropriate methods of raising consciousness about writing strategies need more elaboration. Third, peer feedback (written and spoken) should be implemented in English writing instruction, and the effectiveness of peer feedback on students' subsequent writing, and their own perceptions of its effectiveness, should be examined. Finally, the positive role of L1 use in the L2 academic writing process also needs to be pursued in future research. For example, we should investigate how students use information drawn from L1 materials for L2 writing, and if and how this facilitates their actual L2 writing.

◈ ACKNOWLEDGMENTS

I would like to thank Ilona Leki, William Phillips, and Theresa Austin for their insightful comments on, and suggestions for, this chapter.

◈ CONTRIBUTOR

Keiko Hirose is professor at Aichi Prefectural University, in Japan. Her current research interests include contrastive rhetoric and comparing L1 and L2 writing processes.

PART 2

Connecting L2 Writers to Communities

CHAPTER 4

Making Writing Count in an ESL Learning Community

Marcia Babbitt

◈ INTRODUCTION

At Kingsborough Community College, a large, urban campus that forms part of the City University of New York (CUNY) system, ESL students often take as many as four or more semesters of noncredit ESL and English courses before they qualify for credit-bearing Freshman English Composition and before they are allowed to enter many of the major areas of concentration. Because of changes in CUNY policies regarding time limits for students to complete noncredit courses and restrictions on financial aid, ESL students are under increasing pressure to finish noncredit ESL and English courses as quickly as possible.

Recent research has shown that students achieve higher success rates in college when they are part of a strong academic-social learning community, working together collaboratively on course assignments and gaining new insights and perspectives from each other while forming strong social bonds (see Bruffee, 1993, 1995; Gabelnick, MacGregor, Matthews, & Smith, 1990; Tinto, 1987, 1997; Tinto, Goodsell Love, & Russo, 1993, 1994). When students are block-programmed, taking all their classes with the same students within the framework of an interdisciplinary, content-based curriculum, learning communities can take root. The collaborative aspect of such a program is two-pronged: It requires (a) a cooperative effort on the part of the faculty in the design and implementation of a demanding content-based curriculum structure, and (b) the creation of a learning environment for students in which collaboration, openness, and a willingness to listen to, speak to, and learn from others is encouraged.

◈ CONTEXT

Kingsborough's intensive English program (IEP) was designed as a content-based, collaborative, and interdisciplinary program in which entering ESL students would do extensive academic writing and reading in a supportive environment and work closely with their peers while earning academic credits in a variety of non-ESL courses. The ESL faculty in the program believed that, with this program, we would improve the pass rate of students in our ESL classes, and our results have shown that this is the case. In regular ESL classes, the pass rate had been between 60–70%; in the IEP, it is better than 80%. We knew that by improving the pass rate, we would also improve the retention rate for ESL students.

The block format of the program was designed to take place over one semester and includes (a) an 8-hour, noncredit ESL class; (b) two three-credit courses in other academic disciplines; (c) two one-credit student development (SD) courses; and 4 hours of tutoring for a total of eight college credits and 20 contact hours.

At first, the IEP was optional for new ESL students. Those who chose not to participate were generally students who could not commit to a 5-day-a-week, 9 a.m.–3 p.m. schedule, or who thought the workload would be too daunting. However, because the success rate of students in the intensive blocks was greater than that of other ESL students, we mandated the program for entering full-time students in the fall of 1998.

The IEP courses were designed to give students the opportunity to skip a level. Skipping a course in the ESL sequence was extremely rare before the IEP began. The general goals of Kingsborough's IEP are to

- accelerate ESL students' acquisition of academic written and spoken English
- allow ESL students to take, and to prepare them to succeed in, credit-bearing courses in their first semester and beyond
- significantly improve the retention and graduation rates of ESL students
- encourage and facilitate ESL students' integration into all aspects of college life by providing a solid grounding in the college academic-social community

In this chapter, I discuss four major aspects of our IEP:

1. the context into which our program fits, the student population that we serve, and the student needs that we at the college must meet

2. a description of our program and a rationale for a program of this type, including a brief summary of some relevant research into learning communities and content-based instruction

3. the innovative aspects of our program, including our approach to all aspects of language learning (especially writing) in an academic setting, our faculty development component, and other factors that foster the success of a strong academic learning community

4. practical ideas that readers in other institutions can take from our experience in working in a successful, collaborative program and adapt to their unique circumstances

The community college population, in general, and ESL students, in particular, are, for the most part, a population at high risk of dropping out of college because of their precarious economic and social situations. Therefore, we believe it is vital for them to participate in a program that will accelerate them through the ESL and English course sequence, prepare them with the academic skills necessary to do well in challenging courses in their major programs, help them gain self-confidence, and help them become a part of the wider college community. I will discuss in more detail how our program addresses student needs in the third section of this chapter, which focuses on the distinguishing features of our program.

◈ DESCRIPTION

We have structured our IEP, keeping in mind the four general goals listed in the introduction. The elements of our program, described below, also contribute to its distinctiveness and, therefore, are discussed in the next section of this chapter as well.

Block Program Structure

The IEP has several cohorts at three ESL proficiency levels: low intermediate (ESL 07), intermediate (ESL 09), and high intermediate (ESL 91). ESL classes at all levels integrate academic writing, reading, speaking, and listening skills.

Students in each cohort attend classes as a group and earn eight college credits in academic courses. (ESL courses have equated credits only, which means they count toward full-time status but not toward graduation.)

When they enter the college, full-time day students are placed into one of the three ESL cohorts, depending on their performance on the CUNY-wide reading and writing tests. Students in the program must register for the entire block of courses at their level.

There are generally 15–23 students in each program block. In addition to their classroom hours, students are scheduled for 4 hours of tutoring per week with their assigned tutors in the Reading and Writing Center. Credit courses in the low intermediate block include two speech courses and two SD courses. Intermediate- and high intermediate-level blocks consist of a sociology, psychology, or popular American history course; a speech course; and two SD courses.

Speech and ESL courses, which, of course, are specifically geared toward ESL students, are restricted to the students in the block. SD courses, one of which helps students to understand and maneuver through the college system, and the other, which focuses on career planning, are also limited to the students in a particular block. History, psychology, and sociology courses, however, are also open to students outside the block. There are advantages and disadvantages to these mixed classes, but we believe that, on the whole, IEP students have positive experiences in mixed classes. For one thing, students feel that these courses are the real thing, not a lesser version of the course adapted specifically for the ESL population.

Components That Shape the IEP

Connections With Other Departments

In the first semesters of the program, we needed to develop a working relationship with other department chairs to create our program blocks. We continue to work closely with these chairs every semester to schedule their courses for our program and to decide on faculty to teach these courses. We make an effort to find faculty who would enjoy working collaboratively. Brinton, Snow, and Wesche (1989) note that faculty who teach in a collaborative ESL program setting should be "particularly sensitive to the needs and abilities of second language learners" (p. 21). We meet with instructors to discuss the program. Even those who, at first, are skeptical about the ability of ESL students to do well in their courses find that the students are quite capable and often more highly motivated than their classmates who are not in the program.

We strongly recommend that our non-ESL teachers incorporate writing into their course curriculum and discussion into their class sessions (if they do not already do so). For instance, the sociology professor assigns at least two short papers (3–7 pages each) and includes some questions on her exams that require written responses of several sentences in addition to multiple-choice questions. We encourage non-ESL faculty to give written work a priority in IEP classes, and ESL instructors often read first drafts of short papers and other short written assignments that are later submitted to content-course instructors.

Faculty Development and Collaboration Among Faculty and Tutors

Faculty development activities are a vital component of any IEP. Through regular communication and sharing of ideas, faculty work toward structuring a dynamic and integrated curriculum. Brinton et al. (1989) suggest weekly meetings to facilitate communication between instructors who work together. Faculty development in the IEP takes the form of an initial 3-hour presemester meeting; monthly 90-minute meetings; and frequent team meetings over coffee, during lunch, on the phone, or by e-mail. Most of the time spent in meetings is dedicated to small team workshops: faculty, counselors, and tutors in the same block working together to coordinate course work and deal with problems in courses or with individual students. As Babbitt and Mlynarczyk (2000) point out:

> Teaching in a content-based ESL program does not constitute "business as usual" either for the ESL professors or for faculty in other departments. It is, therefore, essential to offer enough support to help participating teachers implement the program effectively. This faculty development work has two major purposes: (1) providing the teachers (and tutors, if possible) who will be working together with the necessary time to discuss and thoughtfully plan how they will coordinate and interrelate course material and (2) acquainting faculty members with different pedagogical techniques. (p. 31)

As a direct result of attending faculty development workshops and IEP and team meetings, the sociology instructor, for example, has added small-group work to her more traditional class sessions and has changed course requirements (as I have noted above).

Benesch (1992) discusses the necessity for faculty to work together to find ways to help students make difficult concepts their own. One way to do this is for content and ESL teachers to have students write about the difficult concepts, particularly relating these concepts to their own experiences.

At our meetings, we sometimes devise ways for team members to share various aspects of an assignment. The cultural artifact project for sociology is an example of team collaboration so that students can work on one project from different perspectives in different courses. The sociology teacher introduces the assignment and explains and discusses cultural artifacts and their function and fit in the sociological tapestry. In ESL class, students work on the project in groups, with worksheets created by the ESL teacher after discussions with the sociology teacher. In this class, students also work on understanding, explaining, and finding meaningful personal examples of concepts connected with the project in whole-class as well as in group activities. Work on various aspects of the project is continued in tutoring sessions. Students then present their work orally in speech class, and the speech teacher might also work on vocabulary, pronunciation, or other components of the project in her class. The ESL teacher looks over and comments on the worksheet, drafts, and the final written project. Final drafts are given to the sociology teacher to read as well. Interactions such as these among faculty play a vital role in our faculty development component because they yield positive results for our students.

Counseling

Counselors, who are faculty from the Department of Student Development, play an important role in facilitating students' adjustment to the college and in familiarizing them with all aspects of college life. They see students in their block for 2 hours each week in the SD classes and often meet with them outside the classroom as well. Students' problems, of course, can affect their performance in school, and counselors can sometimes assist students in ways that other instructors cannot. Often counselors and teachers on the same team work together to resolve issues that students face.

Tutoring

Tutoring is an important component of our program, and Kingsborough is fortunate to have a reading and writing center that serves students in developmental and other ESL and English courses. In the IEP, we have made extensive use of tutors. In addition to the 4 lab hours per week that they spend working with students, the two tutors assigned to each block also attend the ESL class 2 hours per week; the history, psychology, and sociology classes 2 hours per week; and the speech class 1 or 2 hours per week. In ESL class, tutors mostly facilitate small-group work. In other classes, the tutors take notes and occasionally work in small-group settings. Tutors are also encouraged to attend IEP meetings, workshops, and field trips.

Because of their close contact with students and their close connection with instructors, tutors provide an invaluable service to the program. They truly are liaisons, on practically a daily basis, between students and instructors. Often students feel more comfortable discussing issues with tutors because tutors are not in the same position of authority as instructors.

Collaboration Among Students

The creation of a strong and active learning community among students in each program block is, we believe, of paramount importance in the progress students make in academic writing and reading, analytical thinking, note taking, listening, and speaking. Students spend much ESL class time working in small groups. My intermediate-level class, for example, often spends at least 60% of a 2-hour class in groups. Much of the work students do focuses on their writing, which is often a written response to readings.[1] The group provides the audience for students' writing. Group members discuss, critique, and praise one another's writing; make suggestions; disagree and agree with each other's arguments; and generally support one another. The academic-social communities form: Students begin to feel comfortable with each other, learn to respect each other's views, realize their own views are valuable, and gain confidence in their abilities as learners and writers.

---

[1] Many of the writing activities described here are used in ESL and non-ESL classes in other institutions.

What Happens in the ESL Classroom?

Material covered in academic credit courses that IEP students take is demanding. Students are faced with the task of tackling difficult concepts in a variety of writing styles and genres. To deal with the learning of academic language and academic content, we have adopted a whole language, fluency first approach, developed at City College, CUNY, by MacGowan-Gilhooly and Rorschach, with grant support from the Fund for the Improvement of Post Secondary Education (FIPSE) (see MacGowan-Gilhooly, 1996a, 1996b). Whole language looks at the learning of all aspects of language as a social process, beginning with whole aspects of language and later moving to the smaller parts. Students begin by constructing a whole piece of writing, such as a complete essay, and are often amazed that they are able to do just that, rather than first constructing a sentence and then a paragraph. Much of the writing, particularly at the outset, is done in the supportive classroom environment. Writing begun in class and finished at home is shared with peers, as are drafts written at home.

The academic writing framework in the IEP incorporates extensive and varied writing, including freewriting, dialogic journal writing, point-of-view writing, essay writing with several revised drafts, academic project writing, rewriting of lecture and class discussion notes (from content courses), and reflective writing. The writing is tied to extensive reading of full-length works, generally novels, biographies, or plays; and also to essays, poems, and the texts of the sociology, history, or psychology courses. Readings are chosen to coordinate with themes of the credit courses in the block and, in the low intermediate level, to complement the theme devised by the ESL and speech instructors.

Point-of-View Writing and Freewriting

The activities in my intermediate-level class, most especially the writing activities, illustrate the integration of the whole language approach with a content-based focus. Students begin with Yezierska's (1975) novel, *Bread Givers*, about the struggles of an early 20th-century Russian Jewish family. The book is rich in issues covered in the sociology course, such as gender, economic class, sociological groups, culture shock, acculturation, and discrimination. One typical form of writing connected with this book is point-of-view writing: Students might look at a photo of the young protagonist, Sara, on the book's cover (or choose another character in the book) and write a point-of-view piece taking on the persona of the character. The first time point-of-view writing is done, it should be modeled for the class: Students write a few sentences as if they were the character they have chosen and read their sentences aloud (some are written on the chalkboard). Then they write their point-of-view piece, which they usually can finish in 30–40 minutes. Students read their writings to each other in small groups and discuss the writings. Groups choose a paper or two to read to the whole class. Often following activities such as this, students spend 5–8 minutes freewriting about their reactions to the activity.

Taking on the dual roles of author and respondent allows students to read their work to the peer group and to comment on the work of others, which helps students build self-confidence in their writing. Moreover, because the writing grows out of the readings, the writing activities themselves (e.g., writing, discussion, revision, feedback) force students to grasp the difficult concepts in the readings more firmly.

Journal Writing

Another important writing activity is journal writing, which can take many forms. Although the writing itself is usually individual, there are many social aspects involved in it. One type of journal writing is the double-entry journal (see MacGowan-Gilhooly, 1996a, 1996b). Students discuss what they are reading in *Bread Givers*, for example. They look at passages that interest them (e.g., surprise them, shock them, make them happy, infuriate them), then choose one to write about. They write the quotation on the left-hand side of their paper, along with the page reference of the quote. On the right-hand side of the paper, students write their response to the passage quoted. Responses that tend to be lengthy may include reaction to, and discussion, explanation, and analysis of, the passage. Responses also connect the passage to the students' experiences and to the sociological concepts illustrated in it. Journal writing helps students learn to refer to sources, think more analytically, and develop ideas for more formal essay writing. When I read the journals, I begin a dialogue with the student about the entries. If analysis or explanation is insufficient, I ask questions to elicit thoughtful written response.

Another type of journal writing is based on the sociology text. This journal format is more structured than the one described above. It can consist of questions I write designed to lead students to explore complex sociological issues and concepts discussed in their texts. Some discussion and written work on these journals is done in groups so that students have the opportunity to examine the issues with each other. If tutors are in class when this is done, they can guide students in their work. Again, students are asked to write in-depth responses to these journal questions. Generally, there is one question for each group that other groups do not work on. Each group presents its collective response to the class. Also, students sometimes compose their own sociology journal questions.

Essay Writing

There is an emphasis on essay writing in the IEP. One important purpose of essay writing is for students to focus on the process of writing and the changes they can make from draft to draft to improve what they have written. Although essay writing is individual, it is also a social experience. There are several essay topics based on *Bread Givers*. Students read the topics and discuss them. Then they choose one to write about. Students have a copy of *Bread Givers* with them while they are writing the essay so they can refer to the book in their writing. They are encouraged to use quotes from the book and to paraphrase short passages to support what they say in the essay. Then students give me the essays. The next day, I return their essays with a Peer Response Sheet, which asks questions such as "What did you especially like about this essay?" and "What could be added?" Students then break into small groups. Each student reads her or his essay, and the group discusses it in light of the questions on the Peer Response Sheet. The group recorder fills out the Peer Response Sheet with input from group members before the group moves to the next student's essay, and group roles are changed. After all group members have read their essays and received completed Peer Response Sheets, students respond in writing to the group's comments and discuss on the sheets how they plan to revise their essays. Students write revisions and then turn in their first and second drafts, along with the Peer Response Sheet. Often students make positive changes in their second drafts, based on peer review. I then respond to the essay and to the Peer Response Sheet, and students begin work on a third draft. Grammar is addressed within the context of student writing. Students not only revise essays by refocusing, analyzing, or illustrating their ideas, but also edit what they have written for tense consistency, verb form, sentence structure, and so forth. My students also work with a controlled-composition workbook, and our IEP has adopted a grammar reference book for use throughout the ESL sequence.

Project Writing

Students in my intermediate-level class also work for several weeks on writing projects that have topics with sociological themes. In groups, with a sociology syllabus in hand, students peruse the sociology text and respond to questions on a worksheet to explore possible topics (see Figure 1 for a sample Writing Project Worksheet).

Students narrow their choices, then discuss them with the class. Topics students have chosen include discrimination against Chinese students in a New York City high school; the impact of divorce on women in Iran; and reasons New York City teens join gangs. The writing project does not take the form of one large paper; rather, it is composed of several essays of various types on the same topic. The first essay is a position paper in which students discuss their topic, give reasons for their choice, tell what they know about their topic, and state what they would like to find out about it (see MacGowan-Gilhooly, 1996a, 1996b). Projects can include one or more point-of-view pieces, interviews, expository essays, and essays containing some researched material.

Activities in the ESL classroom are varied, student centered, intensive, challenging, and academically oriented. Students are given a great deal of work to complete for the course. It is sometimes a struggle for students to get all assignments done, but

---

Name: _____

Group members: _____

Writing Project #1

Group work: Choose a group leader for the day. Talk to each other about topics as you go through this worksheet, and read your freewriting to each other.

1. **Look through** the sociology syllabus for topics that interest you. **Write** several topics in the space below and include the chapters/page numbers in the text where these topics are discussed. Then **find** the topics in the sociology text and **read** a little about them.

2. **Discuss** topics you chose for #1 with your group. **Give reasons** for choosing those topics.

3. **Rewrite** your list of topics in the space below. **Add** any other topics you might be interested in writing about for your project. **Remove** any topics from #1 above that you're not particularly interested in.

4. **Freewrite** in the space below for about 7 or 8 minutes on two or three topics from #3. Use the back of this paper if necessary.

FIGURE 1. Writing Project Worksheet

feedback from students about what they have learned and how prepared they feel for college courses has been positive.

⬙ DISTINGUISHING FEATURES

The special aspects of our program, when taken together, serve to distinguish our program from other content-based or linked ESL programs. We believe that our IEP equips our students with the necessary foundation in their first semester to meet the demands of college and to become part of the larger college community.

We help our students achieve the program's goals through our focus on implementing and constantly refining the collaborative, interdisciplinary, block-program structure with its emphasis on learning communities.

Our IEP is based, in part, on the findings of recent research in the area of collaborative learning, most of which deals with non-ESL college students. In explaining the effectiveness of a coordinated studies program at Seattle Central Community College, Tinto et al. (1994) stated that the program "consciously seeks to engage students as full participants in the construction of knowledge" (p. 2). The IEP at Kingsborough Community College is also guided by this philosophy, with an emphasis on writing to learn. The development of our curriculum has also been influenced, as I have stated, by the whole language, fluency first approach to teaching ESL. Both approaches have been integrated into Kingsborough's IEP.

The faculty development component is crucial to our program, just as it is in the programs Tinto et al. (1994) have studied. Instructors from the different departments meet before classes begin to plan a coordinated curriculum of shared intellectual content. A greater number of classroom hours and the inclusion of peer counselors (in our case, we have in-class and out-of-class tutors) is another of Tinto et al.'s (1993) recommendations that we follow. The tutors provide a valuable link among the different courses, facilitating the kind of fine tuning that enables students to connect personally with the concepts they are studying, a process that Jacob, Rottenberg, Patrick, & Wheeler (1996) indicate is necessary if students are to acquire academic English through cooperative learning.

A distinguishing feature of Kingsborough's IEP is the type of extracurricular activities that it offers. Each semester includes a field trip for students that relates in some way to the work they do in their classes. For example, we have taken our students to Ellis Island, where they see a documentary film about the island, explore the museum in small groups, and respond to questions on a worksheet that we have created. Another of our trips is to the Lower East Side Tenement Museum in New York City, where students walk through a preserved apartment building that once housed thousands of immigrants from the late 19th through the early 20th century. This trip is meaningful for all immigrants and is especially interesting to those students who have read *Bread Givers* or Gold's (1996) *Jews Without Money*, which is one of the texts in the high intermediate-level ESL class.

In addition to trips off campus, students attend on-campus events, such as lectures by faculty or guests, during the course of the semester. This semester, my students attended a talk on domestic violence, held in connection with the Clothesline Project (a display of 1,000 hand-designed t-shirts showing the horrors of domestic violence). Students were required to take notes and do some writing about what they had learned about this topic. Several students had chosen this topic for their writing projects, so the discussion was particularly relevant for them. All students were affected by what they saw and heard and were eager to do something to prevent domestic violence. Students were also able to connect what they learned with what they were studying in sociology.

Students in community colleges generally graduate in 3–5 years. ESL students may take even longer. From our results so far, it appears that students who are enrolled in the IEP in their first semester in college, with the many enriching learning experiences they have and the progress they make in academic writing, have a greater chance of graduating within this time frame, if not sooner, or of transferring to other institutions and realizing their academic goals. This is not to suggest that all our IEP students succeed at the end of the semester. Some students, especially at the low intermediate level, must repeat the ESL course. Our program does not have all the answers, but it has improved our students' chances of success.

◈ PRACTICAL IDEAS

All of the ideas and activities discussed in the Description section can be adapted, individually or in combination, to readers' particular situations and institutions. At Kingsborough, the content of the academic credit-bearing courses drives the ESL curriculum. At some institutions, however, block programs that combine ESL with one or more other courses may not be possible to set up.

Consider Theme-Based Writing Courses

Linked courses, such as those in the IEP, which Brinton et al. (1989) refer to as adjunct courses, may be replaced by theme-based courses, or courses that focus on the content of a particular discipline, such as sociology. In the adjunct model, the content, rather than the content course, drives the curriculum, as it does in our ESL courses for continuing students.

Work Toward Creating Student-Centered Learning Communities

Regardless of the structure of the ESL program, instructors can make internal pedagogical shifts that stress student-centered writing activities in the content-based ESL classroom. Examples of such classroom activities previously discussed here include

- group work during a greater percentage of classroom hours
- student written response to readings
- in-depth analytical and interpretive student response to challenging readings
- sharing of writing and doing revisions based on peer and faculty response
- initiating journal writing and other forms of writing in class
- student collaboration on group and individual writing projects

When students become active learners by moving to the center of classroom writing activities and thus assuming responsibility for their own learning, their writing can thrive.

All materials that we use in the block-program courses (see Figure 1 for sample material) can be used as is or adapted to fit the particular content area or classroom situation of a particular institution. The essential element that instructors must strive to create in their classrooms in using the approach described here is a student-centered learning community. Instructors must trust students to work together in groups so that they can bond, collaborate with, support, and help each other. Through concentrated, focused, and meaningful activities, students can become academically empowered through their writing.

◈ CONCLUSION

Results of our IEP have continued to show positive results since its inception in the spring of 1995. As Table 1 illustrates, students do skip at all levels and, on the whole, do well in subsequent semesters at the college.

Table 2 shows the results for intensive ESL and nonintensive students enrolled in the Introduction to Sociology course during a semester when there were equal numbers of students from each group in the course. As Table 2 illustrates, there is a dramatic difference in the percentage of students who passed from each group as well as a significant difference in the grades the students earned. Thus, these results provide clear evidence of the successful impact of the IEP.

Retention, as I have stated, is an important goal of our program, and our students remain in college and continue to succeed long after they have completed their first semester with us. According to a report by Kingsborough's director of institutional research, "the overall grade performance of this group of students, through the Spring 1996 semester, was extraordinary" (Fox, 1996, p. 4). The overall

TABLE 1. INTENSIVE ESL PROGRAM PASS AND ACCELERATION RATES FROM SPRING 1998

	% Passing*	% Advancing 1 Level	% Skipping 1 Level
Low Intermediate Level ESL 07	78.9%	57.9%	21%
Intermediate Level ESL 09	88.23%	53.3%	52.9%
High Intermediate Level ESL 91	87.5%	18.75%	68.8%

*Passing students are those who either advanced to the next level (Column 2) or skipped a level (Column 3).

TABLE 2. COMPARISON OF RESULTS OF INTENSIVE ESL AND NONINTENSIVE STUDENTS IN INTRODUCTION TO SOCIOLOGY, SPRING 1997

Intensive ESL Students N = 15		Nonintensive Students N = 15	
Students who passed	93%	Students who passed	50%
Students who failed	7%	Students who failed	31%
Students who dropped	0%	Students who dropped	19%

grade point average (GPA) then was 3.42, higher than the college average, and 45.6% of the students in the program had a GPA of 3.49 or better. With a grant from the Professional Staff Congress of CUNY, we will follow the IEP students to measure their academic success by studying their academic achievements throughout their college careers.

The framing of the IEP curriculum in a strong content-based, interdisciplinary, and collaborative structure with a whole language, fluency first base fosters the creation of cohesive academic-social learning communities among students in the same block of courses. Our focus on having students develop an analytical thinking and writing base addresses our need to prepare students for the academic mainstream. The strong social network students form also prepares them for the challenges of college life. By developing this essential academic base in their first semester, students begin immediately to tackle the demands of college courses. In this dynamic learning community, which they maintain from class to class in the program, students participate actively, work together, and are listened to and valued by their peers. The learning community empowers students to develop reading, writing, and critical thinking skills through the academic writing they do. The academic-social bonds that students form in the program during their crucial first semester in college seem to facilitate their integration into the larger college community and to lay the foundation for a successful college career.

⬦ CONTRIBUTOR

Marcia Babbitt is codirector of ESL at Kingsborough Community College, New York, in the United States, and director of the IEP, a content-based, interdisciplinary program designed to accelerate the progress of entering ESL students. She is also coordinator of ESL for Kingsborough's College Now Program, which offers college-level courses for high school seniors in New York City. She holds an MA in Spanish language and literature from the University of Iowa and a PhD in linguistics from the CUNY Graduate Center. She is coauthor, with Rebecca Mlynarczyk, of "Keys to successful content-based ESL programs: Administrative perspectives," (in *Content-Based College ESL Instruction*, Lawrence Erlbaum, 2000).

CHAPTER 5

An Interdisciplinary, Interinstitutional, Learning Communities Program: Student Involvement and Student Success

Ann M. Johns

◈ INTRODUCTION

Like many public, postsecondary institutions throughout the world, San Diego State University (SDSU), in California, is concerned with attracting, and retaining, diverse students from within the local region and state. SDSU's students come from varied cultural and language backgrounds and from a variety of socioeconomic classes and literacy backgrounds. When the diverse students enroll, however, certain questions always arise. The faculty and administration ask, "How can we motivate students to learn while still introducing them to the (often unfamiliar) values, practices, and genres of university and professional cultures? How can we guarantee that their cultures, experiences, languages, and texts are valued, while still ensuring that the educational goals of the university are met? How can we ensure student success? And how can we develop, among them, the faculty, and the campus, a sense of community?" This chapter discusses SDSU's attempts to answer these, and other, questions related to the teaching and learning of students from a number of languages and cultures.

In 1991, when SDSU was in turmoil and losing students, the university administration decided it needed to become more student friendly. Part of its plan, the Freshman Success Program (FSP), included expanding an adjunct/learning communities model. By fall 1999, the program was serving more than 1,300 first-time freshmen, many of whom were bilingual or ESL students and the first in their families to attend a university. Although it will never become required of every student, the FSP could expand to include two thirds of the freshmen, or more than 2,000 students. And no wonder. Statistics for the program, kept since 1993, indicate that students enrolled in the FSP achieve significantly higher grade point averages and are more frequently retained[1] than their counterparts who do not enroll in the program.

---

[1] Retention here means remaining in the university. Generally, about 60% of the students at SDSU graduate within 6 years.

◈ CONTEXT

SDSU is one of the largest campuses in the California State University (CSU) system, and one of the largest in the western United States, with an enrollment of more than 28,000 students. One half of the student population is nonmajority (i.e., from an ethnic group that is not European-American), and unless testing and other requirements prevent the growth of the ethnic minority student population on campus, this number will grow over the coming years because the high school population in the area is becoming increasingly diverse.

The city of San Diego, where the university is located, is just 20 miles from the Mexican border town of Tijuana and adjacent to one of the busiest border crossings in the world. Although many of the diverse students within the community and the university are Latino, there are also large numbers of students of Filipino and Pacific Island backgrounds due to the proximity of the Pacific Rim and the presence of a large naval station. Since the 1970s, there has been an increasingly large number of Asian immigrants in the city, principally refugees from Vietnam, Laos, and Cambodia. More recent groups of immigrants have come from African nations, specifically Ethiopia, Eritrea, and Somalia, and a large number of Caldeans, originally from Iraq, live in the area. Russians have been immigrating to this region, and, more recently, San Diego has been welcoming families from the Balkans.

SDSU is located near the Ellis Island[2] area of San Diego, called City Heights, where many new immigrants find inexpensive housing or friends and family with whom to live as they settle in and begin their lives in the United States. The two high schools in the area enroll students from a variety of countries, including speakers of nearly 30 languages; thus, many of the classes offered are sheltered or ESL. SDSU has a special relationship with one of these schools, Hoover High, an issue that will be discussed later in the chapter.

◈ DESCRIPTION

Student Population

First-semester students of various descriptions enter the FSP. There are Educational Opportunity Program (EOP) students who, for financial and other reasons, may need special assistance and counseling throughout their university experience. Most of these are ESL or bilingual students, and the first members of their families to attend university. About half of these students are special admits.[3] A great deal has been written about students such as these, particularly by composition instructors, who are concerned with the continuing moves on the part of university administrations to rely for admissions decisions upon standardized tests that favor middle and

---

[2] Ellis Island, in the New York harbor, was the first stop for many immigrants to the United States during the last half of the 19th century and the beginning of the 20th. The term has become a metaphor for the area of first residences of new immigrants in the San Diego city heights.

[3] Twenty percent of the students each year are special admits, a group that includes EOP students, athletes, disabled students, and others, such as the children of alumni who make contributions. The regular admit student generally has a Scholastic Aptitude Test score of more than 1,000 and a high school grade point average of C+ or better. That is, these students from minority-isolated high schools are motivated students who do not meet the university entrance requirements.

upper class students (see Harklau, Losey, & Siegal, 1999; Mutnick, 1996; see also Rose, 1989, a well-known volume on underprepared students). A second group of FSP students are those who, like some in the EOP group, have not achieved satisfactory scores on the CSU placement examination, an Educational Testing Service instrument that has a multiple-choice reading and composing section and a holistically scored essay.[4] All students who do not achieve passing scores are relegated to remedial classes and required to pass written examinations within their first year of university. A third group of FSP students has passed the placement examination, and they are permitted to enroll in first-year, regular composition classes. Many of these students in the first-year FSP composition classes, like their remedial counterparts, are bilingual and ESL students. Other groups of students in FSP are not assigned to a composition class in the program. In the sciences and engineering, for example, students are enrolled in appropriate mathematics, chemistry, or other core classes, rather than in composition classes.

The Principal Program Option

Students enrolling in the FSP have three options, the most comprehensive of which will be discussed here. In this option, cohorts of 25 students block enroll in a linked/adjunct learning community's cluster of four classes, totaling eight semester units, that are related to each other but maintain distinct foci. There are two one-unit classes, the first of which is the University Seminar, taught by volunteer faculty, staff, or administrators. This course, typical of many freshman-year experience courses offered throughout the United States, meets once a week for an hour and has a maximum student enrollment of 13. It is designed to provide faculty mentoring, orient students to university life, and introduce them to a number of important campus resources, such as Career Services, University Advising, and the library. The second one-unit class, The Study Group, is taught to the 25-student cohort by a graduate student. It is designed to prepare the freshmen not only for their first-semester courses but also for the general study demands in other university classes. A third class is a three-unit, general education (GE) class, selected by the students on the basis of their interest or intended major.[5] There were 34 such GE class options offered in the fall 1999 semester. Finally, the same 25-student cohort enrolls in a three-unit composition class that is designed to focus upon the literacy demands of the GE class and, by extension, the other classes in the university. When students register, they participate together in all eight units.

Orientation and curricular meetings are held for University Seminar and study group faculty, and other faculty in the program are encouraged to coconstruct syllabi and to meet periodically to discuss students, curricula, and other issues relating to

---

[4] As is the case with most standardized tests administered in the United States, there is a close correlation between the scores on this test and socioeconomic class. A recent article in the *San Diego Magazine* (Zimmerman, 1999), for example, showed perfect correlations between wealthy (and poorer) schools and the Scholastic Aptitude Test (SAT) scores. The SAT is a widely administered entrance examination developed by Educational Testing Service, which also markets the Test of English as a Foreign Language (TOEFL) and the Graduate Record Exam (GRE).

[5] GE, often called the breadth requirement, is central to the goals of this campus and many others in the United States. At SDSU, students devote one third of their 124–133 graduation load to GE classes.

the program. It is important here to discuss some of the factors relating to faculty because, along with the students, they are the central players in the program. University Seminar faculty are volunteers; only recently have they been given a small stipend with which to entertain students or buy books and other materials. These faculty are drawn from all divisions of the university: from regular faculty (i.e., those teaching in the disciplines); from various administrative personnel, including the university president and his wife, and several vice presidents; from Student Affairs offices, such as the Advising Center and Student Resource Center; and, in a few cases, from student mentor groups in the various colleges. The faculty who teach the GE classes are generally handpicked because the FSP administration wants to guarantee that they are the best instructors for first-year students. Most are very interested in the challenges involved in teaching these students and in principles of teaching itself. In 1997–1998, several GE faculty joined the composition faculty in a funded Curriculum Transformation Project to provide workshops in reading, writing, and collaborative learning for all interested faculty. The composition instructors are also handpicked, on the basis of their interest in going outside of their own classrooms to explore the demands and rhetorical situations provided in the GE classes. Many composition faculty work very closely with the GE faculty, in some cases coconstructing syllabi and writing tasks for their shared students. (See Johns, 1997, for a more complete discussion of syllabus coconstruction.)

Curriculum

There are several distinguishing features in the FSP, the most unusual of which relate to the linked/adjunct arrangement (see, e.g., Brinton, Snow, & Wesche, 1989, for a complete discussion of adjunct models) and to the portfolio program design in the composition classes. The following is an outline of the eight class units.

General Education Classes (3 Units)

GE classes, in covering various disciplinary areas, are required of first- and second-year students to ensure the breadth of their education. During the past few years, GE classes from the following disciplines have been FSP options: sociology, Africana studies, anthropology, history, geography, Chicano/Chicana studies, political science, speech communication, natural science, chemistry, information and decision sciences, biology, psychology, philosophy, drama, and economics.

The Study Group (1 Unit)

The study group teachers are chosen from among graduate students by the department offering the GE class. Although charged with teaching study habits that can generally be applied to all classes, these graduate students are often most successful working with the content of and specific strategies for the GE class in which the students are enrolled, viewing it as a kind of microcosm for student skills development. Training sessions are held for the study group teachers, and the teachers are counseled and observed by expert faculty who have previously taught these classes.

Composition/Literacy Classes (3 Units)

As noted earlier, these classes are offered at the freshman level and at the remedial (subfreshman) or developmental level, depending upon placement test scores. Since 1985, the curricula for the composition courses have been honed by a group of expert teachers, as described below.

Curricula for the Literacy Classes

For the Developmental Classes

Those students, many of whom are ESL and bilingual students, who do not achieve sufficiently high scores on the university placement examination are required to enroll in one of the developmental classes. Though each of the composition classes is linked to a GE class, all FSP developmental writing classes share common goals, a common portfolio design, and a common examination. The goals are that students will be able to

- produce a variety of texts under varied circumstances
- develop an awareness of a range of discourse styles in public prose, including academic discourses
- increase their repertoire of strategies for approaching different kinds of reading and writing tasks
- demonstrate awareness of the possibilities for multiple interpretations of subject matter and texts by teachers and students
- develop a sense of power and motivation in relation to the language, contexts, topics, and texts of academic disciplines

As can be seen from this list of goals, the curriculum committee for the FSP developmental classes draws from two major approaches to the teaching of literacy: the psycholinguistic, or process, approach and the social constructionist approach (see Johns, 1997). The faculty believe that the contexts and cultures for writing are central and that students need to develop a variety of strategies for approaching rhetorical tasks in an unpredictable number of contexts. Thus, the writing process is not completed in a vacuum; instead, processes depend upon the types of tasks that students are attempting (see, e.g., Horowitz, 1986). Other goals relate to motivation and multiple interpretations of tasks and readings, ways in which students' own experiences and approaches are valued, and reflected upon, in the classroom. Instructors want to enable students to comprehend and critique academic texts and to use their own experiences to construct and analyze their responses to classroom tasks.

Portfolios

To ensure reflection and a variety of texts in the classroom, the FSP developmental class curriculum committee has designed a portfolio that allows for considerable teacher creativity and student input. (See Johns, 1997, pp. 132–150, for a discussion of basic portfolio principles, models, and management.) Students must complete the portfolios to the instructor's satisfaction before they are able to take the final, timed examination. The portfolio consists of the following entries:

Required: (a) summary/abstract/précis or summary response, (b) timed writing completed in the classroom, and (c) semester reflection

Options (three are chosen):

1. paper for which students gather and analyze data (GE related)
2. paper, including observation and report or critique
3. interview (GE discipline related)
4. collaborative writing project (GE related)
5. intertextual project (in which students examine one text in relation to another)
6. argumentative or persuasive essay
7. letter project, focusing on purpose and audience (using GE material)
8. genre-based project, generally analytical (GE related)

The students and faculty select the entries together, over time, after considerable study of the academic requirements of the GE class in which the student cohort is enrolled. In almost every university class, some type of summary or abstract of lecture notes, readings, or data is necessary. Timed writing, especially timed examinations, is the most common type of writing completed in most first- and second-year classes (see Horowitz, 1986). The semester reflection encourages students to look back on their first-semester literacy and social experiences. The options are taken from a list of genres and rhetorical strategies garnered from university classes and faculty since 1985 (see Johns, 1997) and a large body of research on the demands of university classes at the undergraduate level (see, e.g., Carson, Chase, Gibson, & Hargrove, 1992). Instructors have found this developmental class portfolio to be generative, in other words, to be sufficiently broad so that they can exploit the genres and cultures of the GE class to the benefit of their composition class students.

A Final, Timed Examination

In the last analysis, the composition teachers in the developmental classes are coaches. In addition to assisting the students in researching their GE class, preparing a portfolio, and processing a variety of texts, they are also preparing them for the final examination, which, graded holistically by other FSP writing instructors, is the determining factor in whether students will proceed to regular freshman-level composition classes or be required to enroll in a developmental class. The following is one example of the prompt for the 2-hour timed, final examination:

Introduction:

This semester you have been enrolled in a package of classes that focus on a GE class. This GE class has been the subject of many of your writing assignments in your composition class as well as the focus of your study group class.

Question:

In every college class, there are certain terms, concepts, or events that stand out as particularly important: (a) Choose one term, concept, or event discussed in your GE class, and 2) explain it and its importance to the course. Be sure to explain both the term, concept, or event AND its importance to the discipline of the GE course in specific detail. (Remember, your reader is not familiar with your class.)

Directions:

Write an essay discussing the above topic. Make sure your focus is clear, your essay is well organized, and the points you make are well developed. Your essay should show that you are knowledgeable about your Integrated Curriculum GE class. Be sure to provide plenty of specific support.

For the Regular, Freshman-Level Composition Class

The goals for this FSP class include all of the goals for the developmental classes listed above; however, there is much more emphasis upon intertextuality and close reading of difficult texts. Most composition instructors not only exploit the texts and language of the GE class, but they also use a literacy class reader, such as Kiniry and Rose (1993). As is the case in the developmental classes, the freshman-level composition class uses the GE class as a laboratory for students from which they can draw content, practice reading and writing for a specific academic context, and apply what they learn in the writing class.

Portfolio

There is no timed, final examination required for the freshman-level composition class, so the portfolio takes on an even more important role. In most cases, the portfolio entries are graded before they are entered, and, in addition to these grades, the students are given a specific percentage of the class grade (e.g., 15%) for completing and compiling the portfolio and semester reflection. Like the portfolio for the developmental class, this one is based upon a combination of social construction-ist and process approaches.

The required entries in the freshman-level portfolio are the following:

1. personal essay (with analysis)
2. source- or data-driven paper, related to the GE course
3. summary, abstract, or précis
4. genre analysis related to the GE course
5. reflection on the portfolio and the semester's experience in FSP

Of course, this portfolio is a selected collection (see Johns, 1997). Much more reading and writing is completed at this level than the portfolio entries indicate.

The Hoover Project

The FSP also emphasizes faculty cooperation and student involvement. The most ambitious effort so far attempted in these areas involves a community-based learning project with a human migration theme launched in cooperation with a local high school, Hoover High, and taught by the FSP faculty to the cohort of students who have chosen cultural anthropology as their GE class. Eight faculty are involved in this project: three who teach humanities and social sciences to first-year high school students (9th-grade, 13- to 14-year-olds), two composition instructors (for EOP developmental and freshman-level classes), the instructor of the cultural anthropol-ogy class, and the two study group leaders. As was noted earlier, Hoover High, located near SDSU, is in San Diego's Ellis Island area. It has the lowest college entrance scores on the Scholastic Aptitude Test (SAT) of any high school in the large county (788 out of 1,500, with 39% of the students having taken the examination; see Zimmerman, 1999), and, not surprisingly, it has a very high percentage of new immigrants, who represent nearly 30 different language groups. In addition to meeting the curricular goals of the composition classes and the goals of the anthropology class, the FSP faculty involved in this project have developed the following goals so that students in their theme-based project will be able to

- value the diverse experiences of their high school partners and their families, particularly those relating to issues of migration into and within the United States

- develop more sophisticated research skills: interviewing techniques, use of the World Wide Web and the library, note taking, citing, paraphrasing, and other necessary abilities

- complete increasingly difficult tasks, resulting in a complex, intertextual, research paper

- provide academic and personal mentoring for diverse high school students

- demonstrate their knowledge of subject matter and their own writing processes through speeches to the high school students and written reflection

This project is centered on the development of a research paper and a mentoring process throughout an academic semester (15 weeks). Students from each of the schools (Hoover High and SDSU) visit each other's campuses, and the university students model for the high school students a research process and mentor these students about issues of academic life at universities. The following sections present the semester plan for the Hoover Project.

September

Students at both campuses are introduced to the program, and they read materials about human migration and cultural persistence that appear in the high school texts or are provided by the GE instructor at the university. The SDSU students are given expert instruction and readings on conducting ethnographic interviews. After their instruction and reading, they develop a scripted interview that focuses on issues of migration, specifically cultural values and practices that have persisted in the migrating families despite dislocation. The SDSU students practice interviewing, using their scripted questions with their own families and often uncovering information of which they had been unaware. The first text the SDSU students produce is a family tree and interview write-up from their own families' experiences. This interview write-up becomes an entry in the portfolio. At the same time, the Hoover students interview their families about migration histories, using the questions developed by the SDSU students. Late in September, the SDSU students visit the Hoover campus and complete a follow-up interview, generally with students who are not in their own cultural groups, again relying upon the questions developed earlier. The SDSU students write and analyze the Hoover students' interview responses, making attempts to locate particular topics that they can use as the focus of their semester's research paper. Some of these topics have been food, festivals, religious observances, practices relating to family and gender, the mix of old and new at occasions such as Thanksgiving, family literacy practices, and storytelling.

October

In the next month, the Hoover students prepare to interview the SDSU students on related topics. Then they come, with their teachers, to visit the university campus. Often, this is the high school students' first visit to the university, and their reactions can be unusual. In one case, a Hoover student asked his SDSU counterpart whether SDSU was a real university, and in others, Hoover students were amazed that there was so much emphasis on eating and shopping on campus. Many comment on the ethnic diversity of the university and the crowded nature of the campus. While at SDSU, the Hoover students are taken on a campus tour, after which the SDSU students give formal talks on the FSP, the literacy demands of the university, how to obtain scholarships, and how to succeed at the university. Before they leave, the Hoover students interview the SDSU students about their families' migration histories and share lunch with them at one of the university's several fast-food centers. The Hoover students write reflections on their visits, which are later read at the final student meeting in November.

November

Hoover students write up their interview reports from their SDSU visit in October. SDSU students begin to use the Internet, the library, and other sources to pursue the migration topics raised in their interviews with the Hoover students. SDSU students are instructed in the composition classes about the construction of a complex research paper with the following headed sections: (a) an introduction, including the importance and purposes for the study; (b) methodology, including the methods pursued during the interviews and while completing Internet and library research; (c) the results of all of the research; (d) analysis of the results; and (e) a conclusion, including comments on their problems and successes with the research and a critique of the assignment.

December

In the final student-to-student encounter, the SDSU students visit the Hoover campus a second time with trifold displays of their research papers and the drafts for the research paper on which they are currently working. The SDSU students discuss the various steps involved in developing their research papers, to be graded in the anthropology and composition classes. They also meet with the Hoover students in groups to discuss their trifolds and papers. Then the Hoover students present reflections on their experiences with the research process and with their interviews with the SDSU students.

Back at SDSU, the composition instructors and the anthropology instructor grade the final research papers using agreed-upon criteria.

January

At Hoover, the high school students present an exhibition, with trifolds. They also write a reflection on the research conducted in cooperation with the SDSU students.

◈ DISTINGUISHING FEATURES

In addition to distinctive features, such as the emphasis on learning communities and the literacy portfolios with selected, socially produced processes and products, the most ambitious aspect of the FSP is the interinstitutional, theme-based Hoover project. It is time consuming and can also be discouraging for a number of reasons, such as the difficulty of maintaining interview partnerships with Hoover students, whose families are often transient. In addition, most of the Hoover students have no access to computers with Internet and e-mail capability. As a result, the ideal, continuous mentoring arrangements between the students at each school sometimes cannot be maintained.

Despite the difficulties that must be overcome in a project such as this, particularly involving a school as diverse and complicated as Hoover, SDSU faculty's efforts have resulted in achieving a number of goals important to learning communities projects. On the SDSU side, the so-called remedial (developmental) students are empowered by their opportunities to mentor younger students who are like themselves. They and their Hoover counterparts are able to draw from their own experiences and those of their families to produce academic texts, a factor that is central to pedagogies in our multiliterate world (see Cope & Kalantzis, 2000). The university students are introduced to various types of research, complex intertextual demands, and opportunities to use, rather than just be introduced to, the Internet and the technology of the library. The students are able to demonstrate their competencies in ways that are considerably different from standardized tests. Perhaps most impressive are their oral presentations before the Hoover students during the two meetings at the high school. Faculty, administrators, and community members are invited to these sessions, and all are impressed by the abilities of most of these so-called remedial students to make public presentations before a large audience. Also important are the intangibles: The SDSU students form lasting ties and friendships with their peers in the FSP classes and, when possible, with the younger students from the high school.

For the SDSU faculty, there are a number of rewards. The cultural anthropology instructor has found that the student research papers are more sophisticated and better written than those of other freshmen, and she is very pleased with the personal interaction of students within the class and study groups. The composition instructors are able to require excellent final editing, as well as other process elements, because students are graded for process and final product. Faculty are also able to destabilize the students' rather limited theories of genres, an important criterion for student success (Johns, in press).

◈ PRACTICAL IDEAS

I hope that by reading this chapter, particularly the curricular sections, literacy teachers in many parts of the world can glean practical ideas for their classrooms. This section presents a summary of suggestions collected from FSP literacy instructors.

Provide a Variety of Literacy Experiences

Novice students need to have varied textual experiences. More than 10 years of research have shown that students come to universities with very limited genre theories, based upon the curricular requirements of their secondary schools. These experiences may have been principally with literature, personal reflection, and the five-paragraph essay, as is the case in the FSP. In other parts of the world (e.g., parts of Asia and Latin America), the experiences may have been with texts that are useful for test preparation but limited in scope and value for the professional and academic world, particularly in a second or foreign language. Students need to read and write texts from different communities, based upon different assumptions and values, and organized in different ways. There is a very large world beyond the academic essay. Students need to know this and work with texts that are not in this genre. I would argue that portfolio designs such as the ones adopted for the FSP lend themselves to an emphasis upon variety, analysis, and reflection.

Provide Meaningful and Demanding Textual Experiences

Leki and Carson (1997) paint a disturbing picture of students' experiences with texts in ESL composition classes. They found that, in most classes, students were not expected to be text-responsible; in other words, they were asked to react to texts but not to integrate them into their own writing in ways comparable to disciplinary classes. The FSP, because of its linked, adjunct nature and, in the case of the interinstitutional project, the specific ways in which students integrate data, requires text responsibility on the part of these novice students. Students must use a variety of texts, including interview data, for their argumentation, for the presentation of their results, and for their analyses in the conclusion. I heartily agree with Leki and Carson (1997) that these abilities will serve students well throughout their academic careers.

Help Students Develop Technological Literacies

As I have noted, technological expertise is often dependent upon the type of school and socioeconomic class. Thus, universities, and secondary schools, must provide opportunities for all students to use the various technologies available for the classroom (see, e.g., Adam & Artemeva, in press, on the use of newsgroups to discuss a writing task).

Evaluate Students' Work in a Variety of Ways

University and secondary schools' examinations often do not test what students can do. For example, the SDSU remedial students in the interinstitutional program were excellent public speakers, as demonstrated in their presentations to the high school students. In the high school and university FSP classes, these students are graded for their presentations as well as for their traditional reading and writing abilities. It is challenging to interview a student from another culture whom you have never met; however, these students were more than able to warm up the Hoover students to get the information necessary to complete their interview assignment and research paper. Neither public speaking nor interviewing are assessed skills in most university classes.

Encourage Students to Draw From Their Own Cultural and Linguistic Experiences, and Those of Their Families, in Writing and Reading Texts

The students in the FSP wrote very few traditional personal essays. Yet, they used the interview data from their families and their own experiences in writing their research papers and completing analyses of their findings. It appears that students can increase their literacy repertoires and draw from their experiences, and this is what the FSP has attempted to help them achieve, especially in the interinstitutional program described.

Help Students Develop Positive Self-Images

Finally, students who are engaged and who have positive visions of themselves as communicators are better speakers, readers, and writers. The fact that the students who did not pass the freshman examination were able to mentor the high school students in a variety of ways affected text production and student pride in their work. The GE anthropology instructor, and the high school teachers, were very pleased with student engagement—and with the results of the final papers and presentations made in November and January.

◈ CONCLUSION

The kinds of programs possible in one context may not be possible in another, as those of us who have traveled widely and spoken with many of our counterparts in other countries know. However, the principles that are applied to these approaches can be—and have been—applied elsewhere. Thus, I hope that this discussion will be useful to colleagues wherever they live and work.

◈ CONTRIBUTOR

Ann M. Johns is professor of linguistics and writing studies and faculty coordinator for the Center of Teaching and Learning at San Diego State University, in California, in the United States. Her major interest is academic literacy, and she has published and presented for many years on the subject.

CHAPTER 6

Capitalizing on Contacts, Collaboration, and Disciplinary Communities: Academic ESL Options in a Large Research University

Roberta J. Vann and Cynthia Myers

❧ INTRODUCTION

Collaborative learning and genre-based assignments have received much attention in recent years (e.g., Johnson, Johnson, & Smith, 1991; Swales & Feak, 1994), and these trends are especially relevant to university ESL students. These students face challenges in connecting with the larger academic community often because they lack contacts with other university students and professors outside their cultural group or because they fail to connect skills learned in ESL classes with discipline-specific writing needs. At Iowa State University (ISU), these problems have been the catalyst for renovating our academic ESL program through seeking ways in which nonnative-English-speaking (NNS) students can connect with the native-English speakers (NS) on campus and with their own academic disciplines. In this chapter, we describe the challenges facing our students and ways in which our program has used collaborative and inductive approaches to meet these challenges.

Although ISU is located in Ames, a midsized, midwestern U.S. city in which it seems the use of English would be inevitable, some language populations, notably Chinese and Korean, are large enough that a student from one of these countries, especially a graduate student, can go for days without speaking anything except his native language. It is not uncommon for the lingua franca of a lab in one of the sciences to be Chinese and for a student's office mate and roommates to be Chinese. There are Korean and Chinese restaurants, Asian grocery stores, and religious services offered in Korean and Chinese. Unfortunately, some international students report receiving their degrees without having made an American friend. This problem of isolation and its contribution to the communication problems of international students was commented on by several faculty in a recent university survey. One faculty member pointed out that although NNS international students' English language skills improve while they are enrolled in English courses, their skills quickly deteriorate once the students leave the course because of a lack of interaction with English-speaking students. These NNS students, especially at the graduate level, face additional challenges in learning disciplinary-specific writing conventions. Berkenkotter, Huckin, and Ackerman (1991) point out that "students entering academic disciplines need a specialized literacy that consists of the ability to use discipline specific rhetorical and linguistic conventions to serve their purposes as writers" (p. 191). Our academic English program must not only fit with the standards set by the university but also meet students' specialized writing needs in majors as diverse as architecture, accounting, and agricultural science. This chapter illustrates ways in which our academic English program addresses the cultural and discipline-specific needs of our students.

◈ CONTEXT

Almost 2,700 international students are enrolled at ISU (more than 5% of the undergraduates and 33% of the graduates). Refugees and immigrants, whose native languages are not English, add to the diverse backgrounds and varied academic writing needs of the ESL population.

ISU's ESL academic writing program serves undergraduates and graduates who are NNSs. It is designed to help undergraduates meet the writing needs most immediately in their two-semester, first-year writing courses and in subsequent undergraduate courses and to assist graduate students in writing a thesis or dissertation as well as with other academic writing needs.

Students in the program have passed the Test of English as a Foreign Language (TOEFL) requirements for university admission (500 for undergraduates and 500–600 as set by individual departments at the graduate level) but have fallen short on the Iowa State Academic English Placement Test. Students who do not pass the test, as scored by a team of ESL teachers, may be assigned to one or possibly two semesters of ESL writing courses as well as other ESL courses focusing on listening or reading skills. Classes are limited to 17 students and are taught by a combination of tenure-track, adjunct, and graduate student instructors.

◈ DESCRIPTION

Principles of cooperative learning, learner-centered learning, and cross-cultural exchange provide the guiding philosophy for the ESL academic writing program. The following descriptions specify how our goals for the program manifest themselves in the four classes described below.

Academic English I for NNS Undergraduates and Graduates

This class, for NNS undergraduates and graduates who have passed the TOEFL and have been admitted to ISU but still have significant writing problems, focuses on the writing of short academic papers with the goal of developing fluency and self-confidence, controlling troublesome grammatical structures in the context of written assignments, and increasing vocabulary. The class includes grammar and editing exercises in context. Types of assignments include writing business letters and summaries, reading responses, conducting an interview of a professor, and writing journal or notebook entries or e-mail messages.

Because students in this class often lack contact with U.S. students, the program has encouraged interactions through collaborative assignments between this class and a section of an English descriptive grammar course for undergraduates. Students in the grammar course are primarily NSs who are prospective teachers, including elementary education majors and English majors. In one 8-week assignment, for instance, the U.S. grammar students, who were learning about the grammar of their own language, were paired with NNSs in Academic English I. The partners met weekly, working through a series of assignments on aspects of grammar that the NSs knew intuitively (e.g., order of adjectives, time signaling words with verb tense, formation of passive voice, article use) and on assignments that helped raise the awareness of language differences between English and the languages of the international students. (See Figure 1 for a sample assignment.)

For the ESL students, this weekly meeting gave them an opportunity to talk with NSs as well as to practice problematic aspects of grammar that they might use in writing assignments. Many of the NSs in the grammar class became interested in

---

Native Language Comparisons

Many of the difficulties encountered by language learners occur because of differences between their first and second language in the phonology (sound system), syntax (phrase and clause structure), and morphology (word formation). This exercise will allow you to compare some of the differences between English and your partner's native language.

Activity 1

Have your partner express the following sentences in her native language. She should first write the sentence exactly as she would if she were writing a letter to a friend at home, using the same characters or script that she normally uses. Then your partner should try to translate it, word for word, back into English, so that you can see some of the differences.

Example: It is very cold today!

Translated into Spanish: Hace mucho frío hoy.

Literal (word for word) translation back into English: Makes much cold today.

She and I have been studying English grammar this semester.

At 4 o'clock every Thursday, she studies with me in the Union.

I studied chemistry with her last night.

Would you like to study with me?

Tell her that I think she is very nice.

With your partner, try to describe some of the differences you see between your languages. Do the words in both languages come in the same order? How are questions formed? What changes are made to indicate tense (e.g., *study, studied, have been studying, have studied*)? Do you see verb changes depending on person (e.g., In English we say *I study*, but *She studies*.)? Do you notice any difference in pronouns (e.g., *she, her, I, me*)? Are there differences in orthography (the writing system)? Would your partner use different forms if she were writing to a teacher rather than to a friend? What other differences does your partner notice between English and her native language?

FIGURE 1. Sample Collaborative Project Assignment for Academic English I and NS Grammar Course

talking to the international students about issues other than grammar. One U.S. student wrote in her final project evaluation:

> Perhaps the most interesting thing that I am taking away from my meetings with Ling[1] is her . . . interest in American culture. She has been in the United States almost two years, and yet she has had little contact with anyone her own age who is "Americanized." She had loads of questions for me. Since she is a newlywed and I am getting married in July, she was very interested in American wedding customs. We looked at pictures and I showed her a couple of my wedding planning books. Often times we had a few minutes before I had to head to my next class, so we talked about the similarities and differences between China and the U.S.

Though the project was created to heighten the U.S. students' awareness of their internal grammar and as a way to give the ESL students extra practice in several grammatical features, the greatest benefit of the project for both groups appeared to be the opportunity to talk to one another.

Academic English II for NNS Undergraduates

Academic English II focuses on developing the writing and critical reading skills that students will need in their first-year composition and other undergraduate classes, including fluency in writing and command over troublesome grammatical points, as well as utilizing published sources in writing research and persuasive papers, understanding and interpreting essay exam questions, and formulating appropriate responses. Assignments provide writing experience in organizing and developing ideas, summarizing, and synthesizing sources. Other assignments involve practice in responding to essay examination questions and completing journal entries or e-mail messages.

Although Academic English II is composed entirely of NNSs, various assignments in the class encourage them to develop skills for gathering information and communicating with their ESL classmates and NSs outside the ESL classroom. One text used for the course, *Academic English* (Leki, 1995), includes an assignment called "Extracting the Main Idea from Survey Data" (p. 89), which has been effective in encouraging students to collaborate in small groups to find a topic for a survey, create effective questions, interview NSs, and then grapple with organizing complex data. Students learn to negotiate in their small groups to arrive at an appropriate topic for their surveys and to work together to develop good interview questions. The assignment allows students to investigate whatever interests them, and students have chosen topics ranging from U.S. opinions about U.S. President Clinton's impeachment hearings to U.S. attitudes toward junk food. The experience of interviewing others to gather data for the project also gives students valuable practice in asking questions, taking notes, and creating follow-up questions to get more information. Finally, when the groups compile their data from the interviews, they rely on one another's information to write individual papers and work together to decide on effective ways of organizing and presenting the information they have gathered.

---

[1] The student's name is a pseudonym.

Another assignment that helps foster communication among the ESL students in the class is an e-mail journal. Students regularly write and submit journals on e-mail. The journals themselves are a place where students can discuss ideas and improve fluency without focusing on correctness. Each week, students submit their journal entries by e-mail to the instructor and to a classmate; the classmate responds to the journal in a second weekly assignment, again copying the entry to the instructor. Having students read and write to each other is a way of broadening the audience for their writing, and in their responses, students may develop the ideas of the original writer, sometimes providing examples from their own perspective, sometimes disagreeing, sometimes writing about a related experience. Students typically have a choice from several assigned topics that relate to their current major paper, and they usually exchange journals with different partners each week. One student wrote the following as an end-of-course evaluation:

> Although I was disappointed at first to fail the Placement Test, English . . . enlightened me a lot. And the most interesting part of the class was the journal because it let me write my thought without worrying that it would effect the grade. My English surely improved a lot after this course.

Several staff members have developed projects to help connect NS and NNS students. During spring semester 1999, an instructor teaching Academic English II and another teaching first-year composition collaborated to develop a connection between their courses and to provide NSs and NNSs with opportunities for cross-cultural interaction (Hykes & Santiago, 2000). The two teachers began by grouping their students in e-mail discussion groups composed of three U.S. composition students and two ESL students. The students contacted one another by e-mail to get acquainted, and then, because the classes met at the same time, were able to meet jointly several times during the semester for group activities. During the first meeting, the groups began by discussing a list of cultural comparison questions, which served as a prewriting activity for the composition students' cultural comparison papers. After they had narrowed the topics for their papers, the composition students later e-mailed the ESL students in their groups with follow-up questions. Later in the semester, when the ESL class was working on their interview paper, the classes met again, and the ESL students practiced their group-drafted interview questions with members of the composition class. When both classes were working on research papers near the end of the semester, the classes met for a peer evaluation. Finally, during a fourth group meeting, students from the composition class shared excerpts of books they were reading for a final project, explaining why each book would or would not be a good choice for a recommended reading list in the cross-cultural first-year composition class. Two of the criteria for their recommendations, that the book be an accurate portrayal of another culture and that it be at an appropriate reading level and of interest to composition students, were aspects the composition students discussed with the ESL students, who were sometimes able to provide firsthand insights into the cultures described in the books and give feedback on whether the excerpt seemed at an appropriate reading level. In one case, for instance, the composition student had read a book about the cultural revolution in China, and a Chinese student from the ESL class was able to provide more up-to-date descriptions of life in China in the 1990s.

These varied approaches to helping students make connections with other students and to encourage communication with their classmates and those outside the class enrich the Academic English II course for undergraduates.

Cross-Cultural First-Year Composition

ISU requires a two-semester sequence of first-year writing courses for all undergraduates. First-Year Composition I provides an introduction to college-level writing strategies, with an emphasis on critical reading and thinking skills. Writing assignments typically have a personal or narrative focus; students also read and discuss essays from many sources. First-Year Composition II again focuses on developing writing strategies appropriate for university academic needs, but in this semester the emphasis is on expository writing, with a focus on arguing a position, analyzing texts, and using primary and secondary sources.

NNSs in our first-year composition program have, since the 1970s, been integrated with NSs across class sections of the program. Although some of the NNSs take one or two academic ESL writing classes before entering the first-year composition classes, all are expected to take the composition class with NSs and compete on an equal footing.

To reduce the sense of intimidation that ESL students may experience as the minority in mainstream classes, in 1994, the department began offering cross-cultural sections composed of approximately half international and half U.S. students. Since then, the department has continued to offer seven or eight cross-cultural sections each semester. These sections use readings, classroom activities, and assignments that emphasize cross-cultural interaction. Students may choose to register for a section that is cross-cultural or one that is not.

Cross-cultural classes encourage students to be open to the multiple points of view of their classmates. In discussing issues from an international perspective, students learn to tolerate ambiguity and avoid overgeneralizations. In one typical assignment, students in cross-cultural groups interview each other about aspects of culture. In their papers, they write about cultural differences but also find common ground. (See Figure 2 for a sample assignment.)

Students explore topics like dating and marriage, the roles and responsibilities of parents and children, gender roles within families as well as broader issues such as the role of sports in a culture or the values that underlie educational philosophies. Their readings on related topics from a cross-cultural reader (e.g., Hirshberg, 1995; Stamford, 1996; Verberg, 1997), and their discussions of the issues, help the students to see their own society, and that of others, from new perspectives. An assignment as simple as describing a custom from one's own culture for a diverse audience can challenge students to more fully understand unconscious cultural assumptions. For example, in a paper entitled "Chopsticks," a second-generation Vietnamese student explained for her classmates the conflict she felt trying to maintain her Vietnamese roots while being an American. Another student who had written about U.S. weddings commented that she had always thought of her Iowa culture as being modern, yet she realized that many of the customs she was describing had roots in older, established traditions or even superstitions; she found similarities with her group members from Korea and Sweden, who also explained traditional customs.

For this paper, you will compare an aspect of your culture to that of one or more other cultures. Our class discussion and readings will focus on several related topics having to do with the family, relationships, and community; part of your task will be to accurately record information from small group discussions so that you can quote or paraphrase comments made by other group members. You should narrow your topic, develop it with specific detail and examples, and share insights into your or another's culture. Your multicultural classmates are your audience, and your purpose is to clearly explain this aspect of your culture so that classmates from other cultures have a better understanding of how it is different from or similar to the feature in their own culture.

Possible Topics

- Parental roles, children's responsibilities
- Effect of birth order or gender on a family's expectations
- Importance of community beyond the family
- Attitudes toward education
- Homes, neighborhoods, and how physical environments shape or reflect values
- Attitudes toward the elderly
- Childhood games and their meaning

Planning and Drafting

Your research for this paper will include reading several essays from our text and gathering information during class discussions. This interviewing will require some careful questioning on your part as well as accurate recording of your group members' responses. You may find it more effective to phrase your questions in specific terms. The question, "What do people from your culture think of old people?" may not get you very far; a question such as "What role does your grandmother or grandfather play in your life and in your family?" will uncover more information; even better might be specific questions such as "How much time do you spend with your grandparent?" "What advice did your grandparent give you?" or "Where does your grandparent live?" Be sure you know the names and can accurately identify the cultures or nationalities of any classmates you interview. Similarly, when quoting or paraphrasing from our text, make certain you identify the culture accurately and cite the author and page number(s).

Evaluation Criteria

The paper should compare and contrast a specific cultural feature, be developed with interesting and appropriate detail, be explained fully enough that a person from another culture can clearly understand it, include an introduction that forecasts the organization and interests the reader, provide coherent transitions from one idea to another, include direct reference by quote or paraphrase to at least one classmate, show careful attention to proofreading and conventions of standard English.

FIGURE 2. Sample Cultural Comparison Assignment for Cross-Cultural First-Year Composition

Most cross-cultural sections include collaborative projects, giving students from varied backgrounds a chance to work together productively. In some sections, student groups have chosen a reading from the text and teach the reading to the rest of the class. After assigning Tong's (1990/1995) essay, "Bloody Sunday in Tiananmen Square," a group of students acted out a Talk Radio show in which a Chinese student played the role of a public official defending the government's use of troops, while a Malaysian student played the role of a student protester, and a U.S. student moderated questions from the radio audience (class members). In another presentation, focused on a chapter from Salzman's (1986) *Iron and Silk*, which describes the martial arts expert, Pan Qingfu, students brought a martial arts video to class and discussed the values taught by martial arts study. A U.S. student who was on the university swim team compared his relationship with his swimming coach to his relationship with a martial arts teacher, while a Taiwanese classmate discussed seeing Pan Qingfu in an exhibition. This engagement with the readings and involvement of the class members in planning and carrying out class discussion is a valuable experience.

In other collaborative projects, students have designed small research projects on a topic of interest to them. They have examined prejudicial treatment by sales clerks at the local mall where a U.S. and an international student entered a store and observed the amount of time it took for each to be waited on. Another group compiled material on study abroad: The students' final group project included practical sources, addresses, descriptions of programs as well as sections on cultural adjustment and culture shock. In another class, a U.S. student interested in cartoon animation worked with a Japanese student who had an extensive collection of *manga*, Japanese cartoons, to look at the cultural values represented by the cartoons.

The international focus of the cross-cultural class brings new perspectives to research and writing about topical issues. In an assignment used in several cross-cultural sections, group members have chosen a political or social issue to research, comparing coverage of the issue in sources from different countries. Rather than choosing two U.S. sources, groups have looked at international news coverage, examining how the choice of detail, the connotations of the language, the expectations of readers, and the cultural assumptions of the writers shape the coverage of an issue.

Academic English II for NNS Graduates

Academic English II focuses on helping graduate students develop the skills they need to write professional papers and theses, develop fluency in academic correspondence, use published sources appropriately in professional writing, discover expectations for language use (oral and written) in their field of specialization, and clarify troublesome grammar points. The class assignments address typical professional writing needs in the students' fields of study (e.g., descriptions of processes or mechanisms, proposals, progress reports, literature reviews, research reports, critiques) as well as memos, letters, abstracts, curriculum vitae, and one or two oral presentations.

Although cross-cultural communication is a major challenge for the international students in our program, many face an additional problem, that of gaining more discipline-specific writing skills. Because graduate students are writing in their specific disciplines more so than undergraduates, they must therefore grapple with the issues of genre-specific writing (Leki & Carson, 1997). We have approached this problem by involving students in inductive analysis of research writing in their fields. This inductive approach is encouraged by Weissberg and Buker (1990), whose text we use for the graduate courses in Academic English II. Students study each of the conventional sections of a research report by analyzing the format, content, and grammatical and rhetorical conventions of articles in their own fields, and by comparing their findings with those of their classmates. One teacher in the program, Anne Richards, has taken this basic inductive approach one step further by having students reflect on rhetorical analyses of their own disciplinary journals in genre journals. Each week students submit one-page reflections on discipline-specific discourse practices based on the students' observations and analyses of specific features in prominent journals in their fields. Teacher guidelines and questions assist students in analyzing their journals. In one assignment, students reflect on how the journals differ in their treatment of abstracts; in another assignment, they analyze endnotes, footnotes, tables, and figures; students also consider cross-cultural differences in journal features. Especially for beginning graduate students, getting acquainted with and exploring key journals is an important aspect of this assignment. In this way, research on writing practices within a student's field becomes the topic for research in academic English.

One of the problems in teaching academic English to students who are advanced in their disciplines is that few ESL teachers understand the content of students' academic disciplines (e.g., physics, genetics, economics) well enough to help with complex writing problems, such as how to paraphrase without plagiarizing. When students are assigned to write about generic, nondiscipline-related subjects, we find they typically are less interested and involved, perhaps because they fail to see the relevance of these assignments to their eventual needs as an advanced student. How can one provide students with an assignment that the teacher can understand, yet one that connects to the students' disciplinary needs? One approach is to make the research paper topic the investigation of writing needs within the students' chosen discipline.

In one recent class, students responded to a call from the program coordinator for an investigation into the writing needs of Academic English II students. With guidance from the instructor, Dewey Litwiller, students created a survey and used it to assess student writing profiles, including native language, time in the United States, major, academic goals, prior writing experience and study of English, and, most important, current academic writing needs of students in all sections of Academic English II (N = 100). Using the statistical expertise of students in the class, the classes then analyzed the data they had gathered. To gain a more detailed picture of academic and professional writing needs, small discipline-specific groups of students interviewed a professor, a senior graduate, and a postdoctoral student or professional about the writing they did within their particular discipline. A key part of the assignment was utilizing data from multiple sources and comparing the findings. Students then wrote research papers in which they reviewed relevant literature (provided by the instructor), outlined methods, and summarized information from the student survey and the disciplinary writing needs interview. Because the audience for the paper was the ESL academic program coordinator, students were motivated not only by investigating their own future writing needs within their discipline, but additionally by helping to shape the future of the ESL academic program. This assignment not only provided research and writing experience that acquainted students with the format and process of writing up research but also helped students initiate contacts and conversation with experts in their area and make connections between academic writing and their disciplinary needs.

Another project in an Academic English II class was also designed to provide a scenario of conducting, analyzing, and writing up research and to place learning in the framework of an interactive, cooperative effort with cross-cultural interaction. Cooperation between two sections of the class gave students a larger pool of data than would have been possible with a single class. The project began with students discussing whether U.S. students or international students had a superior knowledge of geography, drawing up a study to investigate which was the case on our campus. The project included classes working to design a simple 14-question survey with eight multiple-choice questions such as: "Jakarta is the capital of: (a) Malaysia, (b) Vietnam, (c) Brunei, and (d) Indonesia"; two map questions in which students were asked to decide which land mass was Taiwan and which Korea; and four personal data questions about the respondent's gender, citizenship, age, and whether or not the person had ever traveled abroad. Each student gathered data by randomly sampling peers and conducting brief interviews on campus with five U.S. students and five international students. Data were tabulated and then pooled. A subgroup of students with expertise in statistics did an analysis that was shared in a class presentation. Using the results shared in class, students wrote up individual research papers incorporating source materials provided by their instructor.

In all three of these assignments, the instructors attempted to bridge the gap between English instruction and disciplinary writing needs. In one case, the students simulated collaborative research, and in the other two examples, the instructors moved even closer to the disciplinary needs by making them the center of the students' research.

◈ DISTINGUISHING FEATURES

Using cooperative learning pairs/teams within and across classes, students collaborate on a variety of projects. The communicative focus of our courses helps NNS students find a wider audience for their writing as well as improve their ability to negotiate, discuss ideas, and work in small groups. Because NNS international students often do not have opportunities to interact with NS U.S. students, various assignments, course projects, and even course designs in our writing program foster cross-cultural communication. These cooperative learning initiatives prove effective in broadening the perspectives of students as well as in providing an opportunity for the NNS international students to make meaningful contacts with students in the United States.

In evaluations of the cross-cultural composition sections, students have often written that the class had changed their outlook toward people of other cultures. An international student wrote, "At first I thought that communicate with an American was a difficult thing. But now I realized that it is very easy to interact with an American." Another wrote, "I made some friends in this class." A U.S. student commented:

I came from a sheltered background and a private school where there were not very many minorities. I only saw the Mexicans that lived downtown by my school. My experiences with them weren't very positive ones. When I came to my English class here at Iowa State, I found that the people with backgrounds different than my own were very interesting and great people. I got to ask them questions along with answering the ones they had for me. It really made me think about my culture. When people back home ask me how school is going, I have so many things to tell them about what I learned from being in this class.

U.S. and international students have indicated that the cross-cultural sections reduced their apprehension about interacting with students from different backgrounds. The classes provide a place where the opinions and insights of ESL students are not only valued but sought out by their U.S. classmates. Particularly important in these assignments is the fact that the international students' voices, opinions, and experiences are valued: Their input is necessary for the success of the projects. Thus, the communication between U.S. and international students is not simply a happy by-product of putting them together in a class, but, instead, becomes an essential part of the students' work.

To help students become competent writers in their disciplines, our program also encourages an inductive learner-centered approach. Instead of presenting students with principles and rules first and then having them do exercises to practice the rules, as is typical of a deductive approach, we structure learning so that students gather data and discover principles on their own, often comparing what they discovered with one another. Finally, we encourage students to help shape their own writing curriculum not only through regular needs assessments but by allowing them to do assignments differentiated by their area of study and by having them gather data about the writing needs of students and professionals in their areas, data which is then fed back into the program.

❧ PRACTICAL IDEAS

Certain principles guide our program development and can be applied in other learning situations.

Reach Out to Your Academic Community

We suggest that teachers and administrators begin by analyzing the problems and limitations of their particular situations. In our case, this led to approaching the larger academic community to form intercultural and interdisciplinary partnerships and making students partners in shaping the curriculum.

Create Partnerships Between NNS and NS Students

Curriculum strategies used in our program may apply to other academic settings. For example, smaller schools in which there are too few ESL students in one discipline, or even too few ESL students for single academic English classes, can utilize notions of NS and NNS partnerships. Schools with large international populations where NNS and NS students are not well integrated may want to apply our approaches to incorporating cross-cultural interaction into the curriculum.

Have Students Explore Their Own Disciplines

Likewise, where students feel that academic English courses are somewhat disconnected from their disciplinary goals, and where English teachers lack specific knowledge of disciplines yet team-teaching is not feasible, programs may want to make projects in which students explore discipline-specific writing needs and practices a central part of the curriculum. By expanding traditionally isolated academic English programs to go beyond the classroom to include intercultural and disciplinary communication, students help shape their learning and become more deeply invested in it.

◈ CONCLUSION

Our program remains under construction. Using insights from students and teachers alike, including our colleagues in other disciplines, we are working to move the program beyond its traditional borders by expanding the use of learning technology and by developing cross-cultural cooperative learning teams to better connect our students with the larger academic community.

◈ CONTRIBUTORS

Roberta J. Vann is professor of English at Iowa State University, where she teaches in and coordinates the Academic English Program for Non-Native Speakers of English and also teaches courses in the MATESL program. Her career has focused on making university-level ESL, especially reading and writing skills, effective and enjoyable for teachers and students. This has led to a textbook on reading, research, and publications in learning strategies, and in-service workshops for teachers in the United States and in many other countries.

Cynthia Myers is testing and placement coordinator for academic ESL and adjunct instructor at Iowa State University. She has been involved with ISU's program for international teaching assistants and helped develop the cross-cultural first-year composition program. She is coeditor (with Carolyn Madden) of *Discourse and Performance of International Teaching Assistants* (TESOL, 1994), in which her article on question-based discourse in science labs won the 1996 Malkemes prize from New York University's School of Continuing Education.

CHAPTER 7

Postgraduate Writing: Using Intersecting Genres in a Collaborative, Content-Based Program

Margaret Cargill, Kate Cadman, and Ursula McGowan

◈ INTRODUCTION

In 1994 the ESL team in the Language and Learning Service at Adelaide University initiated an Integrated Bridging Program (IBP) for international postgraduate students as an integral part of the first semester of their postgraduate awards. The IBP is an innovative, language-based, academic induction program that focuses on teaching these students the specific written genres they will need to use in the university. It is designed to assist them to address their special needs in transition to and during their studies in their new learning environments. In particular, the program directly engages students in developing their understanding of postgraduate university culture in the Australian context and their command of the academic English language specific to their area and level of study and research. We chose the name Integrated Bridging Program because we believe that the most effective bridging for international students is an approach that integrates the specific language and learning needs they encounter after they have enrolled in their awards.

Writing in English is crucial within this development and is often the main concern of academic departments. Our experience in developing and teaching the IBP, however, convinces us that we cannot teach postgraduate writing effectively by just teaching writing. Drawing on the work of genre theorists and educational practitioners (see, e.g., Christie & Martin, 1997; Cope & Kalantzis, 1993; Halliday & Hasan, 1985; Halliday & Martin, 1993; Lemke, 1990; Martin, 1989; Martin & Veel, 1998; Swales, 1990; Ventola & Mauranen, 1996), and highlighting the importance of intersecting genres (cf. also Bazerman, 1994; Paltridge, 1998), the IBP focuses on both written and spoken English genres and the relationship of each to the other in developing and presenting academic argument at the postgraduate level. Figure 1 shows how we conceptualize the specific articulations of appropriate language for postgraduates in terms of contexts and forms.

The infrastructure of the IBP that supports the teaching of these genres encompasses several specific features:

- the high level of collaboration between IBP lecturers and those in the students' departments

- the strong teamwork approach of the IBP staff

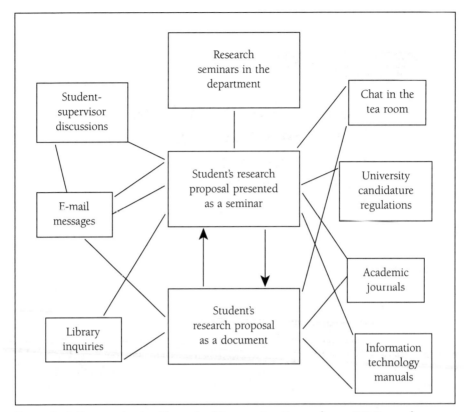

FIGURE 1. A Communication Network of Intersecting Genres for an IBP Group for Research Postgraduates (adapted from Paltridge, 1998, p. 16. Used with permission.)

- the involvement of students and departmental academics in decision making on the curriculum specifications and assessment procedures
- the focus on students' development of skills for analyzing the discourses of their disciplines to facilitate their ongoing development as writers and speakers of new genres

◈ CONTEXT

Adelaide University, named for its location in the capital city of the state of South Australia, has an enrollment of approximately 13,500 students. Of these, 19% are postgraduate students and 1.8% are international postgraduates (Adelaide University, 2000). The university has a strong reputation for research and research training, and recruits postgraduate students from a wide range of countries and language backgrounds. Many are mature professionals, often working in positions of some status at home. They bring with them extensive prior knowledge and well-developed systems for communicating that knowledge appropriately in their first languages. However, although they are required to demonstrate a level of English language proficiency considered appropriate by the university (e.g., a score of 550 on the Test of English as a Foreign Language [TOEFL] or a 6 on the International English Language Testing System [IELTS]) in order to enroll in their awards, these students are generally inexperienced in the specific linguistic and academic contexts of Australian postgraduate course work or research. They have, by definition, excelled academically in other learning environments; however, their previous criteria for success may have been quite different from those they will now encounter. Changing academic contexts is, thus, much more than a language shift; it is a multidimensional experience for them, which very often presents a formidable challenge (Cadman, 1997a, 1997b).

To offer these students effective access to the value systems embedded in Australian postgraduate research and course work programs, the curriculum of the IBP requires that students begin to explore, with their supervisors and lecturers, the cultural relativity of the skills they bring, as a precursor to developing an understanding and a mastery of those skills they now need. This curriculum focus requires tripartite collaboration among the students, the IBP lecturer, and the academic staff member(s) from the department supervising the students' postgraduate studies. The success of this collaborative approach depends to a large extent on the IBP's location within the university's Advisory Centre for University Education (ACUE), which has a brief to work with academic staff in departments and students from all language backgrounds to enhance student learning outcomes across the university. Lecturers appointed to the IBP are well qualified, generally with a higher degree and with qualifications and experience in teaching ESOL. They have the ability to collaborate effectively with staff in the disciplines and successfully claim space for their own applied linguistics knowledge, alongside the content specialties of other departmental academics, through their expertise in genre-based approaches to language teaching within a university context.

◈ DESCRIPTION

The international postgraduate students are placed in IBP classes of up to 15 students according to academic discipline and type of postgraduate program (research only or involving course work[1]). Students whose first language is English or who have extended experience with research in an English language culture may negotiate exemption or reduced participation in the program with their supervisor and the IBP coordinator.

The separation of students into course work classes and research-only classes reflects the different priorities of the two groups of students at the beginning of their candidatures. Research students are writing only on their research topics and the relevant literature; course work students are more focused on producing successful postgraduate-level assignments. In addition, the separation reflects timetable constraints. As course work postgraduates often carry very heavy class loads during the semester, the IBP schedules an intensive 2-week teaching period before the semester

---

[1] In the Australian university system, PhD degrees have no assessed course work component; assessment is by thesis only. Research master's degrees may contain up to 33.3% course work, and course work master's degrees and postgraduate diplomas contain varying proportions of course work, between 66.6% and 100%.

begins for these students, with fewer class hours during the semester. A summary of the program structure for the two types of groups is reproduced in Table 1.

The IBP is designed on a content-based adjunct model (Brinton, Snow, & Wesche, 1989). The curriculum is student centered and based on tasks that are "relevant, rigorous, authentic, and public" (Cadman, 1997b, p. 47). These tasks, however, are quite different for the course work and research strands. For research students, the major tasks are the production of a limited-scope research proposal (including a literature review) and the presentation of a seminar (oral presentation with questions) to justify the proposed research. These students negotiate the topic and scope of their IBP tasks individually with supervisors (as academic advisers of research students are known in the Australian context) and with IBP staff, a process which itself models and allows for reflection on a vital component of the postgraduate process. Tasks are assessed formatively by the IBP lecturer and the student's supervisor, with each providing feedback in their own area of expertise. Course work students begin in their initial intensive class phase by working on group projects requiring negotiation skills and the production of a collaborative piece of writing. During the extensive, semester-long phase, class structure and individual consultations are designed to address the specific assessment genres that students are required to produce.

TABLE 1. SUMMARY OF INTEGRATED BRIDGING PROGRAM STRUCTURE
(CARGILL, 1996, P. 184. USED WITH PERMISSION.)

	Course work students	Research students
Start dates	2–3 weeks before start of course lectures each semester	Second week of teaching each semester
Group teaching	• Intensive 15 hr/week (for 2 weeks) • Extensive 1 hr–90 min/week	3 hr/week
Duration	One semester of 13 weeks	One semester of 13 weeks
Additional modules	As required	As required
Individual consultations	30 min/week	30 min/week
Collaborating academics	Coordinators of postgraduate courses	Supervisors of individual students
Input from collaborating academics	Negotiation on target genres for intensive phase, timing and intensity of extensive phase	Formative comment on content of all written tasks, attendance at student seminars
IBP tasks	As negotiated, to be relevant to initial demands of the students' course(s)	Article summary and critique, limited-scope literature review and research proposal, seminar presentation of proposal, or as negotiated

◈ DISTINGUISHING FEATURES

Basis in Tripartite Negotiation

One of the primary features that distinguishes the IBP from other content-based writing courses is that its curriculum content is designed through tripartite collaboration among IBP lecturers, academic staff in the departments where the students are enrolled, and the international postgraduates themselves, who are mostly nonnative English speakers (NNSs). In the initial setup of the program in 1994, departmental staff identified the key tasks that form the basis for postgraduate course work and research assessment in students' departments. These tasks became nonnegotiable in the program. Assignment marking, attendance at IBP seminar presentations given by students, as well as appropriate directions for language learning, are all negotiated through this tripartite collaboration.

Team Approaches to Holistic Development of International Postgraduate Pedagogy

A key to the success of the IBP is teamwork among the IBP staff, with the coordinator providing academic and professional leadership. The teamwork approach, in fact, extends beyond the IBP staff, as the program is seen as a lynchpin in the university's developing focus on internationalization. Thus, the IBP staff work collaboratively with administrative areas of the university as well as with students' departments to ensure that students and departmental academic staff experience the IBP as being embedded within the administrative and pedagogical processes of the university. For example, administratively, the IBP forms a compulsory part of the first semester of candidature, and completion is required before PhD students proceed to their second year. Pedagogically, professional development for lecturers and research supervisors, which is delivered by another section of the ACUE, benefits from input informed by the experience and the research outcomes of IBP staff. Examples include studies on spoken interaction in face-to-face meetings between research students from language backgrounds other than English and their postgraduate supervisors (Cargill, 1998, 2000), the relationship between the self-concept of international postgraduates and their academic writing (Cadman, 1997a), and metaphor in newspaper articles encountered by economics students (McGowan, 1997).

Within the IBP team, expertise is shared in three ways. First, team teaching of appropriate IBP classes provides a core method of encouraging consistency across the program and inducting new lecturing staff into its ethos and practices. This often occurs at the start of a new semester when several groups are combined for key sessions, such as the Pyramid Discussion described in Practical Ideas. These sessions can serve the additional purposes of engendering group cohesion across the wider IBP cohort and introducing students to some of the similarities and differences between the discourse communities represented by the range of students present.

Second, the IBP staff runs a series of workshops. These enable us to maintain the fundamental thrust of the program, while also developing it in the light of our ongoing research activities, the evaluation information received from students, and the experience of lecturers.

Third, the IBP teaching team also maintains a comprehensive collection of genre examples provided by supervisors or students from previous semesters; all staff add to this collection, annotating their contributions with details of their source and staff contacts. These examples include research proposals, literature reviews, essays, and project reports, as well as published journal articles from across the range of disciplines covered in the university. Some of these examples are used as the basis for detailed teaching materials, which are also kept on file to be used when needed for a particular class. Even the raw documents, however, are a valuable resource for teachers wanting to demonstrate elements of genre analysis or to highlight similarities or differences across genres from different research fields or discourse communities.

Curriculum Design

The IBP's deeply integrated curriculum differentiates it from the more widely found generic academic writing or studies skills courses (which must prepare students for a wide range of target contexts), and from preenrollment English for academic purposes (EAP) courses or those leading to English language proficiency tests for screening purposes. IBP set tasks are nonnegotiable, but before the program begins, the content and timetable for individual students are negotiated with their departmental supervisors. Thus, the program is directly integrated into every postgraduate's departmental requirements. Then, in class discussions, the students negotiate their own priorities as they fill in the semester's IBP timetable leading to their assessment tasks. Gradually, the students take control over the IBP curriculum and direct its teaching orientation themselves, thereby greatly increasing their learner autonomy.

This curriculum model allows international and other NNS students to receive the full support and direction they often need, especially at the start of their postgraduate training (see Cadman & Grey, 2000).

Genre-Based Writing Instruction

The nonnegotiable tasks at the center of the IBP structure are well-established genres in the study programs of postgraduate students. Course work students in medicine, agricultural science, and engineering can be required to complete reports, review essays leading to gap identification, or responses to other kinds of assignment topics, such as case studies. In arts and social sciences, assignments are usually based on the construction of impersonal logical argument, well supported by secondary literature in the field. In women's studies, education, and the critical social sciences, students may be asked to write personal, reflective accounts of experience supported, though not overshadowed, by existing literature, and characterized by thick description and a situated, fully described writer/persona. All these genres can be incorporated into the IBP structure.

Research students throughout Adelaide University are expected in their first year to produce a research proposal that critiques and reviews existing literature, describes a methodology, and clearly sets out the students' research questions and objectives. Again, however, different disciplines interpret these tasks in quite distinct ways, so that the text structures of similar sounding tasks can vary significantly. In contemporary research environments, paradigms of research can have more influence on genres than the disciplines themselves. In some areas, as in some science and engineering fields where paradigms are firmly in place, there is little variation in rhetorical organization that is significant for students. In other areas, such as critical social science or poststructural politics, differences in the communicative purposes and values of research writing can be extremely problematic for those students who have a restricted command of academic English. Examples include whether or not the use of personal pronouns is encouraged and how different methodological approaches affect the way in which evidence is discussed and credibility claimed. The IBP is able to address these issues for students because writing activities are focused on recent authentic models supplied by the relevant departments.

The use of a genre approach with a focus on moving between spoken and written and formal and informal registers to facilitate students' academic writing development is by now widespread and has found many applications in the teaching of writing (Burns, Joyce, & Gollin, 1996; Cope & Kalantzis, 1993; Eggins, 1994; Halliday, 1989; Halliday & Hasan, 1985; Martin, 1989; Swales, 1990). What enriches and distinguishes the IBP is that it has secured the willing and often enthusiastic collaboration of departmental staff, with their students, and our IBP staff, not only in providing the necessary authentic articles and tasks but also in jointly assessing the written products and the accompanying oral presentations. Apart from practice activities, students only write for their own departmental staff, and their drafts are assessed by IBP and departmental lecturers so that discussion of authentic departmental feedback becomes a descriptive, nonvalue-laden learning activity. By this means, students develop awareness of the relationships between language features they have used and meaning as interpreted by a content expert. Thus, the development of students' analysis and composition skills occurs through-out the IBP within the discipline context of their postgraduate study program. In addition, students are introduced to a key resource: the value of seeking out and analyzing examples of any document type they need to produce. Thus, the students embark on a limited-scope apprenticeship as discourse analysts, focusing on their own ongoing needs as lifelong learners.

◈ PRACTICAL IDEAS

Within the conceptual framework bounded by the IBP's philosophy, curriculum structure, and nonnegotiable writing tasks, IBP staff develop a wide range of activities to promote postgraduates' mastery of the genres they must write. Below is a small selection of relevant practical ideas for different contexts.

All Groups: Students Explore Disciplinary Content and Genre Requirements

To help tertiary students develop a shared understanding and mastery of the written genres required of a postgraduate in an English-speaking university environment, we use the steps outlined below. Teaching and learning genres involve a cycle of discussion, modeling, joint construction, and independent construction. The cycle can be entered at any point and each stage repeated as often as necessary (Martin, 1989). The cycle helps students to

- move back and forth between spoken and written language (e.g., by encouraging class discussions about the requirements of a topic and collaboration in writing practice)

- explore the field or content of the academic area they need to write about, with the collaboration of their departmental staff (e.g., by brainstorming or listing on the board all the information that might be required)

- analyze successful examples of genres they need to produce within their own discipline and determine the various stages (Weissberg & Buker, 1990) or moves (Swales, 1990) of the structure of these models, which may be academic assignments, experimental reports, literature reviews, research proposals, or complete dissertations

- note the language features typically associated with the various stages or moves (e.g., the presence or absence of passive voice or personal pronouns; the use of transition markers, such as *however*, *moreover*, and *on the other hand*, or the use of tenses for specific purposes within the text)

In relation to the various stages in model texts, students learn to ask questions such as "What is happening in this stage (or move)?," "Where does the stage end?," and "What is the function of this stage in the text?" For example, in writing that leads into a research proposal, the functions identified might be setting the scene, introducing new information, providing evidence, summarizing literature, stating own opinion or making an evaluative comment, identifying a gap in prior research, stating own research question, and stating purpose or value of proposed research (Weissberg & Buker, 1990).

It is preferable for students to examine several successful texts of the genre they are required to use, rather than relying on just one. This is to expose them to a variety of options within the same general framework and to avoid the temptation of simply paraphrasing (and inadvertently plagiarizing) from the one text that served as a model. By examining a number of texts, students can learn to discover for themselves that in any generic structure there are some obligatory as well as some optional elements.

All Groups: Students Develop Their Own Voice in Writing

The close study of genre examples in the IBP provides an excellent opportunity to highlight the vexed issue of plagiarism in a creative way. Students are encouraged to differentiate between the chunks of technical language specific to their own discipline and field, especially the complex noun phrases, which they need to imitate closely, and the language features that carry the writer's own opinion or voice (see Cadman, 1997a, p. 5). These language structures can be identified and reused by students in different circumstances to construct their own argument. This work helps students move away from inadvertent plagiarism toward independent mastery of generic structures and specific language features within the conventions of their discipline. Student texts are regularly displayed on overhead transparency sheets, and peer evaluation is an integral part of this learning process. The question "Whose voice is saying this, the student writer's or the person they are citing?" recurs throughout the program, asked by students as well as by lecturers.

Use Pyramid Discussions to Develop Students' Awareness of Argumentation

We often begin the writing programs with an oral pyramid discussion activity, which is taken from an original idea from Jordan (1990) and extended, as suggested by

Cadman and Grey (1997). Students take an individual position on what they feel are the three most significant aspects of a topic that has content relevance to them. An example of this activity might be the exercise shown in Figure 2.

Next, by joining into pairs and then into fours, the students try to convince each other of the reasons for their own views and to negotiate a consensus for the group. Groups feed back to a whole-class discussion that requires the students to focus as much on how they have experienced the process of their discussions as on the agreements they have come to (see Cadman & Grey, 1997).

Have Students Manipulate Information to Support Varying Points of View

This task begins with analysis through reading on one or more of students' departmental topics. The students are asked to read a short paragraph taken from a reading appropriate for the assignment, underlining any words or phrases that indicate the writer's point of view on the topic. They then write out the next few lines of the written text, deleting all the expressions carrying persuasive language. Groups redraft the remaining text on overhead transparency sheets, adding their own persuasive language to present a positive or negative view of the topic. One member presents the group's view to the class. Whole-class feedback on each piece of writing leads to lively discussion of how the opinion is being conveyed as well as of how strongly that opinion is reflected in the choice of expressions (see Figure 3). Students always seem to enjoy identifying their colleagues' voices, and they begin to see how the same information can be used to express differing viewpoints.

Reasons Underlying Professional Practice

Consider your own practice as a professional in your field. Select *three* items from the list below which you believe are the most important reasons why you perform your duties as you do:

1. the duties have always been performed that way
2. you have experimented with alternative practices and found them inadequate
3. previous professionals have established good practices
4. your first duty is to obey your superiors
5. there is well-documented theoretical evidence for the procedures that you carry out
6. it is not your place to question the ways in which tasks are performed
7. a professional's confidence and belief in their own practices are more important than evidence to support them
8. cost and time allocation should be prioritized over improving outcomes
9. you have an unshakeable belief that you are working in the best way possible
10. your duties are clearly described in your duty statement
11. allocating money to researching evidence to improve established practices is wasting resources
12. your expertise and experience are sufficient to ensure that you will make the right decisions about your practice
13. changes to existing work practices are disruptive for staff

---

FIGURE 2. A Sample Pyramid Discussion Task

Multinational Enterprises in Indonesia

<u>Although</u> foreign firms have made a <u>significant</u> contribution to Indonesian economic development since 1966, as stated by Hill (1991), *however*, in <u>many</u> aspects foreign firms have *made* <u>negative</u> effects *to* the country. They have *<u>destructed</u>* environment <u>as well as</u> native culture. They <u>also</u> *took* the money back to their countries. <u>Even though</u> MNCs provide training facilities as mentioned by Hill, <u>in fact</u> they <u>really</u> don't have a <u>serious</u> intention *to transfer* technology to Indonesia. In the decision making process, they <u>also</u> do not give <u>any</u> opportunity to domestic partners. <u>Moreover</u>, they <u>always</u> *made* accounting policies, transfer pricing and other techniques which <u>deteriorate</u> the interest of domestic partners and Indonesian government.

FIGURE 3. An Example of Collaboratively Constructed IBP Student Text (Underlined words were identified as carrying writer's voice or opinion, and italicized words as needing attention to grammar.)

Research Groups: Students Turn Personal Profiles Into Research Data

An interesting activity for newly arrived research students that helps them to conceptualize the setting up of a research project can be developed from a productive getting-to-know-you exercise, such as "Milestones," shown in Figure 4.

After the presentations, the students can be directed to think about how all the data they have heard could be grouped under one topic heading. At this point, the parameters of the research topic (suggested in brackets) are discussed in terms of items of vocabulary, singulars and plurals, and appropriate prepositions, for example: *The most significant experiences of [new?] international [postgraduate? mature-age?] students [in Australian universities? an Australian university? in Western universities?].* In pairs or groups, the students can then construct a research question, or possibly two, to which the data they have heard could provide an answer. Oral discussion of the implications of the question form often occurs at several levels, as issues of grammar, register, and logic are raised. The whole process can then be applied to the students'

Milestones

1. What do you think are the three most significant turning points which mark milestones in your life?

2. Prioritize them, putting the least important first.

3. On your overhead transparency, draw a different picture to convey each of the milestones you have chosen, one above the other. Do not use any words.

4. Present a 5 minute talk to the class. Consider carefully how you will introduce your milestones, how you will conclude and how you will link your segments together.

5. Be prepared to answer 2 questions from the floor.

FIGURE 4. The "Milestones" Task (Cadman & Grey, 1997, pp. 101–111). Used with permission.

own fledgling research topics and questions. A topic example could be: *The role[s] of agroindustry[ies?] and the improvement of income distribution in developing countries [in Indonesia? in Kalimantan Province, Indonesia?].*

Research Groups: Students Write About Their Own Personal Research Project

Students can now write about their own research project, recognizing, of course, that it is still in a hesitant and initial form. Working from an analysis of successful authentic departmental models, they can write a topic, research question, and short paragraph about their research project, considering all the implications of the language of their topic and question as well as the audience. Research students enjoy critiquing each other's topics and paragraphs in terms of appropriate register, clarity of expression and logic, and quality of parameter definition of the topic, such as the historical and geographical limitations of the research project. If students are comfortable at this stage that their topic will almost certainly develop and that these initial thoughts may only be embryonic, they raise fruitful questions about grammar, syntax, discipline-specific jargon, and register.

Research Groups: Students Write a Statement on Their Own Personal Research for Different Audiences in a Specific Context

In the initial stages of learning to understand and master the intersecting genres of their discipline, it is sometimes useful for students to practice writing about their research topic for different audiences. Thus, the first task might be as follows: "Write a brief explanation of your research topic for the TESOL lecturer, who is a nonexpert in your field." For this audience, the genre cycle of "discussion, modeling, joint construction, and independent construction" (see McGowan, Seton, & Cargill, 1996, p. 119, for a case study of engineering students illustrating this example) is entered at the point of individual construction. By beginning with their own attempt to write about their research topic, students are alerted to the need for examining examples, or models, of this genre. Once the need for modeling is established, a number of successful examples of well-written brief explanations for a nonspecialist audience can be examined. Then, students practice constructing similar texts. They do this as a whole group, writing on the whiteboard or on an overhead transparency, until they are able to produce a more successful text of their own by themselves.

A further audience is then nominated, for example, a group of engineering students and staff. This time, students might enter the genre cycle at the modeling stage, examining a number of good examples before moving through to either joint or individual construction of a statement that would take into account the more specialized audience. Finally, students prepare to write their research proposals and associated formal seminar papers, to be presented to an audience of their full department.

◈ CONCLUSION

The IBP at Adelaide University was short-listed for the 1998 national Australian Awards for University Teaching in the category of "Support for the Special Needs of International Students." This award recognizes some of the features of the IBP that distinguish it from more narrowly focused skills programs. The IBP curriculum succeeds in bringing together the following elements:

- embedded, genre-based writing instruction for postgraduates
- development of students' mastery of intersecting genres and skills
- ongoing, reflective, independent learning practices
- reciprocal, intercultural dialogues in the postgraduate context

In a safe discourse environment, students can collaboratively explore, reflect on, and learn how to communicate as students in their disciplines. Our goal is to teach students to apply the practical and reflective skills they learn in this environment in all their future study contexts, however different the discourses may be. We feel we are succeeding when students recognize their own development on several levels.

Since its inception in 1995, evaluation of the IBP has been ongoing and has taken several forms. Interim and final evaluations take place for staff and students through open-ended written surveys and open discussions. Some students also complete learning journals where they are encouraged to offer constructive criticism and suggestions for the development of the IBP. At the moment, the primary goals of the IBP staff are to sharpen our team's ability to structure and deliver a curriculum that reflects the particular challenges that international postgraduates themselves want to address and to increase departmental input in so doing. As Western universities escalate all their international marketing programs, we see the role of the IBP as being that of fostering mutual respect among scholars from different cultures and strengthening multilanguage awareness through our specifically targeted English language writing courses.

❧ CONTRIBUTORS

Margaret Cargill is senior lecturer in language and learning in the Advisory Centre for University Education (ACUE) at Adelaide University, South Australia. She played a major role in developing the IBP and now teaches within it. She also has taught EFL/ESL in Switzerland, Asia, and the South Pacific. Her research focuses on the discourse of cross-cultural postgraduate supervision.

Kate Cadman is senior lecturer in language and learning and coordinator of the IBP at Adelaide University. She has taught English language and literature in Great Britain and Australia. She is currently involved in collaborative research on international postgraduate experiences, focusing on the relationship between the self-concept of international postgraduates and their text construction. She has published several papers in this field, especially with respect to thesis and dissertation writing.

Ursula McGowan is coordinator of the Language and Learning Service in the ACUE at Adelaide University. She is senior lecturer in ESL and is responsible for developing and teaching in programs within the Centre and across the Faculties for students with language backgrounds other than English. She collaborated with Margaret Cargill in the implementation of the IBP across Adelaide University. Her research interest is in the analysis of metaphor in spoken and written language within academic contexts.

PART 3

Using L2 Academic Writing to Explore and Learn

CHAPTER 8

Language and Public Life:
Teaching Multiliteracies in ESL

Judy Hunter and Brian Morgan

◈ INTRODUCTION

Language and Public Life (LNG 200) is an advanced university-level ESL course offered primarily to first- and second-year students at a Canadian polytechnic university. The course deals with language use and the public media that flood the lives of many North Americans. As described in the course outline, it examines the ways that "the sophisticated technologies of media and communication networks affect and reflect the way we talk and write to each other and the ways we see the world." Students analyze and discuss a range of media sources, observe and analyze public events, and talk and write about their understandings.

Our starting points for the course come from our perspectives on the place of ESL in the postsecondary academic context; our beliefs about ESL students and their positioning in Canadian education, society, and civic life; our concepts of language and literacy; and our views of the potential of ESL education in society. In contrast to teachers in many English for academic purposes courses, we do not see our role only as serving other traditional disciplines. Rather, we consider the critical study of language use in North American public life as worthy of exploration and discussion by ESL students who may be in their first years of university or who may be interested in improving their academic English proficiency. Our students are involved in the dynamic of public life. They need to develop a critical response or framework, and they need to defend and advance their own interests. LNG 200 illustrates our perspectives.

◈ CONTEXT

Structural and Historical

LNG 200 is a liberal studies elective at Ryerson Polytechnic University, which offers professional and applied undergraduate degrees. It is a one-term course (3 hours per week for 13 weeks), sequenced after Language and Identity, LNG 100. It is advanced in terms of writing assignments and expectations of student work. LNG 200 is offered to full-time degree students for credit and to part-time evening students, who may select it for interest or for an ESL certificate program. But its placement in the university degree structure has determined the curriculum and the kinds of students who may take it. Because of Ryerson's polytechnic mandate, all degree students take a complement of required core professional and professionally related courses along with liberal studies electives in order "to develop the capacity to understand and appraise the social and cultural context in which graduates will work as professionals and live as educated citizens" (Ryerson Polytechnic University, 1998, p. 338). Key requirements of liberal studies courses are substantive social science or humanities subject matter and essay writing assignments.

An important aspect of LNG 200's context is historical, for it illustrates the importance of confronting marginalization of ESL and ESL students' needs. Prior to 1995, a skills-oriented ESL reading and composition course was required for nonnative-English-speaking (NNS) students flagged by English proficiency admissions tests as needing language support. For over a decade, the course had received liberal studies credit on an ad hoc yearly basis, but in 1992, an institutionwide committee was struck with a view to regularizing the course. Bureaucratic and program constraints centered the debate around noncredit, fee-paying, required ESL or formalization of the liberal studies designation. The committee recommended the latter, and in 1995, the course was officially designated a lower level liberal studies elective.

The 3-year process of course acceptance involved debate at several administrative levels, but the issues were consistent. The ESL faculty were already committed to content ESL and to full recognition of the course within the university structure because students in the course had been admitted as full-time degree students. Moreover, we took the position that requiring students to take ESL shifted major responsibility for student language success onto us. In other words, a passing grade in the course could be seen—and often was seen—as our guarantee of their English mastery, an onus that we rejected. As language educators, we knew that language learning is an intensive and extensive process and that university-level academic language is composed of complex disciplinary discourses, which even native English speakers (NSs) have seldom mastered at the entry level.

Consequently, a major part of our argument involved education of the committee, our department, our faculty, and the curriculum and standards committees. We argued against the commonly held beliefs that one language course should fix the ESL problem, that any students can be expected to be fluent in a discourse they have not yet experienced, that our ESL students had done nothing to improve their English before entering school, that an ESL course was a crutch for inferior students, and that a good ESL curriculum should consist only of language items and exercises. We presented at meetings and documented our rationale; we spoke at informal seminars, including the annual in-house teaching and learning conference. We educated colleagues about the nature of language learning, suggesting ways they could adjust their teaching to promote language and subject-matter learning. Articulate ESL students spoke impressively at one committee meeting in favor of the course, explaining how it helped them to achieve their potential. One of us prepared a document with an annotated bibliography on language, context, and culture. Crucial to our success were the receptiveness of the university community and its overall commitment to a highly diverse, multicultural student population.

Student Profile

LNG 200 is open to NNS students by permission of ESL faculty. All students wishing to take the course, whether degree or continuing education students, present a writing sample and participate in an informal interview. The screening process eliminates students who are nativelike speakers and writers, and directs the lower level students to the first-term course, LNG 100. Part-time students attending Ryerson through continuing education undergo the same screening for the evening section of the course and are admitted if they are seen to match the cohort of day students taking the course.

Because the day course is an elective, a wide range of students enroll. Ryerson's minimum scores on the Test of English as a Foreign Language (TOEFL) are 560 for engineering and math-related programs and 580 for others. A preadmissions testing waiver, for applicants with 5 years in an English-speaking country, can backfire. In the large immigrant communities of Metropolitan Toronto, some live comfortably for many years in an environment where they can use their native language. As a result, some first-year students may arrive with relatively low English proficiency and may attend LNG 200 along with students from programs with stiffer language requirements.

Certainly there are clear benefits to a credit, elective status for the course—students do not feel punished for having to take ESL, and we do not carry the major burden of their short- and long-term language achievement. Nonetheless, there are drawbacks. Because it is a credit-bearing course, with grades contributing to students' overall grade point average, some of the neediest students avoid it. Instead, as we have heard anecdotally, they may choose large classes, submit their friends' essays or pay to have their essays edited, and cram for the final exams, thereby avoiding the close attention and language demands of LNG 200. Similarly, some students who believe they are relatively successful at functioning in English enroll in the course for an easy grade and are often resentful when they find the course much more challenging than they anticipated. But generally, the students find the subject matter of this course interesting and relevant to their lives, and they find the language instruction beneficial. The sections fill, and we have to turn students away each term.

In the continuing education section of LNG 200, some students work full time before class. For them, the concentration needed to do the challenging work we request is sometimes in short supply. Yet this group also brings important perspectives and direct experiences of language and power in the workplace to classroom discussions.

Our largest numbers of students are in engineering programs, computer science, hospitality and tourism, business, and social work, with smaller numbers in applied sciences, fashion design, image arts, and theater. Most students have been exposed to extensive traditional English language instruction. Some have taken ESL skills courses, and some have taken ESL in Canadian high schools. Most come from Hong Kong, Sri Lanka, other areas of Asia, and Iran. Others also come from eastern Europe, east Africa, South America, and China. With this student diversity in English proficiency, programs, and language backgrounds, we have attempted to meet everyone's needs through the course design.

❖ DESCRIPTION

LNG 200, as a liberal studies course, focuses on subject matter as well as on language use. The summary description on our course outline reflects these foci:

- Language is not neutral or objective. It is often framed by cultural and institutional perspectives; language represents, creates, and reflects social perspectives of the world, of reality. Along with the importance of agencies like schools and businesses, the sophisticated technologies of media and communication networks affect and reflect the way we talk and write to each other and the ways we see the world.

- This course deals with academic subject matter in a supportive, language-sensitive manner. It asks questions such as: What are the dominant messages in public language? How are they constructed? and How do we take up those messages? In addition to learning about the nature of public language, you will learn strategies for increasing your language fluency, accuracy, and appropriateness. You will have the opportunity to practice a variety of academic tasks, including formal and informal presentations, group discussion, essay writing, timed writing, using and documenting outside resources, and library and Internet research; and to receive feedback and guidance on your progress.

This description establishes the scope of the course and our critical perspective on language use in the public sphere. The course content is organized into themes, with core sources drawn from a customized reading package. The opening theme on language, viewpoint, and power elaborates and illustrates the nonneutral nature of language use and the relation of language and power. We also introduce the alternative perspective the course will take on mainstream media. We discuss the slanting of information in the positions of many of the course readings. This introduction provides students with an initial framework and metalanguage for understanding and talking about the issues we deal with in the class. The three subsequent course themes are

1. language and advertising
2. the news media, language, and public information
3. language, technology, and public life, which includes two subtopics: private talk, public talk, and reality television; and private information, public information, and the Internet

Themes are approached on several levels of class readings and activities, including (a) building on the introductory framework for textual analysis; (b) group analysis of sample texts; (c) discussion of the relationships between the texts, their construction, and society; and (d) written analysis of the students' own media selections. For example, in the section on the news media, we start with the chapter, "Methods of Misrepresentation" (Parenti, 1986), which outlines multiple ways of presenting factual information to manipulate public perceptions. We then read Lee & Solomon's (1992) comparison and analysis of two *New York Times* editorials, one on the Soviet military's 1983 shooting down of a Korean passenger jet, and the other on the U.S. military's 1988 shooting down of an Iranian passenger jet. A class analysis of a recent news item complements this work. We also discuss the possible reasons for the two contrasting perspectives taken by the *Times*. A Canadian National Film Board (NFB) video, *Only the News That Fits* (Crooks, Monro, & Raymont, 1989), closes the unit. The video presents a sociopolitical analysis different from Parenti's, which maintains that bias in the news media reflects dominant political and economic interests. The NFB video traces the process of news gathering, highlighting competition among reporters for air time and competition among the networks for ratings, as important forces in shaping the news. Finally, students individually select a news story to analyze for a short written essay.

Two assignments provide an overview of the whole course. The first is a group panel presentation on a public event that the students attend. This they contrast with the media representations that they typically experience. The second is a multimedia research paper, for which students are trained in the library to search Internet databases. In preparation for this assignment, they also learn and practice the purposes and conventions of academic documentation.

Because our students bring great diversity of backgrounds and knowledge to this subject matter, we acknowledge these differences by framing the course content in a question-posing dialogue that encourages multiple answers. Questioning begins in the course outline, illustrated in the summary description above and in the structure of each themed unit. For example, in the unit on electronic technology, the questions include

- How does television blur the distinction between public and private, reality and fiction?

- What does it mean to us?

- What role does the Internet, as a public information source, play in our lives?

We design class activities similarly. Students work in groups to analyze texts, debate, and build on each others' analyses. They are encouraged to respond to the course materials, drawing on their own knowledge and perspectives. Writing assignments not only require them to apply their analytical skills and argue implications of the media but also allow them to pursue topics of individual interest within the scope of the course.

The course is also individualized through students' language profiles. These consist of a two-part chart for each student, filled in as feedback after each written assignment. One part deals with language use, categorized as vocabulary, grammar, mechanics, and discourse. The other focuses on textual features: content, organization, formatting, and documentation. Along with each returned essay, the teacher hands back the chart, with positive and negative comments written in the language use categories. As students complete assignments, they see not only a pattern of their strengths and weaknesses but also of their areas of progress, for they use the same feedback chart for the entire course. After each essay assignment, students note from the chart their areas of major weakness, make corrections or revisions, analyze the sources of their problems, and propose a strategy for improvement. Some students do very well on this activity and use it to focus their editing and revising. Others, generally those who write at the last minute and do not take the time to proofread and review the accumulated feedback from the chart, find less progress.

Individual language work is supplemented by whole-class instruction in vocabulary, grammar, and editing strategies. Many students, even at the most advanced level, claim benefit from instruction in verb forms, article use, noun phrase construction, vocabulary organized around semantic fields, and expansion of their word knowledge from passive understanding to accurate, active use. These kinds of activities are always done in the contexts of students' evolving papers and ideas drawn from the reading texts (see Leki & Carson, 1997). For example, many of our students, albeit well trained in the use of present and past verb forms, tend to misuse them when drawing on and describing their own experiences in essays. They may initiate a description with reference to childhood, for instance, and use past tense to narrate, but add their interpretation of the subject, all in past tense. If they have written a single paragraph, their reasoning is often based on the rule of verb tense consistency, especially within a single paragraph. Yet this rule, in these cases, results in ambiguous text, and we revisit verb forms as a signal of the writer's organization and meaning. We look at the ways that our course readings use verb tense shifts, together with time and function expressions, to inform the readers about the writer's shifts in perspective, such as from narrative to point of view. We then talk about students' choices in framing their own discussions and the ways they need to use verbs and vocabulary to lead the reader through their text.

In addition to the customized reading package, students are also required to purchase a large monolingual learner's dictionary and a grammar reference. The approximately 15 readings in the package, regularly revised, include a variety of media analyses. Readings are supplemented with videos and current media samples brought in by the instructors. In addition, instructors prepare support materials for the readings. Students find the readings challenging, and to encourage close and extensive analyses, we often assign pairs of students to single sections of a text. They read closely, explain the gist to the class, draw generalizations to other texts and to their own experiences, and field questions. We find this method also gives students practice in translating academic prose to informal spoken English and in speaking to the whole group.

◈ DISTINGUISHING FEATURES

From our strong beliefs that ESL students not be marginalized and that ESL curricula be neither watered down nor infantilized, we have framed LNG 200 in the context of critical literacy. The notion of critical literacy, along with its role in English education, has been widely discussed (e.g., Gee, 1991; Lankshear & McLaren, 1993; New London Group, 1996; Shannon, 1995), and it informs our ESL course goals in LNG 200. In the words of Shannon:

> Critical perspectives push the definition of literacy beyond traditional decoding or encoding of words in order to reproduce the meaning of text or society until it becomes a means for understanding one's own history and culture, to recognize connections between one's life and the social structure, to believe that change in one's life, and the lives of others and society, are possible as well as desirable, and to act on this new knowledge in order to foster equal and just participation in all the decisions that affect and control our lives. (p. 83)

In other words, we hope to inaugurate our students into North American culture not solely as well-adapted new citizens, but as informed, reflective, full participants in democratic society. We recognize that LNG 200 will not transform their lives, but we intend it to contribute to their thinking and their English.

Accordingly, we believe that an academic writing course should not only attend to the formal textual demands of universities but also relate in a substantive way to emerging sociopolitical developments and patterns of communication beyond the university, where our students will be workers and citizens.

At first glance, our dual goals might appear to be at cross-purposes. On the one hand, we are helping second language writers conform to the conventions of one institution, the university. On the other, the course readings focus on language skills that critically examine and potentially challenge public institutions that shape students' lives. Nonetheless, we view these two strands of LNG 200 as being complementary. In this sense, we feel that explicit attention to form—writing for academic success—can actually help provide a conceptual foundation with which students might better connect the texts and genres to social purposes and power relations in Canadian society. We examine, for example, the ways assertions are made in various discourses. We contrast the frequent stand-alone assertions in political discourse with the requirements for ample substantiation in academic discourse.

We also recognize that conceptual links between text and social purpose and power are not natural or inevitable products of students' common sense or personal experiences. Students should not have to figure it (i.e., the relationship) out for themselves. Part of our responsibilities as course instructors include the development of a metalanguage, an analytical framework with which students can make comparisons and generalizations, linking personal experiences to theory, and the particular elements of text types to the social contexts and interests they privilege (see also Benesch, 1998; Janks, 1991; Morgan, 1998; New London Group, 1996).

For such purposes, the New London Group proposes a pedagogy of multiliteracies and sketches out two important arguments for its implementation. The first relates to the increasingly prominent role that new information technologies and media play in creating wealth and disparity in an integrated, globalized economy. As suggested by the New London Group, these "new communication media are reshaping the way we use language" (p. 64). Whereas traditional notions of literacy focused on language as the sole channel of communication, multiliteracies emphasize the "multiplicity and integration of significant modes of meaning-making, where the textual is also related to the visual, the audio, the spatial, the behavioral, and so on. This is particularly important in the mass media, multimedia, and in electronic hypermedia" (p. 64).

Our course is organized in ways that relate language and academic writing skills to the varied semiotic modalities outlined above. Although the students in LNG 200 are initially exposed to and responsible for analytical and critical concepts introduced primarily through print-based texts (cf. "text-responsible prose," in Leki & Carson, 1997, p. 41), they are required to apply these concepts to a variety of other multimedia forms: film and television, magazine advertising, Web sites on the Internet, and public language events taking place in Toronto during the course. For their first writing assignment, for example, students are asked to analyze two ads from magazines, newspapers, or the Internet. They are asked specifically, "How do ads use language, together with format and image, to get their appeal and message across? Refer to the types of language devices discussed in your course readings."

Prior to this assignment, two print-based articles, in particular, provide theoretical concepts such as *selection*, *slanting* (Birk & Birk, 1995), and *weasel words* (Lutz, 1995), which students use to analyze the combination of images, shapes, colors, and words in the ads they have chosen. Also prior to this assignment, students watch a video, either *Pack of Lies: The Advertising of Tobacco* (Kilbourne & Pollay, 1992) or *Still Killing Us Softly* (Kilbourne, 1987), which are critical deconstructions of the advertising industry.

Another distinguishing course feature, organized along the same multiliteracy principles outlined above, comes near the end of the course in the shape of a challenging group assignment and oral presentation. Usually during the last week of classes, students give oral presentations on a public event they have attended or a public place they have visited. Two major goals underlie this assignment. One is to have students conceptualize these events as texts, broadly speaking, conceptually relatable to what they have read in print form, but now transposed into other signifying modes, such as time, space, symbols, and gestures. The second is to encourage students to see themselves as active participants in the meanings produced in public life. In the assignment handout, a set of questions establishes the analytical and critical stance expected: "How were language and other forms of communication used by the participants to achieve their purposes? How is it distinguishable as public communication? (e.g., Is it communication of one person to a large group, rather than face-to-face individual interaction? Is access limited in an invisible way?) What part does it play in urban Canadian society?"

In this assignment, there have been successes as well as failures. Some groups fail to theorize or generalize beyond the straightforward description of empirical events, demonstrating to us either our course shortcomings in developing critical language skills that can be applied outside of university settings, or, alternatively, our students' preoccupation with more immediate academic concerns. In terms of success, one presentation from the summer of 1998 stands out in our mind. Two groups from this class joined a tour through one of Toronto's older neighborhoods known as Bloor-Dovercourt Village, an area characterized by its high concentration of diverse ethnic groups, small businesses, and low-income families. What the students commented on most in their presentation was the direct experience of multiculturalism that the tour provided. Although immigrants or visa students themselves, many of the presenters noted that they had never ventured outside of their own ethnic group before. The multiracial and multicultural reality of Toronto was something they read about but felt detached from in their own daily lives. The group talked about visiting a Sudanese cafe, a Latin American grocery, and an East Indian video store. In each, they met the proprietors, asked them questions, and learned about their products and business operations. The tour ended with a brief visit to the Working Women Community Centre to learn about the support services this organization provides for immigrant women. In their presentation of the tour, the group analyzed how the combination and sequencing of the tour enhanced community awareness.

Notions of local diversity serving larger, collective aspirations are key to the second dimension of multiliteracies proposed by the New London Group (1996). Along with global integration of economies and information systems, the New London Group notes the parallel tendency toward increased fragmentation and hybridity of traditional forms of national and sociocultural identity. It views this growth in social diversity as an important asset with profound implications for both language education and public participation: "Effective citizenship and productive work now require that we interact effectively using multiple languages, multiple Englishes, and communication patterns that more frequently cross cultural, community, and national boundaries . . . . In addressing these issues, literacy educators and students must see themselves as active participants in social change" (p. 64).

Once again, we agree and can find a number of features in our course that corroborate the New London Group's position. First, we recognize that a class of NNSs and writers, with different experiences of language and public life, is an invaluable resource for developing critical language awareness and active citizenship. This does not mean that our students are necessarily more intelligent or civic-minded than more established citizens. But it does mean that as newcomers, they have not been exposed to, nor have they internalized, the dominant discourses and supporting language practices to quite the same degree as long-term residents have. When taking up class readings or discussing topics and research for their writing assignments, students often pose questions that challenge the assumptions of many in the class. Similarly, they raise perspectives and analyses of current events that are often unrepresented in the corporate media.

One course feature that is particularly supportive of multiliteracies has been students' research on the Internet in preparation for their major research essay on a current event covered in the media. The types of questions that help guide this assignment are "What images of your topic do the media present? How are these images constructed and conveyed? What social implications do these images have?" One memorable paper used critical concepts from the course reading by Parenti (1986) to frame and compare media coverage of the 1998 Indonesian crisis as reported by Antara (The Indonesia National Agency) and by Western media sources, such as Reuters, the *Toronto Star*, and the *Washington Post*. This was an exceptional paper, researched entirely on the Internet, drawing on this student's first language abilities in Indonesian and her experiences of growing up in the country to provide the class with a more complete perspective on unfolding events and underlying causes. In fact, several students have demonstrated to us in their final papers an outstanding ability to analyze issues from multiple perspectives.

Not all students saw the press negatively. One recent essay examined the coverage of two populist papers and their role in highlighting a local issue of red-light-running at busy municipal intersections. The issue coalesced around individual rights versus public safety. Whereas provincial leaders had refused to take strong measures to document these driving infractions with video cameras, and thereby attempt to control them, two newspapers extensively covered the issue and slanted their coverage in favor of the mayor's stand on public safety. The student writer showed his understanding not just of the newspapers' role but also of the political battle involved. Such insights, in our opinion, exemplify the distinguishing features that define the LNG 200 course.

Yet not all students succeed at this assignment. The most common failure is that students analyze a topic rather than the media's construction of the topic. We see two likely reasons for this failure. First, this analytical perspective is a great deal more demanding than most students may be accustomed to. For example, whereas most topic coverage is taught and done in rhetorical forms, such as exposition or description, we are encouraging students to analyze the media sources as powerful ideological devices that appear to be factual and objective. Second, the less dedicated students, who may attend class sporadically and avoid the readings, may easily misinterpret the assignment. One student struggling with her small stack of Internet print outs noted that "it's not enough to understand the topic; you really have to think critically to do this assignment."

◈ PRACTICAL IDEAS

As noted by Leki and Carson (1997), serious engagement with texts and commitment to ideas in student compositions tend to be of secondary importance in academic writing courses for NNS students. Indeed, some students in our course are surprised and even a little frustrated at times by the attention we devote to the content of the original articles. The challenge of encouraging "text-responsible writing" (Leki & Carson, 1997, p. 41) is also complicated by the types of critical and analytical skills that we would like students to develop in relation to the texts that they read and produce in class. In short, not only are we asking students to learn the content of LNG 200—an uncommon feature of many academic writing courses for NNS students—but we are also asking them to (re)conceptualize the very notions of learning and of content in ways that might bear little resemblance to their past academic and social experiences.

Use Critical Questions to Encourage Critical Text Analysis

One of the practical ways that we try to initiate metalinguistic and critical language awareness is through the types of questions we formulate around class readings, videos, and student assignments. A useful guide for conceptualizing questions comes from the critical literacy concepts developed by Ada (1988) and modified by Cummins (1996). Ada and Cummins describe reading as not simply the passive reception of fixed meanings encoded in texts, but also as active and creative production, where the reading process necessarily generates other texts, both critical and complementary, and with the potential to inspire transformative practice beyond the classroom.

In Ada's typology, descriptive phase questions elicit information stated explicitly in the text itself. In the Birk and Birk (1995) reading, *slanting* is a key metalinguistic concept. A descriptive phase question that reinforces its importance would be: "Slanting by the use of emphasis: How do language elements such as word order, choice of conjunction, and subordinating clauses provide slanting?" Ada's personal interpretive phase links meanings from texts to personal experiences and feelings shared and explored in the classroom. For this perspective in Birk and Birk, we might ask, "What are some examples of charged language in our day-to-day lives? Why should we be careful about it?" A critical analysis phase involves meanings that pertain to issues and propositions put forward: Are they valid? Whose interests are served here? As a follow-up to the description of slanting above, for example, we would ask students to select two facts about a famous person and show favorable and unfavorable emphasis. Then we would ask students to examine the possible social interests served by either emphasis. A creative action phase focuses on textual meanings that define and initiate potential action outside the classroom (Cummins, 1996). As an example, we would reiterate the kinds of questions that influenced students' participation in and critical analysis of a public event based on course readings (i.e., the oral presentation assignment described above).

Use Question Prompts to Guide Students From Thinking to Writing

When assigning essays, we attempt to build on the reading and discussion work that have preceded. At the same time, we find that students frequently have difficulty moving from their thoughts about a topic to a structured essay. It is at this point we feel that topic sentence rules and other such formulae tend to fail our students. Adapting earlier work of Hunter and Cooke (1989), we provide question prompts for students to help them reconceptualize their ideas as information useful to readers and as questions that they will answer, explain, teach, and argue for in elaboration of their essay. For example, in developing the thesis, or their answer to the essay question, we pose the questions: "Why do you think your answer is reasonable? Where did you get your ideas?" Their answers become the basis for reasoned support of their thesis, the position they take in their essay.

⬦ CONCLUSION

In presenting LNG 200, we have emphasized its dual goals of teaching academic language and literacy and critical multiliteracies. Its position in the university as a credit-bearing course and its substantive content help us avoid the marginalization of our students. Furthermore, we consider the subject matter we teach vital because it requires students to use language that counts in learning. We also hope that it can promote critical awareness in a rapidly changing environment and an ability to resist imbalances of power and language. We approach the language and literacy aspect of our course from an individual and a group problem-posing perspective, designed to include all the students in the course dialogue.

As we complete each term, we realize that the subject matter and the students themselves have posed more questions than we have answered in the course. We sometimes fear that with our demanding, multiple goals, students may not have as much time to internalize what we teach them as they need. Nevertheless, for us it is a dynamic, challenging course, one that we continually revise, update, and improve.

⬦ ACKNOWLEDGMENT

We would like to thank David Cooke for his critical comments during the preparation of this chapter.

⬦ CONTRIBUTORS

Judy Hunter is assistant professor of English and coordinator of the Language Centre at Ryerson Polytechnic University in Toronto, Canada, where she has taught since 1992. She teaches writing to native English speakers as well as ESL.

Brian Morgan, in addition to teaching LNG 200, is an adult ESL instructor for the Toronto Catholic District School Board.

CHAPTER 9

A Task-Based Composition Course for Resident L2 Writers

Jessica Williams

◈ INTRODUCTION

The University of Illinois at Chicago (UIC) is a large, urban, state university that draws its undergraduate population mainly from Chicago and its surrounding counties. Until recently, it has been almost completely a commuter school at the undergraduate level, and, although the number of resident students has grown recently, most students still live at home and work part time. The diversity of this population has increased in the past 10 years, with European American students no longer a majority. UIC now has a large number of undergraduates who identify themselves as having a home language other than English. A portion of these students is identified, on the basis of a placement essay test, as ESL students and in need of one or more preparatory ESL courses prior to enrolling in required composition courses. Most of the students who are placed in these courses are Asian, although there is also a significant number of Hispanics and some Eastern Europeans. It has become increasingly apparent that these students have a specific set of needs that are different from those of either underprepared native-English-speakers (NSs) or international students, such as those who might be found in a writing course at an intensive English program or in many colleges and universities (Blanton, 1999; Frodesen & Starna, 1999; Harklau, 1999).

◈ CONTEXT

The demographics of second language (L2) writers at U.S. academic institutions have changed a great deal in the past 25 years, but the programs that provide for their needs and the commercial materials available to them often have not. These changes have been particularly dramatic on the campuses of large, urban, state universities, such as UIC. The students who enroll in undergraduate ESL writing classes at these institutions are not, for the most part, foreign students intending to return to their own countries. Most are permanent residents of the United States and many are citizens. Many have lived in this country for most of their lives, some, all of their lives. They do not take the Test of English as a Foreign Language (TOEFL) because they are graduates of U.S. high schools. Some have been through ESL or bilingual programs in those schools, though many have been mainstreamed. It is often difficult to say what their first language (L1) is. They speak a language other than English in their homes, their command of which varies a great deal. Their command of spoken English ranges from hesitant to that of a native speaker. It is always hard to make generalizations about the proficiency of such speakers in either language, and it is equally difficult to make generalizations regarding their background in writing. Students who have been limited to ESL or bilingual programs often have little experience writing in English beyond the sentence level. Those who were enrolled in NS English classes have often done rather well: They work hard, are well behaved, and complete their assignments. Many report that they were high achieving students in high school English and are surprised, often angry, that they have been placed in ESL composition classes. At UIC, one feature that is common to almost all of these students is that they have very little or no experience in writing in their other (home) language.

Upon examining writing samples produced by these students, it quickly becomes apparent that their writing contains a variety of problems. These include many of the features we often associate with developmental writers, from global problems of focus, organization, and development, to more local issues, such as sentence boundaries. At the same time, they clearly include what are usually perceived as ESL errors; indeed, it is these sorts of errors on the students' placement essays that have landed them in ESL composition classes. Again, the errors range from global issues, such as what constitutes an argument or an appropriate introduction (ironically often attributed to contrasting rhetorical conventions in their L1), to numerous sentence-level problems involving basic syntax and word order, tense choice and formation, and word form, to name but a few. In short, these students face the double challenge of developmental and ESL writers. They are underprepared in so many ways to face the challenges of academic writing that many universities have launched special programs to stanch their attrition rate. The situation is a challenge for students, teachers, and administrators alike.

Because the writing ability of these students so often falls short of what is required in academic writing classes, it is tempting to simply call for more remediation and focus on the deficits in their educational background (see Benesch, 1988, for a discussion of this point). In fact, these students are bright; they have been accepted into good schools. Yet, they are often unprepared to deal with the demands of classes that involve analysis and synthesis of information, written expression in general, and argumentation in particular. As a result, many cling to quantitative courses and shun social sciences and humanities. It is a strategy that works for some, but not all, L2 writers. In designing programs for these students, it is important to ask what they can already do and what they really need. Clearly, they need practice and guidance in writing, but the level of their current academic language and writing skills often hampers them in courses that require them to do research; analyze the information they find; and present an argument, a point of view, or even a report. It is as if they need to learn to do these academic tasks, but in order to practice them, they need prerequisite language skills that they do not have (Adamson, 1993). For instance, they would find almost insurmountable a task that requires them to go to the library or the Internet, find a few journal articles on an assigned or self-chosen topic, read them, summarize them, and include the information in an argument of their own devising. Indeed, this is precisely what they are required to do in subsequent courses, and, even with one or more extra semesters of writing classes under their belts, they find such assignments daunting. On the other hand, asking them to write about a holiday in their supposed home country, or even to write a personal narrative, does little to prepare them for the academic tasks ahead of them. Instead, this group of L2 writers needs to gain experience in academic skills, including writing, by practicing realistic tasks that are challenging, yet within the range of their abilities. This has been the goal of our ESL composition program: to begin with what students can do and build toward more authentic tasks that reflect what will be demanded of them in their later course work.

◈ DESCRIPTION

The ESL composition course described here is designed to prepare L2 writers for NS composition. After completing this course, students go on to a bridge course, followed by the two semesters of composition required of all UIC students. It is difficult to offer an arbitrary label, such as *intermediate*, for these students, and no scores on a standardized test, such as the TOEFL, exist for them. They are placed in this class on the basis of a panel's evaluation of an essay they write when they arrive on campus. The panel is made up of composition and ESL composition instructors. In the judgment of these instructors, the combination of limited writing skills and L2 errors would prevent these students from succeeding in freshman composition. They are therefore placed in this prerequisite class that does not carry graduation credit.

Instructors for the course are drawn from the graduate students in the MA TESOL program at UIC. All have had prior teaching experience, but not all have had extensive experience in the teaching of L2 writing. Thus, this course is generally an educational experience for the teachers as well as the students. Instructors are prepared, observed, and supervised by the director of ESL, who is a member of the TESOL/linguistics faculty.

The ESL composition class meets twice a week for 2 hours over a 15-week semester and is required for those whose UIC placement test scores indicate they need an ESL class. Promotion to the next level is determined solely by the class instructor. In many ways, this class is no different from other university ESL composition classes. The approach to writing is the by-now-traditional process approach, with students expected to complete four or five multidraft assignments. During the course of the semester, the class focuses on various aspects of the writing process, such as idea generation, drafting, and editing, as well as on other important considerations, such as audience, writing purpose, and reader-friendly organization. Some time is also spent on the sentence-level errors that are consistent problems for these learners.

All of the writing assignments in this class revolve around tasks. This task orientation means that students have to do something, not just write something, although, of course, the task always culminates in a writing assignment. These assignments include personal narratives, write-ups of surveys, oral interviews, and data collection and analysis activities. To help students complete these tasks, we have broken them down into component activities, beginning with relatively simple ones, such as listing and relating personal experiences, and building toward more complex problem-solving activities, which involve analytical skills, such as interpretation, evaluation, and synthesis, all of which are crucial to success in other academic classes.

Because this group of L2 writers has had minimal experience using analytical skills, the course begins at a very basic level. In fact, we begin with the notion of writing purpose, using skills they already have. We discovered in developing this course that many of our learners have not yet realized that one writes with a purpose beyond the fulfillment of their assignment. The use of life stories is a good example of this. From time to time, we survey our students about the kind of writing they have done in high school. For the most part, they have done very little, and what little they have done is usually narrative, based on personal experience. Alone, these narratives generally have little place in academia outside the composition classroom, but if they are used to illustrate a more general issue, they make an excellent starting point for students like ours. In our course, a topic that has worked well for this purpose is a narrative about stereotyping or ethnic prejudice. Most learners have had some personal experience with this and can provide an anecdote without much difficulty. Clearly, though, an anecdote is not enough; it must be used as an illustration of a point the writer is trying to make. This task provides a clear demonstration of the difference between the narration students are accustomed to and the use of narration in academic writing. We have used narrative writing successfully as a bridging activity to other, more typical academic writing tasks.

Another common academic task consists of gathering information, finding a logical way to organize it, and then extracting some trend or generalization from it. Indeed, this is not just an academic task, nor even just a writing task. It is the process behind market research, business and political decision making, and much of social science research. It is, quite simply, a basic skill that every college student must learn. For the academically underprepared, however, especially for those trying to do these tasks in a L2, this can be a difficult undertaking. Some sort of transitional task is required. We make use of graphic organizers (see, e.g., Mohan, 1986; Tang, 1992–1993), familiar written material, and orally gathered data to moderate the difficulty of these bridging activities. Two examples of such task-based activities are described below, the first, in some detail.

Information Gathering and Analysis

A more detailed example of the kinds of tasks included in our curriculum is an analysis of marketing strategies. The following description illustrates the information gathering and analytical process learners go through in completing the task.[1]

Students begin by doing some background reading to familiarize themselves with the purposes and techniques of marketing and advertising. Then, they collect their data. This can be done simply by watching TV commercials, leafing through advertisements in magazines, or surfing the Internet to review commercial Web sites. There is no need for students to go to the library, or even do much reading. Although we do not mean in any way to imply that reading is unimportant or should be avoided, we do maintain that it is crucial for students such as the L2 writers in our courses to practice academic skills first. Generally, this practice waits until students' reading skills are at a level to allow them to carry out the research for a writing task independently. Without a doubt, good critical reading skills will be crucial to their academic success, but we believe it is a mistake to delay the development of other academically oriented thinking and writing skills until students can read and

---

[1] More examples of these activities can be found in Williams and Evans (2000).

understand sophisticated texts. They can employ the same analytical skills they use to watch commercials or read advertisements that they will need in more traditional academic work in other courses, in which assignments are often based on analysis of extended written texts.

As they gather their information, students consider the overt message contained in the advertisement or commercial, specifically, what the ad touts as the consequence of using their product, for example, younger looking skin, a greener lawn, or a happier child. After they have done this, we ask the students to think about what the advertising message, or pitch, of the company might be. Initially, many students find this concept difficult to grasp. For this purpose, it is useful to use extensive examples as an introduction. Print ads work well for this purpose because their messages are necessarily succinct. For instance, a magazine ad for makeup might contain the overt message that a particular mascara will enhance the wearer's eyelashes, but clearly the message is a bit more than that. With an ad such as this, learners can fairly quickly articulate the notion that the advertisers are trying to convince readers of the following: *If women use this mascara, they will become more attractive to men.* Not all ads are so easily translated into words, however. An ad for a luxury car might contain a picture of the car in front of a country estate with a sweeping drive. The pitch might be something like: *If you drive this car, it shows that you have high status, and others will respect you.*

After a discussion of sample ads and commercials, students should be able to write *if-then* statements that succinctly articulate advertising pitches, based on the ads they have already read or watched:

> If you use product X, you will . . . .
>
> If you buy product Y, it shows . . . .
>
> If you don't use product Z, people will (not) . . . .

Understanding the advertising pitch is only the first step in the analysis of a marketing strategy, however. Students must work their way from the advertisers' message to the broader marketing plan. To do this, they need to go back to their advertisements or commercials and consider where they saw them. A chart is useful for this purpose. We usually start students off with some examples, such as those presented in Table 1, and then give them a blank chart of their own.

After students collect the data, they continue to analyze their information. The raw data at first may seem unwieldy to them, yet it is possible for them to make generalizations with a little help. Specifically, they need to find out what audience the

TABLE 1. UNDERSTANDING TARGET POPULATION OF ADVERTISEMENTS

Product	Advertising message	Source	Target Population
Ortega taco shells	Your family will love the food you make.	*Family Circle* (magazine)	mothers
Gatorade	You will play basketball like Michael Jordan.	*Sports Illustrated* (magazine)	(young) men
Federal Express			
Sears			

company is trying to reach with these ads or commercials. Who is the target population, and what steps is the company taking to try to reach them? Again, examples are helpful. It is particularly useful to present a single product and then discuss its appeal to different segments of the consumer market, as in this example for fast food:

- Who might care that fast food is cheap?
- Who might care that fast food is fast?
- Who might care that fast food means no cooking?
- Who might care that fast food includes toys from popular movies?

Students can then put themselves in the shoes of the company's marketing department by asking questions such as the following:

If you were in charge of marketing for Burger Heaven, a fast food chain,

- how would you advertise and where and when would you do it?
- whom would you try to reach and how?
- would you create television commercials? Print ads?
- what might they say?

With these questions in mind, students can begin to imagine which populations are being targeted for the products they have looked at in their own research. They can then incorporate this information into the final column for target population on their charts, as in the example for magazine advertisements shown in Table 1.

One of the things that students find the most difficult is the next step: turning the information they have collected into claims they can support. Having the information down in tabular form makes it somewhat easier for them to express these claims in their writing. Again, however, some support is required, and guiding questions such as these can be helpful:

- Why do companies choose to advertise in certain magazines?
- Who is buying and reading *Newsweek? People? GQ? PCWeek?*
- Why do companies choose certain TV shows for their advertisements?
- Who is watching *Jerry Springer? ER? Monday Night Football?*
- Why do companies use specific advertising pitches?

Our students then generally can come up with claims much like the following simulated example about television ads:

> Children are the main people eating breakfast cereal. Therefore, cereal manufacturers show most of their ads during cartoons because that is when children are watching television. Some ads show that the cereal is good tasting; others show famous sports stars eating it; some show the toys that are inside the box. Children like all of those things.

Developing Expertise and Audience Awareness

A second task-based unit included in the curriculum focuses on audience awareness and writing purpose. In this unit, which appears later in the course, students choose a university service to research and present. These services can range from tutoring, student employment, intramural sports, housing, or the university records office or health service. They might choose the service because of a negative experience they have had or because they never knew about a service that might have proven helpful. They gather their information in a variety of ways. First, they may draw on their own personal experience. They can interview others who have used the service to find out what went wrong or how best to access the service. They might interview directors, coordinators, or even the person at the front desk. Finally, they must analyze the written texts that the service distributes to publicize itself. Johns (1997) stresses the importance of increasing students' awareness of a variety of text genres, especially those that assume a shared knowledge of the discourse community in which these students are expected to participate. In particular, our students focus on what in the text might confuse or exclude its readers. As Johns suggests, this analysis can also be used to explore issues of genre and discourse community. For instance, why does a pamphlet about the many services of the university computer center baffle so many potential users? What does it assume readers already know? What are its goals? How well does it achieve them?

All of this information is brought together into an essay that sometimes surprises beginning composition students. Many have become accustomed to expository and persuasive writing in which they must introduce and present a series of (three) well-supported claims. In this task, students must combine personal narrative, text analysis, and advice in one piece of writing. This is real writing with a real purpose and a real audience. Incoming freshman in our composition classes have found the essays of previous students very useful in the initial weeks of their first semester. Toward the end of the semester, when we ask students to write an essay of their own, their role as advisors and their audience is already established.

◈ DISTINGUISHING FEATURES

Our approach to task development has been based on concerns for authenticity, learner autonomy, and learner support. Long and Crookes (1992) maintain that a task focuses "on something that is done, not something that is said" (p. 43). They argue that pedagogic tasks should be based on analysis of target tasks and sequenced in increasingly complex approximations of those target tasks. This is exactly what we have tried to do. An analysis of the task types typical of beginning students at UIC has yielded a set of target writing and analysis tasks on which we have based our composition course. These pedagogic tasks are as authentic as possible, approximating the kinds of analytic and writing activities that are typical outside of the composition classroom. They include a range of activities that, initially, are carefully guided and later allow a great deal more learner autonomy. The goal of increasing learner independence and task authenticity must be balanced with the learners' need for support in embarking on academic writing.

What distinguishes this course from many other ESL composition classes is its task orientation and the concentration on the skills necessary to complete a writing assignment that are required before, during, and after the actual writing. The guiding principle has been the completion of tasks that require increasing cognitive complexity across the 15 weeks, yet do not necessarily involve increasing language proficiency. Skehan (1998) provides an analytical scheme for describing tasks, based on cognitive complexity, code complexity, and communicative pressure. Within his framework, we have attempted to steadily increase the cognitive complexity, without increasing code (language) complexity. The components of cognitive complexity in Skehan's scheme include the degree of cognitive familiarity and amount of cognitive processing required. We have attempted to manipulate these by decreasing the former and increasing the latter over the course of the semester.

The challenge of creating materials for our students is to get them to engage in academic tasks and academic writing before they are usually considered to have the linguistic resources to actually do so. They find it difficult to go to the library or the Internet, find texts, or write from sources, as well as interpret them; yet soon they will be asked to do just that. Thus, this preparatory class models some of these activities by requiring similar, but more accessible, tasks. It builds from less demanding activities to ones that begin to approximate the academic writing requirements of other content courses.

Our goal in the unit on information gathering and analysis described above is to have students engage in an information gathering task that does not involve extended written texts. We therefore looked to visual media for possibilities. In this unit, students must gather, organize, analyze, and present information on marketing strategies. This is cognitively very complex; however, because the material is familiar and gathered in simple ways, the task becomes accessible. In addition, because of the complexity of the task and our learners' inexperience in doing this kind of analysis, we provide a fair amount of guidance. This unit goes on to explore paragraph development, again using the data students have gathered to support the claims they have made, and occurs around the middle of the semester, when students still need considerable support. At the end of the semester, they have completed a task that has all the elements of a fairly typical academic writing task. Yet, it remains within the range of the ability of these L2 writers. Earlier units contain even more guided tasks, whereas later units tend to allow greater learner autonomy.

In the second unit described above, students produce a guide to using a specific university service for future students at UIC. Many specialists in the teaching of writing have stressed that it is important for student writers to develop expertise. Leki (1991–1992) describes how this might be done with L2 writers. For those with low language proficiency and minimal writing experience, however, this is not easy to accomplish. In what, other than their personal experience, can they claim expertise? The key is to turn that personal experience into something that can realistically prepare them for academic writing. One area in which freshman L2 writers often can claim expertise is in dealing with a large and unfamiliar university bureaucracy. This is the basis for the information gathering and writing in this unit. Our students attempt to turn their own, often negative, experiences into constructive advice for future and prospective students. In this assignment, the students' personal experience with adjustment to university life provides the information for a task that showcases their expertise, while providing them with an opportunity for real writing for a real audience for a real purpose. Thus, these learners have engaged in another preparatory academic task of considerable complexity, yet one that is well within their ability and resonates to their own experience.

In our view, our time is best spent in helping learners develop their abilities in all of the analytical and writing processes that will lead to academic success. For instance, learners in this class spend as much time collecting and analyzing data as they do writing. They also devote time and energy to developing their own error correction strategies, ones that they will use in writing papers in the future. The focus of the material presented here is on the early part of the writing process: data collection, analysis, and organization; however, the same approach may be taken to later stages of the writing process. For example, peer response and revision, which occur later in the writing process, are complex activities that need a great deal of initial support before learners can work effectively and independently (see Williams & Evans, 2000).

PRACTICAL IDEAS

We have tailored our tasks to meet the needs of students at UIC. There are many universities throughout the United States, and perhaps in other countries, that have similar L2 populations, and we therefore expect that their needs would be quite similar to ours. However, the more closely the course can be adjusted to meet the needs and interests of the specific population, the more successful it is likely to be. The following are some suggestions for similar pedagogic tasks.

Task 1: Gather Information and Extract Generalizations

Any number of possibilities present themselves here. A less complex task might be a survey activity, in which students gather information about the opinions, attitudes, or practices of their peers. It could be about parental discipline and authority, computer use, attitudes toward dating, or an intended major. Some students may be able and willing to select their own topic. This kind of activity would be less complex than the first one offered in this report, in that the central task after data collection would be to extract a generalization based on the data, whereas the marketing strategy task required a more sophisticated analysis of strategy and motivation. Thus, in Skehan's (1998) terms, a survey and reporting task is somewhat less complex in terms of both cognitive familiarity and cognitive processing.

Task 2: Develop Expertise and Audience Awareness

New students can always use advice and upperclassmen are usually ready to give it. A possible variation on the task described in this article would be to tackle a campus issue. Again, this could include personal experience, interviews, and text analysis, but could also take on an advocacy purpose. Potential issues might include food services on campus, campus parking policies, or registration procedures. This activity could be made more complex by adding a solution component. In the task included in this report, students had only to offer advice to other students on how best to avail themselves of campus services. A more demanding assignment would be to offer possible improvements, thus decreasing cognitive familiarity and increasing cognitive processing requirements. It could also include a more critical component, in which the writers actively seek to bring about positive change in their community through their writing.

CONCLUSION

UIC's ESL composition program takes a task-based approach to the teaching of writing and academic skills. We have attempted to sequence pedagogic tasks of increasing complexity that are reflections of the kinds of academic work our students will confront in subsequent classes. In the future, we hope to be able to extend this task-based approach to lower level ESL composition classes.

❖ ACKNOWLEDGMENT

I would like to thank Jacqueline Evans, who was an equal partner in developing the curriculum for the composition course described here.

❖ CONTRIBUTOR

Jessica Williams is director of ESL Composition and of the University Writing Center at the University of Illinois at Chicago, in the United States, where she also teaches in the MA Linguistics-TESOL program. Her most recent publications are *Focus on Form in Classroom Second Language Acquisition* (with Catherine Doughty; Cambridge University Press, 1998) and *Getting There: Tasks for Academic Writing* (with Jacqueline Evans; Holt Rinehart, 2000).

CHAPTER 10

Academic Writing for University Examinations

Sara Cushing Weigle and Gayle Nelson

◈ INTRODUCTION

In 1990, three Georgia State University (GSU) faculty members were awarded a 3-year grant by the U.S. Department of Education's Fund for the Improvement of Postsecondary Education (FIPSE). One of the goals of the grant was to study the academic demands of undergraduate courses at GSU, in particular, the reading, writing, and oral/aural demands of entry-level courses in four disciplines:

1. American history

2. political science

3. biology

4. freshman composition (Carson, Chase, Gibson, & Hargrove, 1992)

An important outcome of the FIPSE research was a description of the academic literacy requirements of these courses—that is, what students were actually expected to do with language to be successful. One purpose of gathering this information was to inform the curriculum of GSU's preuniversity ESL program so that courses could be closely tailored to the actual needs of students entering undergraduate programs. In some instances, the findings of the study contradicted our assumptions about language use in undergraduate courses. For instance, the analysis of the FIPSE data revealed that GSU freshmen and sophomore students are seldom required to write out-of-class research papers; in fact, freshman composition is virtually the only class of those studied that asks students to do extensive out-of-class writing. Contrary to our assumptions, the purpose of most writing in the classes studied was to demonstrate mastery of course content (e.g., facts, theories, concepts) on tests.

As a result of the findings from the FIPSE study, complemented by additional research that demonstrated the importance of short, in-class writing tasks in university courses (Hale, Taylor, Bridgeman, Carson, Kroll, & Kantor, 1996), the curriculum of the ESL program at GSU was reconfigured, with the goal of aligning the courses more closely with the actual language demands of the university. The curriculum revision was guided by two important principles:

1. Courses were to be structured around the academic language tasks required in university courses.

2. Courses were to simulate entry-level university courses as much as possible, in particular, by using sustained content and authentic text-books and materials.

In the revised curriculum, there are two separate courses at each proficiency level that deal with writing. The first, Structure and Composition, focuses primarily on out-of-class, extensive writing and introduces students to the processes of writing, revising, and editing a text over an extended time period, with a complementary focus on improving students' mastery of English grammar. The other course, and the subject of this chapter, is entitled Academic Writing for University Examinations[1] and was designed specifically to address the need for students to cope with text-responsible writing tasks (Leki & Carson, 1997) of the kind identified by Carson et al. (1992). This course has three primary distinctive features. First, the course focuses on the kinds of writing tasks most often required in lower division university classes (i.e., written responses to test questions of various kinds). Second, the course features an integration of reading and writing through sustained content, that is, a single academic content area that provides the conceptual and linguistic input for the writing tasks. Finally, assessment of students' writing in the course is based on students' mastery of the content material as well as on their ability to respond to identification, short answer, and essay questions in an appropriate way.

◈ CONTEXT

The Intensive English Program (IEP) at GSU is a preuniversity English for academic purposes program that offers courses at five levels of proficiency. Full-time students in the IEP are in class 18 hours per week for a 15-week semester.

Students in the IEP come from a variety of backgrounds. In spring semester 1999, 160 students from 46 countries were enrolled either full or part time in the IEP, with the largest numbers of students coming from Vietnam (22%) and Korea (12%). Most students enroll in the IEP with the intent to continue their studies at GSU or another U.S. university.

◈ DESCRIPTION

Academic Writing for University Exams is a course that meets 3 hours a week for 15 weeks. The course is taught at the highest three levels of the IEP: Level 3 (intermediate), Level 4 (high intermediate), and Level 5 (advanced). Each course is tied to a single academic content area. The Level 3 course uses materials from earth science, Level 4 deals with anthropology, and Level 5 uses U.S. history. The materials for the course include a packet of readings taken from authentic academic texts in the content area and a study guide, which includes a variety of supporting materials.

The five main goals of the course are to

1. practice writing skills needed to understand, synthesize, and apply the reading material (i.e., writing to learn), including note taking, using graphic organizers (e.g., charts and/or diagrams), and paraphrasing

---

[1] This chapter is a description of three levels of one ESL writing course at Georgia State University. An in-depth description of one level of the course can be found in Nelson (1999).

2. identify, analyze, and practice organization techniques used by academic writers to express ideas and their interrelationships, including chronological order, comparison, classification, and cause-effect

3. study the format of and write answers to the types of exam questions used in the university, including identification, short answer, short essay (up to half a page), and longer essay (1–2 pages)

4. learn the appropriate language that should be used to answer each type of question, including the language of assertion, attribution, exemplification, definition, classification, causality, and comparison

5. improve computer skills, for example, by using e-mail journals as course assignments

Course activities are organized around academic tasks and pedagogical tasks. Academic tasks are those that support the learning of content information through a combination of reading and writing experiences: That is, they are tasks that a student would ordinarily perform in a regular university class to learn and demonstrate mastery of course material, such as taking reading notes or writing responses to short-answer test items. Pedagogical tasks are those that would not necessarily be required of students in an academic course but, rather, support the learning of academic tasks. Examples of pedagogical tasks are completing graphic organizers, keeping vocabulary logs, and studying academic language structures. Academic tasks and pedagogical tasks are similar at all three levels of the program, although the materials become more complex, cognitively and linguistically, as students advance through the program. The major academic and pedagogical tasks are outlined below.

Academic Tasks

The primary academic tasks are taking reading notes and writing answers to identification, short-answer, and essay questions, the three question types that have been identified as the most frequently used in university courses (Carson et al., 1992). Reading notes are introduced beginning at Level 3 as an important way to manage the extensive reading load of university courses, specifically, to help students understand the reading materials and prepare for class discussions and tests. Students are given guidelines for taking reading notes and are provided with model notes as well. Figure 1 shows an excerpt from model reading notes at Level 4. This model demonstrates several successful strategies for taking reading notes emphasized in the course: for example, the use of abbreviations, an outline format, and a simple chart comparing information about humans and animals. Several times during the semester, students' reading notes are collected and evaluated by the instructor in terms of their completeness and efficiency. It is important that students recognize that taking reading notes is, in fact, a kind of writing that will be useful to them in their university careers, even if it is writing that does not follow the conventions and rules of what we ordinarily think of as academic writing.

A good deal of class time is spent discussing, analyzing, and writing responses to the three types of test items. Identification (ID) questions are the first type of question taught. They tend to be the shortest type of written test question, often asking for definitions of key terms or information about important people, places, or theories. ID questions are important for learning the content area's key terms, concepts, and

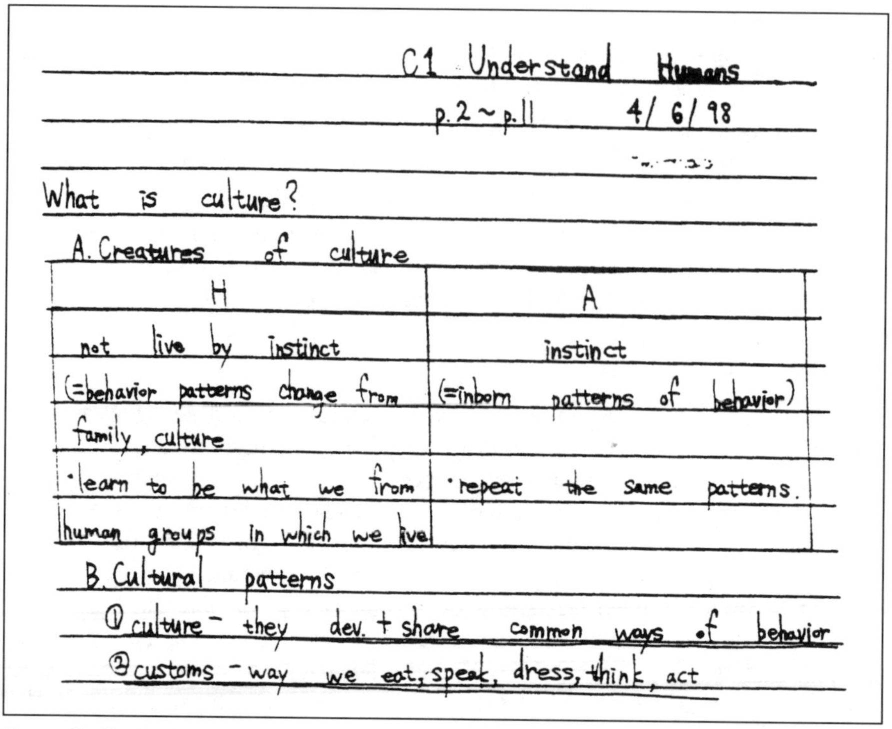

C1 Understand Humans
p.2 ~ p.11 4/ 6/ 98

What is culture?

A. Creatures of culture

H	A
not live by instinct	instinct
(=behavior patterns change from	(=inborn patterns of behavior)
family, culture	
·learn to be what we from	·repeat the same patterns.
human groups in which we live	

B. Cultural patterns

① culture – they dev. + share common ways of behavior

② customs – way we eat, speak, dress, think, act

FIGURE 1. Excerpt From Student Reading Notes (Level 4) (Note: H = Humans, A = Animals)

events, and for determining which ones are important. In responding to ID questions, students also learn how to write definitions. Information about ID questions and a sample test item and answer from the Level 3 course are shown in Figure 2.

Responding to short-answer questions requires similar skills needed for answering ID questions, but, in addition, students must learn how to manage and organize

ID questions

- ask for definitions (important terms)
- ask about important people or places
- require that you state why the person or place is important to the field you are studying
- require a written response of a phrase or a sentence
- are often worth about 2 points each on a test

Sample ID Test Item and Answer

Niels Bohr

scientist—proposed a model of the atom in 1913

FIGURE 2. Information About ID Questions and Sample Test Item and Answer (Level 3)

Type of Test Question: Short-Answer Questions

Short-answer questions usually ask for more information or more complex information than simple ID questions. They often require a written response of approximately four–eight *complete* sentences. They are usually called "short-answer questions," although different instructors use different terms. Short-answer questions

- ask you to compare two concepts or to define or explain a concept and give an example
- do not ask for a lot of detail or explanation
- are usually about 5–10 points each
- begin with a general statement (often a restatement of the question) and then become more specific

Directions for answering short-answer questions usually contain words and exact instructions that guide your answer (e.g., *define, what, compare*). You must pay attention to the language used in the question.

FIGURE 3. Guidelines for Answering Short-Answer Questions (Level 4)

larger amounts of information. Students are taught the type of information called for in short-answer questions and a common organizational pattern to use in answering these questions. The types of information and organizational patterns taught to students in Level 4 are presented in Figure 3.

Figure 4 provides a sample short-answer question and response from the Level 4 course. This short-answer response is included in the students' course packet as an example of an effective student response, along with comments from the instructor about what makes it effective.

Essay questions are similar to short-answer questions but tend to be longer and often call for a larger range of rhetorical patterns and more details or evidence to

---

Test Question

What is *conspicuous consumption*? Give an example of conspicuous consumption.

Possible Answer	Analysis
Conspicuous consumption is a behavior where you show off or display your wealth. For example, the Kwakiutl tribe of the Canadian coast has a special ceremony (a *potlatch*). In a potlatch, an owner burns his belongings in front of others. The purpose of a potlatch is to show a person's wealth and shame his rivals. In the United States, people wear brand name clothing and shoes to show that they have money.	Began with an assertion. Strengthened the assertion by providing an example. Provided even more detail by explaining the example. Provided an example from U.S. society.

FIGURE 4. Sample Short-Answer Question and Response (Level 4)

support students' assertions. To answer essay questions, students need to learn the rhetorical structures inherent in the questions (e.g., cause and effect, comparison/contrast, description, classification). Although students learn the rhetorical conventions of a specific academic discipline, the conventions are widely applicable to other disciplines and contexts. Students become aware of the transferability of the conventions as they move up through the levels and apply the same writing strategies to new materials in different content areas. Figure 5 provides guidelines given to Level 4 students to help them in answering essay questions.

Type of Test Question: Essay Questions

Essay questions

- require a more detailed response than ID or short-answer questions. Your essay response should be 8–15 sentences in length. (The number of sentences will vary, depending on the sentence structures you use. For example, if you write mostly compound and complex sentences, you might have closer to 8 sentences. If you write mostly simple sentences, you will need to write more sentences.)

- are usually worth 15–30 points each.

Essay questions usually ask students to

- explain a concept, event, or procedure in detail

- show the relationship between two or more concepts, events, or procedures

- describe or summarize a theory, invention, or event

- discuss the importance or advantages/disadvantages of an idea, invention, event, or theory

Directions for essay questions usually contain words and exact instructions that guide your answer (e.g., *define*, *what*, *compare*). You must pay attention to the language used in the question. Guidelines for writing responses to essay questions are provided in the boxes below.

> Begin with an assertion (a restatement of the question or a general statement).

↕

> Strengthen your assertion by adding supporting details. You might describe an event and then give reasons for that event, explain an idea and then provide examples to make that idea clear, define a concept and then explain its importance, or explain a procedure and then compare it to something else.

↕

> Sometimes you might end with a closing statement that is general in nature or that restates your main idea. It is also possible to include predictions.

FIGURE 5. Guidelines for Answering Essay Questions (Level 4)

An example of an essay question from Level 4 and a student's response to the question are given in Figure 6. Note that, as before, the instructor has provided specific details about what makes this response particularly effective.

Pedagogical Tasks

Three main pedagogical tasks are used to prepare students for the academic tasks: student-generated questions and answers, graphic organizers, and charts for academic language structures. In addition, students keep vocabulary notebooks and, in some classes, use journals to reflect on the course content and integrate it with their own previous knowledge.

Student-Generated Answers and Questions

After students study each question type, they practice answering and writing each type of question. At the beginning of the course, instructors write the ID questions, and students write the answers. The instructor shows the class particularly good responses on the overhead projector (OHP) so they can see the qualities that make them successful responses. Later, students begin writing their own ID questions, either on paper or on a transparency, and exchange them with partners or group members. Again, examples of answers are shown on the OHP and explained. This

---

Test Question

The Dobu, Zuni, and Kwakiutl cultures each produced a different personality type among its members. How would you explain this? In other words, why do these differences exist?

Student Response	*Analysis*
The Dobu are hate-filled, the Zuni are restrained, and the Kwakiutl are go-getters. According to Dr. Benedict's study, each culture produced a different personality type among its members. There are many factors which contribute to shaping each personality. One of them is cultural determinism. Culture can determine what a person can or cannot become. For instance, a Kwakiutl cannot gain prestige without having the potlatch ceremony because his culture asks him to follow such ceremonies to show off his status among the people of the tribe. Another factor which is equally important is the physical environment. People must adapt themselves to the land and the climate. Each tribe has its own culture and environment, and this explains why each tribe is different from each other.	Began with an assertion by restating the question. Used an attribution structure in the assertion. Used a classification sentence to organize ideas. (coherence: *one of them*) Used a specific example with an example structure. (coherence: *another factor*) Included concluding statements.

FIGURE 6. Essay Question Student Response (Level 4)

method is valuable not only because it enables the instructor to point out the qualities that make up a good answer but because it also helps the instructor assess the areas with which students are having trouble. Student-generated questions are also useful in helping students develop the skill of distinguishing essential information from less important details.

Short-answer and essay questions follow the same format: Students write and answer each other's questions and also the teacher's questions. The class discusses the quality of the questions as well as the answers. Students also evaluate their own responses with a self-assessment checklist.

Graphic Organizers

Graphic organizers provide a way to record and organize information from the text as a supplement to reading notes or as an aid in studying for a test. They are more visual than traditional outline-form notes and clearly achieve several of the goals of sustained content, such as identifying key ideas in reading and the relationships among key and supporting ideas, and learning and practicing argumentation and rhetorical conventions (e.g., cause/effect, comparison/contrast). At the beginning of the semester, the instructor gives the students graphic organizers to fill out, but as the course progresses, students take on the responsibility of preparing their own graphic organizers to help them make sense of the materials. Graphic organizers can take the form of charts, conceptual maps, or any display that visually represents relationships among ideas from the readings.

Charts for Academic Language Structures

In addition to learning how to identify key information in a text, students have many opportunities to learn and practice academic language structures. In the course packets, students find clear, simple charts containing words and structures for fulfilling a particular function (e.g., classification, definition, attribution). These charts are the same for all three levels (with the addition of some more complex structures at the advanced level) so that the material can be recycled from term to term. In this way, students become more familiar with the language structures and can also see clearly how these structures are used across disciplines. For example, the chart presenting language of comparison and contrast contains coordinators, transition words, subordinators, and other words and phrases that show how two things are alike or different. Students work with the charts in several different ways, such as finding examples of the various language structures from their text and creating their own examples using course content. Students also use the charts when writing their own answers to essay questions, and to evaluate their own answers in terms of how well they have incorporated academic language.

Typical Unit

A typical unit begins with one or more prereading activities to build background knowledge to help students to comprehend the reading assignment. Students read a portion of the chapter and take reading notes. Even though they have read the material, they generally come to class with questions, and these are discussed in class. The content is explored through the use of graphic organizers, and the language of the text is analyzed using the academic language structure charts. Before being tested on the materials, students generate their own sample test questions and answers, and these are discussed with the whole class in terms of their relevance, accuracy, and use of academic language structures. Finally, the test for the unit consists of the three types of questions discussed previously: ID, short answer, and short essay (with some longer essays at Level 5). Test responses are graded on content, format, and language use.

◈ DISTINGUISHING FEATURES

Although Academic Writing for University Examinations is distinctive in a number of ways, three features of the program are particularly noteworthy. First, the focus of the course is on text-responsible writing of the sort that students actually need to master in their university courses. Second, sustained content is used to simulate university classes and to give students multiple opportunities to build content and discourse schemata relevant to a single academic discipline. Finally, the approach to writing instruction is carried through to evaluation, in that students are tested, not just on how well they are able to write, but on how well they have mastered the discipline-specific content they have studied throughout the term. Each of these distinguishing features is discussed in further detail below.

Focus on Connecting Reading, Writing, and Critical Thinking

The curriculum for Academic Writing for University Examinations is based upon research into what students actually need to accomplish with writing during their first 2 years of undergraduate study. The existence of two separate writing courses in the curriculum—one dealing primarily with out-of-class writing assignments and the other with in-class essay examinations—signals to students the importance of writing in undergraduate studies and highlights the fact that these two different kinds of writing are used for different purposes and audiences and require different skills on the part of the student.

Even though the title of the course clearly states the focus of the course, it should not be assumed that Academic Writing for University Examinations is simply a test preparation course. In fact, although students may see this approach to teaching writing as primarily beneficial in terms of their ability to get better grades in courses (by understanding what it is that the professor is looking for), the value of the course goes well beyond that. Students are learning to become critical readers and writers and are mastering strategies that will help them with future learning situations. In generating ID questions, students are learning to discern not just what questions the professor is likely to ask on the exam, but what information is relevant and important to know and why. Similarly, in responding appropriately to ID questions, students are not simply learning a collection of facts about history or earth science, but how to identify why a concept, fact, or person is important.

For example, a Level 5 student studying the early colonization of the New World in U.S. history answered an ID question about tobacco as follows: "A plant that grows in the south, for example in Maryland and Virginia." This example illustrates a problem that occurs repeatedly with ID questions: Students have difficulty selecting the key information from the reading. Therefore, the instructor prompted the class for further information by responding, "That's true, but a lot of crops were grown in

Maryland and Virginia. Why was tobacco important?" The student replied, "Because the early colonists of Maryland and Virginia wouldn't have survived without it. They needed the money from selling the tobacco." The instructor continued, "Great! And what time period are we studying?," to which the student responded, "the 1600s." The student eventually wrote, "Tobacco was the main crop in Virginia and Maryland in the 1600s. Without it, the colonists probably wouldn't have survived. The colonists sold it in Europe to make money to live on." Working with ID questions, students become aware of the need to pinpoint what made a person, product, or event important (i.e., worth studying) and to state that importance in their answers.

This process of identifying key information to answer questions reflects the link between reading, writing, and critical thinking. Students read the material; take notes on what they perceive to be key terms, concepts, people, and events; and use that information to answer test questions. To identify key information, however, students must think critically. They must choose what information from the text is worthy of note taking and studying. These processes involve critical decision making: what material is important and what information is needed to correctly complete the task.

The process of reading, writing, and answering questions also reflects the progressive and cyclical nature of learning. In the tobacco example, the student learned some information, but not the most essential information. As a result of the class discussion and revisiting the text, the student learned why tobacco was important to the colonists, how to identify key information, and, perhaps, that the process of reading and writing is cyclical: Students read, then write, and then read some more (their own writing as well as the writing in the text) to determine if they have said what they want to say, understood the text, and correctly completed the task.

Sustained Content

Another key feature of the course is the use of sustained content, not just over a period of several weeks, but over the entire 15-week semester. By reading one content area, students become familiar with the vocabulary, grammatical structures, and rhetorical patterns of the academic discipline. In the beginning of the course, they write short answers, giving them time to become familiar with the rhetorical conventions and background of the discipline that is needed for writing answers to more complex essay questions. Without sustained content, students would not have the opportunity to gradually acquire (through reading) an in-depth understanding of the language and conventions used in one discipline, the kind of understanding that is expected of them in academic and workplace settings.

As students move from answering ID to essay questions, the tasks become more complicated and the need for sustained content more important. If students are faced with processing new information, vocabulary, and rhetorical conventions from numerous thematic units as well as learning new academic tasks, the cognitive demand is extremely high. Also, learning to synthesize, compare, and contrast is problematic if the content changes from one thematic unit to another. If the content remains constant, however, new information builds on previous information, patterns of knowledge emerge (e.g., in U.S. history, similarity in patterns of settling the colonies), and rhetorical conventions remain stable. Consequently, students learn content and skills that they will use later.

Smith's (1988) metaphor of the literacy club may be helpful here. Smith compares academic disciplines to clubs (e.g., tennis or gardening clubs). Like other clubs, the literacy club has members, rules, conventions, traditions, and membership criteria. Smith argues that for students to become a member of a particular literacy club, they must participate in the literacy of that community, including the linguistic and rhetorical practices of the community. Similarly, Bartholomae (1988) contends that a student has "to try on the particular ways of knowing, selecting, evaluating, reporting, concluding, and arguing that define the discourse" (p. 273) of a particular discipline. The kind of knowledge acquisition that Smith and Bartholomae are referring to is difficult, if not impossible, without multiple opportunities to encounter, read, talk, think, and write about a single content area throughout an academic term.

One important consideration that went into decisions about course content was the desire to balance cognitive load with linguistic load. Students at lower levels of language proficiency require materials with a lower cognitive load so that they can focus on acquiring the language they need to be able to deal with more difficult material later on. As proficiency levels increase, so does the cognitive load of the reading materials. All of the materials used in our courses are authentic in the sense that they are textbooks intended for use by native speakers of English. However, to achieve the appropriate level of cognitive versus linguistic load, we use materials intended for middle school students at Level 3, for high school students at Level 4, and for lower division university students at Level 5. The content areas themselves were also chosen with cognitive load in mind. Earth science at Level 3 was chosen because the topics and concepts are concrete and require a minimum of background knowledge, particularly culture-specific background knowledge. Earth science also lends itself well to the patterns of organization of compare/contrast, classification, cause/effect, and process. At Level 4, the materials from anthropology are somewhat more abstract, yet provide opportunities to recycle many of the same academic language structures and organizational patterns as at Level 3. At the same time, anthropology is made personally meaningful to students because it allows them to reflect on a variety of cultural differences that they may have experienced in their own lives.

Finally, at Level 5, U.S. history is studied, using chapters from the same textbook used in introductory courses at GSU. U.S. history is a particularly difficult course for ESL students at GSU (Carson et al., 1992). ESL students often know little about U.S. history when they begin the course and therefore have little background knowledge on which to build. To take just one example, the religious issues that are central to understanding the colonization of North America by different groups can be bewildering to students from non-Western cultures, for whom the distinction between Catholicism and Protestantism is as opaque as the difference between sects of Buddhism would be to most U.S. college students. Another reason that U.S. history can be particularly difficult for ESL students is that university history courses typically have a reading load of up to 85 pages a week (Carson et al., 1992). Because nonnative speakers of English frequently read at a much slower rate than the 200 words per minute generally considered to be minimally necessary for adequate comprehension (Eskey, 1986; Smith, 1982), students need strategies to manage and organize this much reading. Providing background knowledge and strategy training in the academic writing class arms students with the skills they need to take the regular university history class upon exiting the IEP.

Assessment and Evaluation

As Weigle and Jensen (1997) point out, one of the key issues in testing in content-based language programs is the extent to which assessment is based on mastery of the content, mastery of the language, or both. At GSU, students are evaluated on how well they have mastered the rhetorical and linguistic conventions of the specific test item types taught in the course and the accuracy of their answers based on the course readings. Essay questions at all levels are scored on a 25-point scale, with 10 points for correct content, 10 for organization, and 5 for language use. During a mandatory orientation at the beginning of each semester, new instructors are trained by an experienced instructor in the use of the scoring rubric so that similar standards are used to evaluate essays across different sections of the same course. The instructors give the students the scoring rubric so they are aware of the criteria on which their writing will be judged.

Another important aspect of the evaluation process is that the tests simulate university exams in that the question types (ID, short-answer, and essay) are those that have been shown to be the most common test types outside of objective items (e.g., multiple-choice, true/false) used in lower division university courses. Students thus become very familiar with the kinds of examinations they will have to face at the university and learn explicit strategies for dealing with these kinds of tests.

Similarly, students are never tested on things they have not had ample opportunity to work on in class. For example, students are never asked to write an impromptu essay on a topic they have not discussed in class, or to read and answer comprehension questions on an unfamiliar passage. On the contrary, students are only tested on material they have read, discussed, and written about extensively in class.

◈ PRACTICAL IDEAS

In many situations, it may not be feasible or even desirable to structure an entire course around the writing tasks discussed in this chapter. However, many of the activities and tasks from our course can be adapted for use in other settings. The examples of academic language structures, descriptions of test item types, graphic organizers, and in-class activities described above can easily be used with different content areas and at varying levels of proficiency. To aid practitioners in adapting the ideas from our course, what follows is a description of how various activities can be sequenced to integrate reading, using appropriate academic language, and writing essays.

Use Graphic Organizers

With the help of computers, it is not difficult to create graphic organizers that help students organize the content of a reading passage in a way that makes relationships clearer to them. Graphic organizers can be seen as a note-taking, organizing, and prewriting activity. Before filling out the example graphic organizer in Figure 7, students in the Level 3 class read a portion of the textbook on plains and plateaus.

Activity 3: Graphic Organizer

Landforms: Plains and Plateaus

In Boxes 1 and 2, list phrases and words to describe plains and plateaus. Then, in Box 3, list the similarities and the differences between them. (What is the same and what is different?)

Box 1: Plains

Box 2: Plateaus

Box 3

Similarities	Differences

FIGURE 7. Example Graphic Organizer (Level 3)

After they have read it once, they read it again while filling out the boxes. The teacher may ask them to share their work with another student or in a group.

Help Students to Become Familiar With Appropriate Academic Vocabulary

Continuing with the same lesson on plains and plateaus, students practice the academic language of comparison and contrast in their course packet by completing sentences requiring the use of this language (e.g., "Plains, _____ _____, are landforms.").

Let Students Self-Assess

The third step in the lesson is actually writing a short essay on the prompt: compare and contrast plains and plateaus (see Figure 8). The graphic organizer is used to help students plan and organize the content of their essay, while the academic language chart helps them structure the language of the essay in an appropriate way. After they have completed their essays, students can assess their own writing by using the checklist shown in the figure. This structure can be applied to virtually any content area, and we have found it to be quite successful.

Activity 5: Practice Essay Writing

Plains and Plateaus

Write an answer to the following essay question: Compare and contrast plains and plateaus. Answer the question using your reading notes and not the textbook. After you have written your essay response, ask yourself these questions:

- Is my form correct?

   Did I use complete sentences?

   Does my response move from general to specific?

   Did I restate the question at the beginning?

   Did I provide examples or detail where necessary?

- Is my information accurate?

FIGURE 8. Practice Essay Prompt and Self-Assessment (Level 3)

◈ CONCLUSION

Academic Writing for University Exams has been taught using the current materials for several semesters. Based on the experiences of instructors teaching the course and feedback from students, the course has been largely successful. Students particularly appreciate the emphasis on writing for examinations. As one Level 5 student wrote, "Now we won't be shocked when we get to the university." Students also recognize the value of using sustained content and, particularly at Level 5, an authentic university-level textbook.

Despite the overall positive evaluations given of the course by students and our strong commitment to the philosophy and structure of the course, there are still challenges to face in further developing the curriculum and course materials. Two of these challenges deserve mention:

1. the amount of content knowledge needed by instructors
2. the time and resources required to develop materials

Instructors who have taught the Level 5 course, in particular, have found that they needed a thorough grounding in U.S. history beyond what is actually in the course text to answer students' questions. However, instructors who have taught the course more than once build up a body of knowledge in the content area, which can be passed on to other instructors.

The amount of time required to develop support materials for a content-area textbook is also a challenge. When the curriculum was first developed, three faculty members were given course release time to create materials for the three levels of the course. Ongoing curricular development is also essential, as the textbooks become outdated or as instructors find innovative approaches to the study of writing. The investment of time and resources involved in this kind of materials development must not be underestimated.

Despite these challenges, we believe that the quality of the curriculum makes the investment more than worthwhile. One advantage of developing the materials in-house is the instructors' sense of ownership in the curriculum. Faculty members involved in the curriculum development are energized by the creative challenges of writing materials and take particular pride in seeing their students' writing improve through use of these materials. Students also experience creative pleasure in writing their own test items and graphic organizers—their own creations that help them learn. More important, they learn reading and writing skills that are directly relevant to the world of the university they are about to enter, and their success in that world is the best measure of our success as course developers and teachers.

⬧ ACKNOWLEDGMENTS

We would like to thank Sharon Cavusgil and Debra Snell for developing most of the materials used as examples in this chapter and for allowing us to use them here. We would also like to thank Jill Burns, who developed many of the materials for the Level 5 course, and Joan Carson for initiating the curriculum revision project and for her unswerving support.

⬧ CONTRIBUTORS

Sara Cushing Weigle is assistant professor of applied linguistics and ESL, and director of the ESL service courses and testing at Georgia State University, in the United States. Her research interests include writing assessment, quantitative and qualitative methods in language testing, and content-based language teaching.

Gayle Nelson is associate professor of applied linguistics and ESL at Georgia State University, where she teaches graduate courses in second language writing and intercultural communication, and ESL courses in writing. She has published in journals, including *Journal of Second Language Writing*, *TESOL Quarterly*, *International Journal of Intercultural Relations*, and *Applied Linguistics*, and is the author of numerous book chapters. Her research interests include cultural differences in pedagogy, cross-cultural speech acts, and second language writing.

CHAPTER 11

"This Course is Giving Me Cephalalgia . . .": Linking ESL Writing and the Greek and Latin Roots of English

Trudy Smoke, Tamara M. Green, and Elizabeth Isenstead

❖ INTRODUCTION

ESL students bring a wealth of knowledge and intelligence to their classes that may be overlooked when schools focus so much on standards that they perceive ESL students only in terms of their limitations or deficiencies in English. The pedagogical model that was developed in this project builds instead on the strengths of ESL students by creating an interdisciplinary link between two departments at Hunter College, a large urban college in New York City, in the United States. The project involves linking an intermediate-level ESL writing class taught in the English Department with an etymology class, The Greek and Latin Roots of English (hereafter referred to as Roots), taught in the Classics Department. While learning powerful tools to acquire and use new vocabulary, ESL students are also introduced to linguistic concepts so that they can discuss features of their first language and write a short research paper describing the language with which they are most familiar. The ESL writing and Roots classes have language as a theme and give students an opportunity to function as experts in their own languages, as they use what they already know about how languages work to develop their abilities in English.

❖ CONTEXT

The linguistic demography of Hunter College, a college of the City University of New York (CUNY), is an accurate reflection of the changing patterns of immigration to the United States. More than 50% of its 19,000 students are nonnative speakers of English (NNS) and represent more than 60 languages; for many, entrance into Hunter is their first U.S. educational experience. When we first developed this project, more than 1,000 students at our college enrolled in English for Bilingual Students II and III (ESL writing classes) in the Department of English each year. Most classes at Hunter are closed to students who have not yet taken expository writing, so those students identified as ESL students are limited in terms of the number and type of classes open to them. Moreover, although the ESL writing course, English for Bilingual Students II (ENGL 004), meets for 6 hours a week, students receive only one credit; the next level of this course, English for Bilingual Students III (ENGL

005), meets for 3 hours and students receive two credits for it. Thus, after a year of college, students may have earned as few as 14 credits toward their degree. As a result, too often ESL students feel isolated from the larger community and may be concerned that they are not doing what they understand as real college work. Many become discouraged by their slow rate of progress in accumulating academic credits; others feel frustrated by their inability to match newly acquired language skills with academically demanding class work. Finally, the learning of these language skills is frequently viewed by students and faculty as separate from what goes on in the subject-area classroom and thus may not be adequately reinforced outside the ESL class. All of these factors led to the development of this project linking the classics course with the English Department's intermediate-level ESL writing course. The linkage serves a vital role in assisting ESL students in acquiring and developing their English language abilities, while enabling them to be retained, gain credits, and make progress in their college studies.

Our focus on vocabulary and language made pedagogic sense and is supported by surveys such as Leki and Carson's (1994), in which ESL student respondents felt that ESL classes should have focused more on language skills and specifically on vocabulary building. Parry (1991) tells us that in ESL classes, "little vocabulary building gets done through our own direct agency . . . . we seem, rather, to act on the assumption that if we teach our students grammar, and reading and writing skills, they will build vocabularies on their own as they engage in other activities; and that this will happen particularly in the context of academic reading" (p. 630). In her research with ESL learners, Parry found that students benefit from learning a variety of vocabulary building strategies, and helping students build these strategies is part of the goal of the links created in this project.

Creating links between ESL classes and discipline-specific courses throughout the college has been found to be pedagogically effective by many ESL instructors and researchers (Benesch, 1988, 1998; Brinton, Snow, & Wesche, 1989; Crandall, 1993; Haas, Hernández, & Smoke, 1991; Smoke & Haas, 1995; Snow & Brinton, 1988; Snow & Kamhi-Stein, 1996). The field has moved from viewing the acquisition of English language skills as distinct from a mastery of academic course content to recognizing that these two competencies are the product of an interactive process. Language education, it has been recognized, must be seen as taking place not only in the ESL classroom but in all courses across the curriculum, as students learn the techniques and strategies of mastering academic content.

As a result, recent efforts in college-level ESL instruction, the English for academic purposes movement, are grounded in the understanding that not only can successful language learning be an outgrowth of content instruction but that it is an integral component of discipline-based learning.

◈ DESCRIPTION

The syllabus used for the Roots course was first developed about 15 years ago and has since evolved into the textbook that is used by all instructors (Green, 1994). This three-credit lecture course meets for 3 hours a week for 15 weeks and enrolls 800–1,000 students in 12–14 sections each year. The two main goals of the course are to help students to

1. build and enrich their vocabulary
2. develop an awareness of the power of language to shape their lives

Although Roots is open to all students who have completed the first level of developmental English, it also attracts a large number of students who have never needed to take basic skills courses but use it in partial fulfillment of a nine-credit humanities distribution requirement. It is also a very popular course for ESL students who want to improve their vocabulary and who are interested in learning more about the etymology of words

However, despite the fact that most ESL students who have taken Roots complete the course successfully, prior to the linkage project, it was difficult to assess its long-term benefits. We had not attempted to determine the impact that Roots had on the performance of the ESL students in classes in which they were simultaneously enrolled or the extent to which ESL students subsequently used and built upon this newly acquired vocabulary in other discipline-based courses. What all the instructors of Roots had noted informally, however, was that although most ESL students were successful in mastering the Greek and Latin roots of English vocabulary, they often had difficulty using these words in context and in choosing the correct form of the word for use in English sentences.

To determine whether the goals of the course could be more accurately tailored to meet these specific needs of ESL students without any compromise of content, the English and Classics Departments offered an experimental section of Roots in the fall 1993 semester for NNSs only. The experimental program was linked to a section of ENGL 004, the intermediate-level ESL course, a one-credit course that meets 6 hours a week for a 15-week semester and whose enrollment is capped at 22 students. The 19 students who enrolled in that first linked section of developmental English had to register also for the designated Roots class. To ensure the coherence of these paired classes, the English instructor attended most sessions of the etymology course, and she and the etymology instructor met weekly to plan classes, devise assignments, and monitor the progress of individual students.

Although each course had its own goals and expectations, their common aim was to strengthen English language skills within the context of college-level academic work. In the Roots class, the primary goals were (a) developing word analysis skills, (b) recognizing and using new vocabulary words in context and in grammatically correct form, and (c) refining students' ability to define vocabulary. Special emphasis was placed not only on word formation, prefixes, and suffixes, but also on providing multiple examples of usage within specific context. In addition, because the Roots textbook is organized thematically, with chapters on the Latin- and Greek-based English vocabulary used in politics, psychology, medicine and the sciences, literature, and the fine arts, students were introduced to discipline-specific language and terminology that they might use in other academic settings. Finally, an ongoing discussion of the various language families and their relationships provided an opportunity for the students to consider the similarities and differences between English and their native languages (which have included, among others, Spanish, French, Haitian Creole, Russian, Hebrew, Japanese, Chinese [Mandarin and Cantonese], Korean, Cambodian, Azerbaijani, Arabic, Igbo, Greek, and Tagalog).

Students did homework assignments for each class in which they wrote sentences or paragraphs using the words they discussed in class as various parts of speech, such as verbs, adjectives, and adverbs. Or they examined a Latin or Greek word, for example the Latin *audax* or *audacis,* and, with help from the textbook and the required dictionary, identified the English word (bold), the stem (*audac*), the derivative (audacity), the meaning (boldness or daring), and then used the English word in a sentence. The homework assignments were discussed so that students understood why one answer was a better choice than another. There were weekly quizzes and discussions following each quiz. Finally, although the class was largely lecture, students were invited to participate and to ask questions about unfamiliar words. A Foundation for the Improvement of Post Secondary Education (FIPSE) grant funding the link between the ESL and Roots classes enabled the college to limit the Roots class to 25 students, rather than enrolling the normal 50 or more students. The smaller class size allowed for more interactions between the teacher and students. The ESL students were invited to offer illustrations of vocabulary, usage, and syntax drawn from their native languages. Thus, speakers of French and Spanish were able to see the intimate connections between Latin structure and vocabulary and that of the Romance languages; speakers of other Indo-European languages perceived the broader linguistic connections among the various branches of the family; and those who spoke Asian, African, or other languages were able to consider the complexities of such points of comparison, such as verb tenses, the use of articles, and word order. Finally, and most broadly, the instructors tried to demonstrate in a variety of ways that ideas take on life only when they are expressed; and one of the ways in which people express ideas is through their ability to use language.

We found that the weekly quizzes in Roots not only tested mastery of new vocabulary but also helped pinpoint specific problem areas, such as the identification of parts of speech, verb tenses, and number, that could then be worked on in the ESL writing class. In general, however, the main focus of the ENGL 004 class was the writing of essays, with special emphasis on description, narration, and explication as well as on organization, grammatical usage, and sentence structure. In the linked ESL class, the writing assignments were specifically designed to give the students an opportunity to use newly learned vocabulary. Each week, the ESL instructor distributed a list of words that had been introduced in the Roots class, from which students would construct sentences for classroom analysis. As part of the reciprocal arrangement, the ESL writing teacher shared her readings with the Roots teacher, who chose words from the readings to work on in her class as well. These exercises provided a means of further measuring students' understanding of the word roots they were learning, while providing an immediate evaluation for the Roots instructor of the levels of comprehension and retention of materials in the content area. They also provided the ESL writing instructor with the opportunity to discover how well students could use words and correct word forms in their writing.

Students in the ESL writing classes typically read a selection of essays or short stories as a stimulus for discussion and development of paper topics, and the teachers in the linked classes usually focused the readings on the issues raised by learning a new language and, with it, a new culture. Thus, most of the reading assignments dealt with language learning and included magazine articles on bilingual education and language as an expression of identity as well as short selections from Plato's *Phaedras* (1960), in which Socrates relates the ancient Egyptian myth of the invention of the alphabet and its consequences, and Hoffman's (1989) memoir, *Lost in Translation*, in which she describes her sense of acute cultural deprivation and alienation when she moved to Canada from Poland as an adolescent, not knowing any English. In some semesters, students also read *Hunger of Memory* (Rodriguez, 1982). Because the reading selections were unabridged, all assignments were discussed and analyzed in the ESL writing class to ensure comprehension.

The students were, from the beginning, enthusiastic about the linked classes, and the student evaluations of the courses at the end of the term were overwhelmingly positive. Not only did the students feel that the skills acquired in each class were complementary and mutually reinforcing, but they felt the content-based approach to ESL writing also acknowledged that they were, in fact, doing college-level academic work. Furthermore, the affirmation that the various readings related to the students' own struggles with the mastery of a new language and culture was especially gratifying to them in that the texts chosen articulated what many had experienced but were unable to express because they lacked the proficiency in English to do so. Through classroom discussions and writing assignments based on the selected readings, the students were able to become one another's teachers by drawing upon their own linguistic experiences, and thus they engaged more actively in the process of their own language learning. As one student wrote on her final exam, "I definitely think language has miraculous power!! Thank you very much from the bottom of my heart. P.S. *An American Heritage Dictionary* is my favorite friend."

Thinking that this assignment would help build confidence, the teachers began assigning a short documented paper during the first semester of their collaboration. They knew that ESL students often felt marginalized in classes and infantilized by limitations in their vocabulary and understanding of English, but that through writing and teaching their peers about their languages, the students would have the opportunity to become experts. This proved to be the case; students talked and wrote about their languages with more ease and motivation than they did about other topics. The Roots teacher started each semester with an introduction to linguistic concepts, which included a broad discussion about language families as well as a brief introduction to the history of languages in general, and English in particular. In these very interactive lectures, she included students by asking them to relate their languages to whatever she was discussing. The writing teacher reinforced this work in her class by helping students to identify discrete linguistic features of their languages, such as the positioning of adjectives, the use of the interrogative, and the use and marking of tense. Students' knowledge about their languages made them an integral part of the dialogue in the class.

In this reaffirming atmosphere, students begin to perceive their language as a member of the world's family of languages. Each language was treated with respect, and every student had something to contribute to the class. English became more accessible because in its history it shares much with all of the other languages of the world. Students learned that English owes some of its grammar to Latin and some of its difficult spelling to French, and that English has borrowed words from almost every language in the world. Students enjoyed learning about words borrowed from their languages and sharing this information with classmates. A special result of this experience was that students discovered that by taking careful notes, reading the textbook, completing all exercises, and memorizing prefixes and suffixes, they were able to learn this body of knowledge.

For some students, however, learning to write in English was not an easy process. The Roots class complemented the ESL writing class by giving students tools that helped them understand and overcome their writing difficulties. As students began to speak about their own languages and about how their languages differed from English in the Roots class, they were able to use this information in their ESL writing class to pinpoint and discuss aspects of English they had trouble understanding. "You know," a student from Uzbekistan offered, "we don't use articles in Russian language." In private conferences or in whole class error identification and correction exercises taken from student writing, students volunteered their insights about their own errors. "We use *what* after *something* in Russian." "We use *but* after *although* in Chinese." "We put the adjective after the noun in Spanish." By recognizing and verbalizing these differences, students were able to retain their linguistic identity while adapting to a new culture and to become more fluent in a new language.

Along with class discussions, students in the ESL writing class also read about language. In some semesters, reading assignments emphasized culture in stories such as "The All-American Slurp," by Lensey (Namioka, 1996), and in books, such as *The Woman Warrior* (Kingston, 1976) and *How the Garcia Girls Lost Their Accents* (Alvarez, 1991). In others, students were more interested in language acquisition and read "Mother Tongue" (Tan, 1990), in addition to the Hoffman or Rodriguez book. In classes that emphasized the development of language, students read essays from newspapers, such as "You Say Begin, I Say Commence: To the Victor Belongs the Language" (Brown, 1987) and "Linguists Debating Deepest Roots of Language" (Johnson, 1995), along with short excerpts from books, such as *The Language Instinct* (Pinker, 1994), *The Study of Language* (Yule, 1985), or *The Story of English* (McCrum, Cran, & MacNeil, 1993). ESL writing teachers put together a packet of short readings and a list of recommended novels, memoirs, and books. Such readings stimulated lively discussions and interesting compositions based on the issues these readings raised. This packet continues to grow as different instructors teach the linked writing classes.

Discussions about language are rich and varied. One teacher discovered that, for several students, English was not their second or even their third language. In another class, a student volunteered that he spoke several first languages (L1s): Uzbek, a dialect he could not name, and Russian. Later, encouraged by the discussion, he said he could also read Hebrew and speak some Pushtu as well as a little Urdu and some Turkish. The competition had begun. Students began offering details on how many languages they could communicate in, how many different languages were spoken in their families, and so on. The class defined L1 as a language that the student remembered always speaking. Five out of the 18 students in that class spoke more than two L1s, and of those 5 students, 2 of them had three L1s. Students who spoke only one L1 were surprised. Several Japanese students explained about the different registers of Japanese that are used when speaking with an elder, an authority figure, a younger person, or a peer. Some of the Chinese students explained that Chinese has one system for writing, but many different spoken dialects. They told the class that someone who spoke Mandarin, for instance, might not understand someone who spoke Hakka, but they could read one another's writing.

Student enthusiasm may not be a measurable item, but success on the exit exam is. The pass rate in ENGL 004 is normally 70–80%, including multiple repeaters; the pass rate for students enrolled in these linked sections, however, is always more than

90%. Each time we offer these linked classes, we are pleased that the success rate remains high; even if all students do not always pass, most do, and they are retained in the college at higher numbers as well.

Certainly, content-based ESL teaching is not an easily administered panacea for the multitude of issues that NNSs have in the college classroom setting. Although linking discipline-based courses with ESL instruction generally has enhanced student success in those particular courses, analyses of content-based ESL teaching have pointed out the following difficulties.

- In courses that combine subject mastery and ESL, it is sometimes hard to maintain a balance between the demands of content learning and the acquisition of language proficiency. Advocates of content-based ESL instruction have recognized that in the development of such courses, it is essential to choose content areas in which the volume and level of subject-area reading and writing assignments do not overwhelm the ESL student. At the same time, how much and what level of subject mastery is necessary in order to constitute a real content course can become problematic for students and instructors alike.

- When content-based courses are linked to ESL classes, the latter often are considered as adjunct to what goes on in the discipline-based class because the primary goal remains mastery of the subject. Although paired ESL and subject-area courses are in theory interactive, the content-based class rarely reshapes its curriculum or format to acknowledge issues of language skill acquisition, whereas the ESL class must meet the demands of the discipline and, thus, may be regarded as merely a service course. As a result, not only do the students tend to view increased language proficiency as less important than mastery of the subject area, but the ESL instructor may also feel that he or she has been relegated to second-class status in the classroom.

◈ DISTINGUISHING FEATURES

We believe that the pairing of Roots and ESL writing represents an approach that answers these difficulties, for the following reasons.

1. Roots and ESL writing share the common goal of enhancing language proficiency through a variety of instructional techniques that, although different, are mutually reinforcing.

2. Because both courses have as their focus the acquisition of English language skills, including more precise manipulation of vocabulary, there are no artificial divisions of learning tasks; thus, students and instructors are made to feel that the work in both classes is equally important.

3. The instructors of the two classes are proficient in the teaching of language because, traditionally, courses in etymology have been given by classics faculty, whose training has been grounded in the study of philology. Experience in teaching the classical languages at the introductory level makes the Roots instructor aware of the problems ESL students may encounter in learning the grammar and structure of English.

4. Rather than the content-based course determining which skills are to be mastered in an adjunct ESL course, language acquisition and content learning are going on in both classes. Newly acquired vocabulary that is reinforced through contextual use helps students improve their language-processing abilities in other academic subject areas.

5. The linking of Roots and ESL writing allows the students to learn about the role of language in determining their cultural identity by drawing upon their own knowledge, simultaneous to acquiring English language skills. The vocabulary that they master in Roots gives them the means to express the ideas generated by the readings in ENGL 004, while the continued use of that vocabulary in their writing reinforces its contextual function. Through talking, reading, and writing about the function of language in culture and their own cultural experiences of language, students are then able to make connections between the familiar and the unfamiliar.

6. The instructors in the Roots and ESL writing courses feel that linkage provides a truly collaborative teaching and learning experience because the interactive structure of the linked classes prevents either course (or either instructor) from being viewed as dominant or peripheral to the essential needs of the students. Teachers attend one another's classes frequently and sometimes team teach specific lessons.

7. The linking of ESL writing and Roots can provide teachers with another opportunity to illustrate that multiculturalism and multilingualism need to be seen as assets, not liabilities.

8. These courses forge long-lasting relationships among teachers and peers that may promote higher student retention.

◈ PRACTICAL IDEAS

Our experience with the linked ESL writing and Roots classes has convinced us of the efficacy of this model; however, we are aware that some schools may not yet offer Roots-type classes. For these schools, we offer the following suggestions.

Teach Language Issues as Content for Writing Courses

Vocabulary acquisition, specifically through the teaching of the Greek and Latin roots of English, can provide a tool that will be invaluable for students studying English. Books that are thematic and cumulative, with exercises that students can do on their own, are preferable (see Green, 1994). ESL teachers can also incorporate language and language acquisition as a theme for writing courses. Our students come to us with varying degrees of knowledge about the languages they speak. Using that knowledge, they can teach their classmates and their teachers particular features of those languages, thus becoming the experts. For many students, this is the key to their success in the acquisition of English.

Use a Step-By-Step Approach in Assigning Research Papers

The decision to require a short research paper met with opposition from some of our colleagues, who felt that students at the intermediate level needed to focus on learning English rather than on doing academic writing assignments. Our experience indicated that students in these classes were often taking another college course and had to do academic reading, writing, and research. A step-by-step approach to writing the research paper helped them in those courses as well. Students were instructed to write a two- to three-page, double-spaced, typed paper. Some of them wrote longer papers; all of them wrote multiple drafts. Most used this as an opportunity to use the college library and computer facilities, thereby gaining some experience doing research, word processing, and printing with the computer—skills that would be useful to them as they progressed throughout their college years.

Give Students Access to Other Students' Papers

The ESL writing instructors often shared examples of papers students had written in previous semesters with the class. After students read the papers in small groups and in pairs, the class as a whole discussed what worked or did not work in the various papers. They discussed how students used source material to support their ideas or to answer their questions, and they looked at the "Works Cited" section to see how students cited papers and on-line sources. They often enjoyed the creative spirit with which other students responded to the assignment. Some of the titles of papers written in past classes include: "My Own Language—Tajiki," "The Language of Love: Haitian Creole," "The History and Structure of the Korean Language," and "Slang Used by Teen-Aged Japanese Girls."

Take Full Advantage of Students' Knowledge of Their L1s

One of the most successful follow ups to the students' papers was the class when the Roots and ESL writing teacher met and divided the students into groups of four, trying to ensure that each member of the groups spoke a different language. Students shared their papers with each other and then taught the other members of the group something from their language. Using students in this way to teach and learn from one another was a productive model that produced a great deal of enthusiasm among the participants. Students in these linked classes often formed enduring friendships with their peers and with the teachers of the two classes.

Consider the Following Successful Topics for Your Own Class

The following are some of the topics that were most successful in the linked classes:

1. Find out about your own language and write a short paper (two- to three-page, double-spaced pages) in which you answer some of the following questions. To which language family does your language belong? How many people speak it worldwide? What makes it difficult for someone to learn? Is it harder to speak, read, or write? Why? What is one of your favorite words or phrases in your language? What does it mean in English?

2. Interview a classmate, a friend, or a family member, and find out what strategies the person used to learn a new language. Ask the person what

worked and what did not and why. What would the person recommend to someone who was trying to learn a new language? What aspects of the new language were especially hard? Which were easy? Why? Write a paper in which you describe the interview and what you learned from it. Be sure to include some quotations from your interviewee so your reader will have a sense of the person.

3. Interview someone in the class whose native language is not the same as yours. Ask him or her to teach you how to make a statement, make it negative, ask a question, and make a simple greeting in his or her language. What rules about the language can you learn from this experience? After you have written your assumptions about the new language, ask your classmate if they are correct. Talk together until you have a better sense of the new language. Write about what you learned.

◈ CONCLUSION

Working together with other part-time teachers, we developed linked classes that not only emphasized the acquisition of vocabulary, specialized and general, and the acquisition of writing abilities, but, equally important, provided students with the opportunity to be experts in understanding and teaching others about their own languages.

Deepening students' awareness of language, its history, and how it is acquired created a classroom in which all languages are respected, are interesting, and can offer insight into human ways of knowing. English becomes a tool for gaining entrance into the U.S. academic system and not a barrier to success.

◈ CONTRIBUTORS

Trudy Smoke is professor in the English Department at Hunter College, CUNY, in the United States, where she coordinates the Freshman and Developmental English Programs and teaches courses in writing and multicultural literature. She is the author of *A Writer's Workbook* (Cambridge University Press), *A Writer's World* (St. Martin's Press), and *Adult ESL: Politics, Pedagogy, and Participation in Classroom and Community Programs* (Lawrence Erlbaum). She has presented at TESOL, the 4Cs, and many other local and national conferences, writes frequently on ESL and writing in public higher education, and coedits *Journal of Basic Writing*.

Tamara M. Green is professor of classics and chair of the Department of Classical and Oriental Studies at Hunter College, CUNY. She is the author of *The Greek and Latin Roots of English* and was the originator and director of a 3-year FIPSE grant focusing on "Improving Success Rates of ESL Students Through Paired Courses."

Elizabeth Isenstead received her MA in TESOL at Hunter College, CUNY, in 1994, and has been teaching developmental English there since that time. Her class was linked with Tamara Green's Greek and Latin Roots of English for 2 years. She has degrees in German and comparative literature and a strong professional background in the performing arts, all of which led her to develop a method of tailoring content for musicians. Using this method, she has been teaching ESL and a freshman humanities core section for NNSs at the Hunter School of Music since 1990.

CHAPTER 12

Relinquishing Teacher Control: Learners as Generators of Course Content

David Hall

◈ INTRODUCTION

The National Centre for English Language Teaching and Research (NCELTR), part of the Division of Linguistics and Psychology at Macquarie University, in Sydney, Australia, conducts a variety of language and professional development courses for different client groups, including immigrants to Australia, workplace groups, overseas students, teachers taking short intensive courses, and Macquarie University undergraduates and postgraduates.

Among its offerings is a course entitled English for Academic and Professional Development (EAPD). This course, which actually consists of a series of nine 5-week modules offered throughout the year, is designed for two main groups:

1. overseas students who need to improve their English before being admitted to an Australian university

2. overseas or local professionals who need to improve their English for their work

An initial configuration of four 10-week courses was instituted in late 1992 with an eye particularly on the necessity to comply with Australian visa conditions for overseas students, which specify a break of no more than 4 weeks between courses. In response to a combination of student demand for flexibility of entry dates, similar university pressure for flexibility, a widening range of student needs, and the economics of resource usage, the schedule was changed to nine 5-week modules in 1996. However, the course described in this chapter details only the final 10 weeks before students enter their university or college study. It assumes that students will score somewhere around 525 on their Test of English as a Foreign Language or Level 5 on the International English Language Testing System before they begin the module, although in practice, levels can be very variable, and that they will stay for the full 10 weeks.

The course is designed to allow students to learn how to cope successfully with the demands of academic and professional life. Writing is a major part of this, but as will be seen from the description that follows, there is no single course component called writing, nor is there one specific kind of writing, such as essay or précis writing. Instead, the course takes a holistic view of the learning process, and activities typically include learners interacting with various kinds of spoken and written text, often, as in poster sessions or collaborative writing, combining the two.

The EAPD course, like all other courses at NCELTR, had, from its inception, an element of student negotiation of curriculum, influenced particularly by the presence of David Nunan and his colleagues within the Adult Migrant Education Program (see Nunan, 1988, and Parkinson & O'Sullivan, 1990). In the main, this negotiating consisted of weekly meetings at which students might request a redistribution of emphasis—more writing, more examination practice, less technical reading, and so on. In other words, students were exercising autonomy to the extent of selecting from a predetermined menu of activity types.

Despite this flexibility, EAPD teachers consistently reported that they and the students were dissatisfied with the course. Two problems in particular were raised repeatedly:

1. The range of linguistic ability within the class frustrated both teachers and learners, demoralizing the weaker students and exasperating the stronger ones.

2. The range of purposes within the class meant that it was difficult to find texts and topics that were relevant to everyone. The class had postgraduate and undergraduate students intending to study in a large number of different fields as well as participants who intended to return to their respective professions on completing the course.

For a solution, the teachers and I turned to a radically different student-generated methodology, now known as Talkbase, developed in response to a similar, though not identical, set of problems at the Asian Institute of Technology (AIT) in Bangkok, Thailand.

This chapter describes the Talkbase approach and its underlying assumptions, and gives a detailed description of how the course runs at Macquarie.

◈ CONTEXT

This section presents a very brief overview of the theoretical and philosophical underpinnings of the Talkbase methodology before describing in more detail in the following section the framework of the 10-week NCELTR course. Although discussions may be found elsewhere on the implications and applications of Talkbase (Champagne et al., in press; Clayton & Shaw, 1997; Hall, 1994; Hall & Kenny, 1988, 1995; Kenny, 1993a, 1993b; Kenny & Laszewski, 1997; Savage & Storer, 1992), this chapter represents the first attempt to give a practical account of the course in enough detail to allow practitioners to try it in other contexts.

The underlying aim of the Talkbase methodology is to equip participants with the self-confidence and skills to continue improving their ability to communicate after leaving the course. This self-confidence will include, in particular, the will to initiate communicative encounters and the determination to persist despite difficulties.

The view of learning implied by the methodology is that language develops through the need for communication, and that learning takes place especially at those points where there are communicative difficulties to be overcome.

For genuine communication to take place, there are three prerequisites:

1. There must be something to communicate.

2. There must be someone to communicate with.

3. Participants must have a personal interest in the outcome of the communication.

Few classroom activities have these prerequisites, even those that are labeled as communicative. In information gap and simulation exercises, for example, the thing to be communicated is often dictated by the teacher, the textbook, or the materials, and there is no personal involvement in the outcome.

It is the aim of Talkbase that participants should provide their own content to the course, thereby helping to ensure that the above three conditions are met.

An underlying assumption is that the overall aim of education is to produce independent, autonomous thinkers and learners. This aspect of the Talkbase philosophy is explored particularly in Kenny (1993a, 1993b).

◈ DESCRIPTION

Plan, Do, Report, Evaluate, Plan

The Talkbase syllabus does not consist of traditional slots, such as writing, study skills, and grammar. Instead, learners undertake a series of activities focusing on the investigation of an area or areas of interest to them and involving looking for information from a variety of sources (e.g., the library, the World Wide Web, other lecturers and researchers on campus, interviews with home-stay families, local business people). Interim reports on these investigations in the form of posters, more formal writing, or more formal spoken presentations (or often a mixture of all of these) are then open to comment from other course participants. Learners have to articulate what work they have done, how they have done it, what they have discovered, and what conclusions they have come to. What is important here is that what each learner has done is subjected to a process of group scrutiny so that the evaluation stage is not simply a personal evaluation but an evaluation based on feedback and reflection. Through this process, where feedback may be positive as well as negative and may come from teachers and peer learners, learners reappraise their work, identify what further work or revisions need to be done, and plan the next stage accordingly.

In a way, the work being done resembles small-scale research projects, although we avoid the word *research* because it sounds difficult and scares students, especially if they are undergraduates or not intending to enter university at all. We also avoid the word *project* because we want to focus on the process rather than suggest that there is a final finished product toward which learners are working. Nevertheless, the process of collecting and analyzing data, presenting results, and evaluating the effectiveness of one's own presentation are extremely useful skills in preparation for university entry or for personal development.

Field, Problem, Solution, Evaluation

The second pattern underlying course organization is that of field, problem, solution, and evaluation. The words come from the move-structure tradition of discourse and genre analysis, with an emphasis on examining the function of a stretch of text, whether written or spoken, in the context of the goals of the whole text.

The most well-known application of this pattern is in Swales's analysis of research article introductions, initially (Swales, 1981) analyzed as a four-move pattern (establish the field, refer to previous work in the field, identify a gap in the field, introduce the present research) and later (Swales, 1990) refined to the three-move Creating a Research Space (CARS) model. Learners are introduced to this model at the beginning of Week 2 of the course, with a focus particularly on how people establish their field. Weeks 3–5 then focus on problems, solutions, and evaluations, respectively.

Each week starts with the analysis of an appropriate text chosen by the teacher, but learners are then asked to find texts of their own. They find two sorts of text to analyze:

1. written texts from their own field of interest
2. spoken texts from interviews they conduct either on audio- or videotape with research students or research associates around the campus

Although interviews and journal articles are clearly two different genres, what they have in common for the purposes of this course is that, in both cases, we are interested in examining how other people explain what they are doing and why they are doing it.

Learners use the move analysis tools they have acquired to examine these texts, to analyze, in particular, how well the authors or speakers have been able to establish their field for the audience, explain their motivation for doing the research (i.e., identify the gap), outline what they hope to achieve or have achieved, and so on. Students are often afraid of criticizing the quality of a written text because they assume it must be well written if it is published and because they lack confidence in their own proficiency. The analytical framework provides a way into critical reading. Similarly, students are not often predisposed to critically evaluate one another in the way that the course demands, but there are fewer inhibitions about examining the performance of disembodied voices on audiotape or talking heads on videotape, and this establishes a foundation on which robust engagement can later take place between members of the class.

Students present to their colleagues the texts they have found or the interviews they have recorded, highlighting what they think are salient features of the discourse. Some presentations may be at a whole-class level, particularly at the beginning of the course, so that the teacher can monitor students' understanding of the process and encourage participation, but small-group work is more effective in terms of time management and student attentiveness and engagement. Small groups may be established along disciplinary lines so that one group might consist only of students interested in, say, construction engineering, all of them looking at texts related to their own discipline. In many contexts, however, this sort of division may be impractical, and there are advantages also in having mixed-interest groups because this tends to bring out the importance of taking the audience and its shared assumptions into account when establishing a field or explaining the significance of a piece of research.

Week 1: Getting Started

The course quickly develops into one in which learners are responsible for most materials and nearly all of the actual content, and by about the third week, learners are completely comfortable with this expectation. But getting to that stage is no easy matter, and the first week is needed to convince learners that this is going to be different from anything they have done before. Although it might be argued that a good way to begin would be to give an overview of the course, outline the methodology, explain why this is an effective way of learning language, and ask learners to select a topic or topics that interest them for use on a series of projects, this would merely reinforce learners' previous experience of the teacher as the transmitter of knowledge. It maintains the learner in the position of consumer of prepackaged ideas. Something more radical than this is needed if learners are to be allowed to start to question preconceived ideas and to try out their own voice. There is an apparent paradox in that teachers may appear to be pushing students into what, for many, will be a new way of thinking about their language learning—an autonomy that many will not initially be inclined to seek. But the paradox (ironically often voiced by teachers who wish to retain more teacher control) is one that cannot be avoided. The teacher is initially in a position of power and does have control, and the course is all about relinquishing that power to allow students to learn.

For reasons that will become clear, Week 1 is known as the *Deep End week*. The goal is to allow learners to discover for themselves the importance of motivated study, independent data collection and analysis, and critical evaluation. On their arrival in class, participants are welcomed and introduced to staff, and then they are given a piece of paper with a single word or phrase written on it. *Drying, water, unexpected outcomes, autonomy, contraction,* and *protection* are examples of such words. Participants are then asked to go away and return 2 hours later, ready to talk to the rest of the class about their word.

Although they are bewildered at first and seek confirmation from the teachers and then from their classmates that they have actually understood what is required, participants eventually venture to the library to try to find something out about their word, often beginning with reference materials.

When they return to class, students present what they have learned about their word. These presentations vary from the enlightening (occasionally) to the uninspiring (frequently), but the teacher refrains from intervening, and it gradually becomes clear to students that the long silences are not going to be filled by the teacher. This kind of session is known as a *reportback*, and this first session normally requires two class periods. Because the reports are generally quite short, they can usually be presented to the whole class if the class size is small enough; however, small-group presentations might be more suitable, especially for students who are still too self-conscious to speak to the whole class. There is no advantage in forcing learners to speak before they are ready and confident and feel they have something interesting to say. By the end of the first series of reportbacks, there is an emerging realization among students that there are several different ways of going about data collection, and that the more successful presentations tend to be those where the presenter has sought out some personal relevance. Note that the words are deliberately vague and capable of being applied to many different fields of investigation. By this stage, some participants have already discovered what the others will eventually discover: that this language, which most of them have probably never used except in formal classroom exercises, can actually be used for real communication.

After the first reportback, participants are asked to replan their presentations based on feedback from fellow participants and teachers and on what they have learned from other presentations. They are also encouraged to work with other students who had the same word, although this is by no means obligatory, as learners may have quite different interests. This time, students are expected to do the preparation outside normal class time, using the resources and study facilities of our Independent Learning Centre if necessary.

The aim of the second presentation is to consolidate the lessons learned from the first presentation, the most obvious of which is the application of a much more divergent approach to the task. Imaginations and possibilities are opened up over the course of the first reportbacks, and this is very clear when the second round of reportbacks takes place. It is useful to give students about half an hour of class time to finalize their second reports and then to proceed with presentations in groups of six.

Students are then asked to produce their reports in written form. Where they have worked together to produce an oral report, they may now work together to produce the written version. These written versions are then distributed to other participants for comments and modifications. Comments are not limited to content; they often focus on formal aspects of the language. The teacher also may often be asked at this stage to say whether something is correct English or not. In this way, awareness of grammar and lexis arises out of a communicative need rather than being taught as an abstract system. The final written version—arrived at through a process of integrating all the skills—is then handed in for the teacher to make further comments as appropriate.

Participants are also asked for a written evaluation of the first week. This is not a questionnaire but a free-form essay. These can vary widely in tone, from wildly enthusiastic to quite hostile, and responses show that some students are still insecure at this stage. The purpose of the activity is to raise students' awareness about the learning process and why they are doing what they are doing. Typically, this activity will lead to discussion with the teacher of how language is learned.

The week ends with the first weekly meeting. The meeting is closed to teachers and administrative staff, but minutes are required and decisions or recommendations are recorded. NCELTR staff return at the end of the meeting to hear a report and to answer questions where necessary.

The weekly meetings are wide ranging, covering such things as social planning (e.g., parties, weekend activities, field trips), course housekeeping (e.g., buying of coffee and biscuits, election of chair and secretary for the week), and discussion about the course and its methodology, including requests for particular items to be covered. (We leave a number of slots in the course outline where specific activities, such as computer training, test practice [for those who are required to take external tests], and bibliographic database usage can be carried out on request).

Week 3: A Representative First-Half Week in Class

The first morning of the third week starts with text analysis, as it does for each of Weeks 2–5. The teacher leads the class through an analysis of a research or journal article introduction and then tells participants to go and find examples of texts in their area of interest: one text that they think is clearly written and one that is not. They are to bring the texts back ready to present a move-structure analysis to their classmates, which they do in small groups of no more than three or four students.

Not all participants return to class with academic articles; after all, not all students are going to study at university. Some find chapters from books or magazine articles. This is not a disadvantage because the process of critical analysis still takes place, and the activity raises awareness of the different features that make different genres distinctive.

The next stage is for participants to find someone in their own area of interest, normally a research student or staff member, and audiotape an interview. Students bring this interview back to class and analyze it in much the same way as the written text, with participants playing key passages of the interview for their classmates. Participants do need to spend rather more time selecting passages to play than they do on the written text; otherwise, listening to an audiotape can become tedious. The teacher should suggest a time limit on audiotape extracts to be played: for example, 2 minutes from a 10-minute interview.

In the final stage in the week, participants prepare what is referred to as a *piece of work* (e.g., Kenny, 1993a; Hall & Kenny, 1988). Participants make their first attempt to write an introduction to a piece of work of personal interest. Because participants are, by this stage, used to the idea of conducting investigations in small groups, they often choose to work in cooperation with others. Teachers encourage this because the process of negotiation required in cowriting, coinvestigating, and copresenting involves considerable motivated use of language. The work is not seen as just another language exercise. Rather, the results are taken seriously, there is genuine discussion and argument in class, and the work may well end up as the foundation for a future thesis or dissertation.

The introduction is the privileged (sub)genre at this stage because it exhibits discourse features beyond the research article, allows learners to define their own motivations, and, if clearly written, makes everything else about the work much easier. Collecting data, writing a literature review, analyzing data, and stating conclusions and recommendations all can be related to how well the problem has been defined in the first instance.

During the first 5 weeks of the course, participants become gradually more expert in choosing and analyzing texts, conducting coherent interviews, challenging one another, and, in general, communicating their own ideas. The difference between specialist-to-specialist and specialist-to-nonspecialist communication becomes apparent (see Hall, 1994) because the implicit assumptions of the specialist culture often have to be made explicit in the exchanges.

Week 8: A Representative Second-Half Week in Class

In the second half of the course, participants develop their own piece of work, either individually or in small teams, following the plan-do-report-evaluate-plan pattern outlined earlier. The culmination of this effort is an open poster session of work in progress. Presentations in the weeks leading up to the open poster session may consist of formal written work, formal spoken presentations, or, most often, poster presentations.

Poster presentations, used throughout the course, are similar to those now common at conferences. Students use poster boards, wall space, or tables to display the progress of their work. In this way, all students get a chance to see everyone else's work as well as a chance to field comments and questions on their own work in a relatively short time, without the time and fatigue associated with many consecutive formal presentations. If presentations are done by a group, learners can take turns staying with the poster display while the others visit the other displays. In the case of individual pieces of work, there has to be a balance between visiting and standing, but this is not difficult to manage. The advantages of posters are that they (a) allow each team (or individual) to present simultaneously; (b) encourage spoken inter-action, requests for clarification, and close questioning in a relatively nonthreatening way; and (c) clearly represent an interim record rather than a completed project so that their format and content may be changed as the weeks go by in response to feedback and further investigation. Learners are much more willing to change what they have written, discard items, add new items, even change the title, than they are with more formal writing.

Week 8 begins with a few student presentations to the whole class—not all groups do this every week, but they will all present in this way approximately two or three times during Weeks 6–9. What happens on the first day will depend to some extent on how much discussion takes place on the topics presented, but there will also be a short report from all groups (either in small groups or to the whole class) on where they are with their work (e.g., what has been done, what is the next step). The output from this will be a plan for research work to be done during the week.

The second day has a slot for a special activity (as mentioned earlier in the description of Week 1) and for further presentations. On Day 3, students write up their research in small collaborative groups and evaluate each other's writing, typically making suggestions on both the content and the form. During this activity, the teacher may be asked to comment on the correctness of the language, and although there is no formal language teaching of the traditional sentence-based kind built into the course, much of the discussion at this stage may be precisely on this area. The difference between this approach and traditional grammar teaching, however, is that questions arise from the particular communicative needs of the moment rather than representing an abstract system illustrated and practiced with decontextualized exemplars. Discussion among students during cowriting focuses on choice among different ways of trying to say what is meant, and this explicit discussion raises awareness about what choices are available in language.

Day 4 is given to poster preparation, followed by poster presentations, then group evaluation and planning. The process of negotiation of content that accompa-nies the preparation, and the effort put into selection and ordering of material, is not only a useful experience in and of itself, it is also a highly motivating process over which participants have a strong sense of ownership. Linguistically weaker students are just as likely as stronger students to claim the floor to try to get their point across, simply because their determination to get their point across has overcome their fear of using English (see Hall, 1994, for a detailed example). Initially, they may have the confidence to do this only in the more private discussion surrounding the poster presentation, but by Week 8, this is already evident in whole-class events.

Day 5 starts with writing of a more individual kind, where students complete their diary of what they think they have achieved during the week and their impressions of their individual progress and difficulties, while the teacher conducts individual or small-group feedback sessions. This is followed by the weekly meeting and class feedback.

◈ DISTINGUISHING FEATURES

The main distinguishing feature of the course is not just that it is learner centered and devoted to learner autonomy; it is that the course content, to a very large degree, is generated by the learners themselves. Learners get to choose the topics and to develop topics in cooperation with each other. The course encourages learner interdependence—rather than just independence—as language use is clearly cooperative and goal-directed. Learners go beyond the assimilation of information into their own mental systems to a point where they can confidently articulate and evaluate their own and others' points of view, can assess their own and others' clarity of expression, and are willing to submit opinions to the critical scrutiny of others. Most important, they can do all this in English.

The most common reactions we get from visitors to the course include claims that

- we are in a particularly privileged situation, with a good deal of professional autonomy and highly motivated students, and we can therefore conduct activities that would not be possible in other institutions

- the visitor has tried something similar but it failed

- many students would not accept this sort of methodology because it is culturally inappropriate

- many teachers would not accept this sort of methodology because it is culturally inappropriate

What underlies these reactions is a fear of committing to a wholly different methodology, a fear of abandoning control, not just for a certain specified and severely circumscribed section of the course, but giving over the major responsibility for course content to the learners themselves. Often when we merely describe the course, people will store it mentally in the autonomy basket and think of strategy training or self-access facilities. It is only when they visit the class and actually experience the changed relationships between participants that they begin to understand the difference between an accommodation of autonomy in traditional teaching practices and this approach, which begins with the notion of communication rather than with the notion of language.

That the approach is so different from the prior expectations of participants does produce its own problems, which can be dealt with under the headings of teacher resistance and learner resistance.

Introducing new teachers to the Talkbase methodology and maintaining the consistency of approach that is necessary for the course to succeed have always been particular areas of concern (see Hall & Kenny, 1995). One teacher's remark that "it's very intimidating to walk into a class with no materials under your arm and to be totally dependent on what the students will come up with" is indicative of this unease. The approach challenges teachers' as well as students' views and previous experience of how classrooms and teacher-student interactions work. The move away from a pattern of teacher initiation, student response, and teacher evaluation can be as challenging and intimidating for students as for teachers. As Lewis (1993) points out:

> A new language . . . can threaten identity. Any perceived threat will have a profound influence on the student's openness to the new language . . . . It is easy to recognise the uncomfortable feeling that comes when we cannot get what we want, say what we mean, or explain a difficulty. Many activities in the traditional language classroom do not put the student in the position of using language in this way . . . . These activities may not necessarily contribute to the student's long-term language ability, but in the short term they do not represent a psychological threat. It comes, therefore, as no surprise that students frequently ask for such activities. (p. 64)

Students sometimes ask for safe activities, such as grammar, spelling, and dictation, especially in the first week of the course. Student resistance occurs typically at the initial hurdle of attempting genuine communication beyond the formulaic. However, once this hurdle is passed, students make rapid progress and are aware of their own progress.

A student challenge to the methodology—where the very possibility of such a challenge is facilitated by course procedures—can be undermining to teacher confidence. And confidence—that the teacher will not be left stranded, looking defensive or ignorant or incompetent—is essential to success. The opportunity for teachers to discuss in an informal way the challenges faced in running a course of this kind is extremely important, and, for that reason, there are always two teachers sharing a class.

Invariably, however, learners and teachers become enthusiastic supporters of the course. The most common comment from teachers who have experienced a course of this kind is that they feel dissatisfied and impatient with courses run in any other way.

◈ PRACTICAL IDEAS

Realize That Learner Autonomy Cannot Be Achieved Piecemeal

The approach described in this chapter is not one that lends itself to individual activities adapted for use in another context. It is very much an integrated approach that suffers when it is diluted by a return to teacher-led activities. This is why it is possible for people to say that they have tried something similar and it has failed. To practice autonomy as just one component in a course is to reduce it to a series of things to be learned, just like the other course components. Learners in such a case never seem to get to the point where they can interact and develop using their own meanings. Much of traditional methodology infantilizes learners, keeping them in a state of dependence (e.g., on the teacher, the textbook, the examiner, the materials) for what can be said, and how, when, and where it can be said. The Talkbase approach is fundamentally different, so although it is possible to envisage the opening activity described above—the one-word-on-a-slip-of-paper activity—as one activity among others (e.g., information gap tasks, drills, role plays, reading comprehension exercises), the activity would be perceived by learners in a quite different way, as just another trick in the teacher's repertoire. The activity would become an exercise with no real-life meaning, as opposed to an act of communication in its own right, an act that is valorized by the seriousness (by which I do not mean solemnity) with which the findings of the learner are subsequently treated.

Consider Carefully Whether Your Context Will Permit Implementation of This Approach

The EAPD course was developed in the context of a full-time intensive English program (IEP): It consists of 20 hours of face-to-face interaction each week, plus at least an additional 5 hours of private study. Class size is subject to the mandatory maximum for Australian IEPs of 18 students. The consequences of trying to adapt the approach to a more extensive program, where learners meet for language learning for only a handful of hours each week, or for much larger classes, would have to be very seriously considered, though teachers of large classes could look profitably at the work done by Sharwar (1991) in Pakistan.

◈ CONCLUSION

Having experienced the transformation in student confidence brought about by the Talkbase approach, I would make very strong claims about its effectiveness. In this chapter, I have tried to describe the methodology and its underlying assumptions in a practical way that may help others to establish similar courses. I have also pointed out some of the pitfalls and dangers of the approach—it is not for teachers who want to retain control, nor for those who work in systems where teacher evaluation favors those who keep their heads down. As an approach, it is full of risks for teachers and students, but at the end of a course, students have the confidence to continue improving and developing their language proficiency. When comparison is made with the distressingly mediocre products of most formal language teaching operations, the risks are insignificant.

◈ CONTRIBUTOR

David Hall is senior lecturer in linguistics at Macquarie University in Sydney, in Australia, where he also manages the English language services section of the National Centre for English Language Teaching and Research, is coordinator of postgraduate programs in linguistics, and manages distance learning programs in linguistics. He has lived and worked in England, France, Rwanda, Iran, Malaysia, Thailand, and Australia, and has conducted consultancies and workshops in Algeria, Yugoslavia, Laos, Vietnam, Thailand, the Philippines, Indonesia, Japan, and Brunei. He has published several textbooks on English for specific purposes, and is joint general editor of a new Applied Linguistics series for Addison Wesley Longman. His main interests are teacher training, learner autonomy, technical writing, and distance learning.

References

Ada, A. F. (1988). Creative reading: A relevant methodology for language minority children. In L. M. Malave (Ed.), *NABE '87. Theory, research and application: Selected papers* (pp. 97–111). Buffalo, NY: SUNY Press.

Adam, C., & Artemeva, N. (in press). Writing instruction in EAP and disciplinary classes: Building bridges. In A. Johns (Ed.), *Genre and pedagogy*. Mahwah, NJ: Lawrence Erlbaum.

Adamson. D. (1993). *Academic competence.* New York: Longman.

Adams-Smith, D. E. (1984). Planning a university language center in Oman: Problems and proposals. In J. Swales & H. Mustafa (Eds.), *English for specific purposes in the Arab world* (pp. 197–211). Birmingham, England: University of Aston, Language Studies Unit.

Adelaide University. (2000). *Adelaide University annual report 1999.* Adelaide, Australia: Author.

Alvarez, J. (1991). *How the Garcia girls lost their accents.* New York: Penguin.

Babbitt, M., & Mlynarczyk, R. W. (2000). Keys to successful content-based ESL programs: Administrative perspectives. In L. Kasper (Ed.), *Content-based college ESL instruction* (pp. 26–47). Mahwah, NJ: Lawrence Erlbaum.

Bartholomae, D. (1988). Inventing the university. In E. R. Kintgen, B. M. Kroll, & M. Rose (Eds.), *Perspectives on literacy* (pp. 273–285). Carbondale: Southern Illinois University Press.

Bates, M., & Dudley-Evans, T. (1976). *Nucleus: English for science and technology.* London: Longman.

Bazerman, C. (1994). System of genre and the enactment of social intentions. In A. Freedman & P. Medway (Eds.), *Rethinking genre* (pp. 79–101). London: Taylor & Francis.

Benesch, S. (1988). *Ending remediation: Linking ESL and content in higher education.* Washington, DC: TESOL.

Benesch, S. (1992). Sharing responsibilities: An alternative to the adjunct model. *College ESL, 2*(1), 1–10.

Benesch, S. (1993). ESL, ideology, and the politics of pragmatism. *TESOL Quarterly, 27,* 705–717.

Benesch, S. (1998). Anorexia: A feminist ESP curriculum. In T. Smoke (Ed.), *Adult ESL: Politics, pedagogy, and participation in classrooms and community programs* (pp. 101–114). Mahwah, NJ: Lawrence Erlbaum.

Berkenkotter, C., Huckin, T., & Ackerman, J. (1991). Social context and socially constructed texts: The initiation of a graduate student into a writing research community. In C. Bazerman & J. Paradis (Eds.), *Textual dynamics in the professions: Historical and contemporary studies of writing in professional communities* (pp. 191–215). Madison: University of Wisconsin Press.

Bint, P. (1982). *Report on the English language programme for Qaboos University*. Muscat, Oman: Sultanate of Oman, Ministry of Education, ELT Unit.

Birk, N., & Birk, G. (1995). Selection, slanting, and charged language. In G. Goshgarian (Ed.), *Exploring language* (pp. 113–121). New York: HarperCollins.

Blanton, L. (1999). Classroom instruction and language minority students: On teaching to "smarter" readers and writers. In L. Harklau, K. M. Losey, & M. Siegal (Eds.), *Generation 1.5 meets college composition: Issues in the teaching of writing to U.S.-educated learners of ESL* (pp. 119–142). Mahwah, NJ: Lawrence Erlbaum.

Bloor, M., & Bloor, T. (1986). *Language for specific purposes: Practice and theory*. (OLCS Occasional Paper No. 19). Dublin, Ireland: Trinity College.

Brinton, D. M., Snow, M. A., & Wesche, M. B. (1989). *Content-based second language instruction*. Boston: Heinle & Heinle (formerly New York: Newbury House).

Brown, R. M. (1987, December 20). You say begin, I say commence: To the victor belongs the language. *New York Times Book Review*, pp. 12–13.

Bruffee, K. A. (1993). Collaboration, conversation, and reacculturation. In K. A. Bruffee (Ed.), *Collaborative learning: Higher education, interdependence, and the authority of knowledge* (pp. 15–27). Baltimore, MD: Johns Hopkins University Press.

Bruffee, K. A. (1995). Sharing our toys: Cooperative learning versus collaborative learning. *Change* (January/February), 12–18.

Burns, A., Joyce, H., & Gollin, S. (1996). *I see what you mean: Using spoken discourse in the classroom*. Sydney, Australia: National Centre for English Language Teaching and Research.

Cadman, K. (1997a). Thesis writing for international postgraduates: A question of identity? *English for Specific Purposes, 16*(1), 3–14.

Cadman, K. (1997b). The "songlines" of academic writing: Integrating the voices of international and NESB students into their texts. In R. Murray-Harvey & H. Silins (Eds.), *Learning and teaching in higher education: Advancing international perspectives* [Proceedings of the HERDSA National Conference, July 7–10, Adelaide] (pp. 37–50). Adelaide, Australia: Flinders University Press.

Cadman, K., & Grey, M. (1997). *Action teaching: Student-managed English for academic contexts*. Gold Coast, Australia: Antipodean Educational Enterprises.

Cadman, K., & Grey, M. (2000). The "Action Teaching" model of curriculum design: EAP students managing their own learning in an academic conference course. *EA Journal, 17*(2), 21–36. (ELICOS Association).

Cargill, M. (1996). An integrated bridging program for international postgraduate students. *Higher Education Research and Development, 15*, 177–188.

Cargill, M. (1998). Cross-cultural postgraduate supervision meetings as intercultural communication. In M. Kiley & G. Mullins (Eds.), *Quality in postgraduate research: Managing the new agenda* [Proceedings of the 1998 Conference on Quality in Postgraduate Research, 23–24 April] (pp. 175–188). Adelaide, Australia: Adelaide University, Advisory Centre for University Education.

Cargill, M. (2000). Inter-cultural postgraduate supervision meetings: An exploratory discourse study. *Prospect: A Journal of Australian TESOL, 15*(2), 28–38.

Carson, J. G., Chase, N. D., Gibson, S. U., & Hargrove, M. (1992). Literacy demands of the undergraduate curriculum. *Reading Research and Instruction, 31*(4), 25–50.

Champagne, M-F., Clayton, T., Dimmit, N., Laszewski, M., Savage, W., Shaw, J., Stroupe, R., Thein, M. M., & Walter, P. (in press). Talkbase, tasks and the assessment of learner autonomy and language learning. *AILA Review* (Association Internationale de Linguistique Appliquee), *14*.

Christie, F., & Martin, J. R. (Eds.). (1997). *Genre and institutions: Social processes in the workplace and school*. London: Cassell.

Clayton, T., & Shaw, J. (1997). Discovering resources in Ho Chi Minh City. In B. Kenny & W. Savage (Eds.), *Language and Development* (pp. 151–163). Harlow, England: Addison Wesley Longman.

Cobb, T., & Horst, M. (2001). Reading academic English: Carrying learners across the lexical threshold. In J. Flowerdew & M. Peacock (Eds.), *Research perspectives on English for academic purposes* (pp. 315–329). Cambridge: Cambridge University Press.

Cope, B., & Kalantzis, M. (1993). How a genre approach to literacy can transform the way literacy is taught. In B. Cope & M. Kalantzis (Eds.), *The powers of literacy: A genre approach to the teaching of writing* (pp. 1–21). London: Falmer Press.

Cope, B., & Kalantzis, M. (2000). *Multiliteracies: Literacy learning and the design of social futures.* London: Routledge.

Crandall, J. (1993). Content-centered learning in the United States. *Annual Review of Applied Linguistics, 13,* 111–126.

Crooks, H., Monro, J., & Raymont, P. (Producers). (1989). *Only the news that fits* [Videotape]. Toronto, Canada: National Film Board.

Crystal, D., & Davy, D. (1969). *Investigating English style.* London: Longman.

Cummins, J. (1996). *Negotiating identities: Education for empowerment in a diverse society.* Ontario, CA: California Association for Bilingual Education.

Eggins, S. (1994). *An introduction to systemic functional linguistics.* London: Pinter.

Eskey, D. (1986). Theoretical considerations. In F. Dubin, D. Eskey, & W. Grabe (Eds.), *Teaching second language reading for academic purposes* (pp. 3–23). Reading, MA: Addison-Wesley.

Fox, R. N. (1996). *Intensive ESL program spring 1996 outcomes* (Institutional Research Report No. 114). Brooklyn, NY: Kingsborough Community College, Office of Institutional Research.

Frodesen, J., & Starna, N. (1999). Distinguishing incipient and functional bilingual writers: Assessment and instructional insights gained through second-language writer profiles. In L. Harklau, K. M. Losey, & M. Siegal (Eds.), *Generation 1.5 meets college composition: Issues in the teaching of writing to U.S.-educated learners of ESL* (pp. 61–79). Mahwah, NJ: Lawrence Erlbaum.

Fu, G. S. (1987). The Hong Kong bilingual. In R. Lord & H. N. L. Cheng (Eds.), *Language education in Hong Kong* (pp. 27–50). Hong Kong, SAR: Chinese University Press.

Gabelnick, F., MacGregor, J., Matthews, R., & Smith, B. (1990). *Learning communities: Creating connections among students, faculty, and disciplines.* San Francisco: Jossey-Bass.

Gee, J. (1991). *Social linguistics and literacies: Ideology in discourses.* London: Falmer Press.

Gold, M. (1996). *Jews without money.* New York: Carroll & Graf.

Goldstein, L. M., & Conrad, S. M. (1990). Student input and negotiation of meaning in ESL writing conferences. *TESOL Quarterly, 24,* 443–460.

Green, T. M. (1994). *The Greek and Latin roots of English* (2nd ed.). New York: Ardsley House.

Haas, T., Hernández, J., & Smoke, T. (1991). A collaborative model for empowering nontraditional students. In S. Benesch (Ed.), *ESL in America: Myths and possibilities.* (pp. 112–129). Portsmouth, NH: Heinemann.

Hale, G., Taylor, C., Bridgeman, B., Carson, J., Kroll, B., & Kantor, R. (1996). *A study of writing tasks assigned in academic degree programs* (TOEFL Research Report No. 44). Princeton, NJ: Educational Testing Service.

Hall, D. (1994). The advantages for the LSP teacher of having different specialisations in the same class. In R. Khoo (Ed.), *The practice of LSP: Perspectives, programmes and projects* (pp. 209–217). Singapore: South-East Asia Ministers of Education Organisation—Regional English Language Centre [SEAMEO-RELC] Anthology Series 34.

Hall, D., & Kenny, B. (1988). An approach to a truly communicative methodology: The AIT pre-sessional course. *English for Specific Purposes, 7*(1), 19–32.

Hall, D., & Kenny, B. (1995). Evolution of a language centre: Pursuing autonomy in a collegial context. In A. Pincas (Ed.), *Spreading English: ELT projects in international development* (pp. 26–42). Hemel Hempstead, England: Phoenix ELT.

Halliday, M. A. K. (1989). *Spoken and written language.* Oxford: Oxford University Press.

Halliday, M. A. K., & Hasan, R. (1985). *Language, context and text: Aspects of language in a social semiotic perspective.* Geelong, Australia: Deakin University Press.

Halliday, M. A. K., & Martin, J. R. (Eds.). (1993). *Writing science: Literacy and discursive power.* London: Falmer Press.

Harklau, L. (1999). Representing culture in the ESL classroom. In E. Hinkel (Ed.), *Culture in second language teaching and learning* (pp. 109–130). Cambridge: Cambridge University Press.

Harklau, L., Losey, K. M., & Siegal, M. (Eds.). (1999). *Generation 1.5 meets college composition: Issues in the teaching of writing to U.S.-educated learners of ESL.* Mahwah, NJ: Lawrence Erlbaum.

Harris, D. P., & Palmer, L. A. (1986). *CELT: Examiners' instructions and technical manual.* New York: McGraw-Hill.

Harris, M. (1997). Cultural conflicts in the writing center: Expectations and assumptions of ESL students. In C. Severino, J. C. Guerra, & J. E. Butler (Eds.), *Writing in multicultural settings* (pp. 220–233). New York: Modern Language Association.

Harris, M., & Silva, T. (1993). Tutoring ESL students: Issues and options. *College Composition and Communication, 44,* 525–537.

Hirshberg, S. (1995). *One world, many cultures.* Needham Heights, MA: Allyn & Bacon.

Hoffman, E. (1989). *Lost in translation.* New York: Dutton.

Holes, C. D. (1985). *Report on a consultancy visit to Sultan Qaboos University Project* [Mimeograph]. Muscat, Oman: Sultan Qaboos University.

Horowitz, D. M. (1986). Essay examination prompts and the teaching of academic writing. *English for Specific Purposes, 5,* 107–120.

Hunter, J., & Cooke, D. (1989). Dealing with argument: Content and skills in ESL. In E. Harris & H. McGarrell (Eds.), *TESL '88: Raising the profile* (pp. 103–110). Toronto, Canada: TESL Ontario.

Hykes, J., & Santiago, S. (2000). *ESL and NS collaboration in composition classes.* Paper presented at the 34th Annual TESOL Convention, Vancouver, Canada.

Jacob, E., Rottenberg, L., Patrick, S., & Wheeler, E. (1996). Cooperative learning: Context and opportunities for acquiring academic English. *TESOL Quarterly, 30,* 253–280.

Janks, H. (1991). A critical approach to the teaching of language. *Educational Review, 43,* 191–199.

Johns, A. M. (1997). *Text, role, and context: Developing academic literacies.* Cambridge: Cambridge University Press.

Johns, A. M. (Ed.). (in press). *Genre and pedagogy.* Mahwah, NJ: Lawrence Erlbaum.

Johns, T. (1989). Whence and whither classroom concordancing? In T. Bongaerts, et al., (Eds.), *Computer applications in language learning* (pp. 9–33). Dordrecht, The Netherlands: Foris.

Johns, T., & Dudley-Evans, A. (1980). An experiment in team-teaching of overseas postgraduate students of transportation and plant biology. In British Council (Ed.), *ELT Documents 106, Team teaching in ESP* (pp. 6–23). London: British Council.

Johnson, D., Johnson R., & Smith, K. (1991). *Active learning: Cooperation in the college classroom.* Edina, MN: Interaction Book Company.

Johnson, G. (1995, June 27). Linguists debating deepest roots of language. *The New York Times,* pp. C1, C13.

Jordan R. R. (1990). Pyramid discussions. *ELT Journal, 44,* 46–54.

Kenny, B. (1993a). Investigative research: How it changes learner status. *TESOL Quarterly, 27,* 217–223.

Kenny, B. (1993b). For more autonomy. *System, 21*(4), 431–442.

Kenny, B., & Laszewski, M. (1997). Talkbase in Vientiane. In B. Kenny & W. Savage (Eds.), *Language and Development* (pp. 129–140). Harlow, England: Addison Wesley Longman.

Kilbourne, J. (Producer). (1987). *Still killing us softly* [Videotape]. Boston: Cambridge Films.

Kilbourne, J., & Pollay, R. (Producers). (1992). *Pack of lies: The advertising of tobacco* [Videotape]. New York: Media Education Foundation.

Kingston, M. H. (1976). *The woman warrior.* New York: Alfred A. Knopf.

Kiniry, M., & Rose, M. (1993). *Critical strategies for academic thinking and writing* (2nd ed.). Boston: St. Martin's Press.

Kobayashi, H., & Rinnert, C. (1992). Effects of first language on second language writing: Translation versus direct composition. *Language Learning, 42,* 183–215.

Koike, I., Ando, S., Furukawa, S., Haraoka, S., Ibe, S., Ito, K., Ishida, M., Kuniyoshi, T., Masukawa, K., Nishimura, Y., Tada, M., & Tanabe, Y. (1983). *Daigaku eigo kyoiku ni kansuru jittai to shoraizo no sogoteki kenkyu (I): Kyoin no tachiba* [General survey of English language teaching at colleges and universities in Japan: Teachers' view]. Tokyo: Research Group for College English Teaching in Japan.

Koike, I., Ando, S., Furukawa, S., Haraoka, S., Ibe, S., Ito, K., Ishida, M., Ishikawa, S., Kuniyoshi, T., Matsuyama, M. Narisawa, Y., Nishimura, Y., Tada, M., Tajima, K., Tanabe, Y., & Yoshioka, M. (1985). *Daigaku eigo kyoiku ni kansuru jittai to shoraizo no sogoteki kenkyu (II): Gakusei no tachiba* [General survey of English language teaching at colleges and universities in Japan: Students' view]. Tokyo: Research Group for College English Teaching in Japan.

Krashen, S. (1981). *Second language acquisition and second language teaching.* Oxford: Pergamon.

Krashen, S. (1982). *Principles and practice in second language acquisition.* Oxford: Pergamon.

Lankshear, C., & McLaren, P. (Eds.). (1993). *Critical literacy.* Albany, NY: SUNY Press.

Lee, M., & Solomon, N. (1992). *Unreliable sources.* New York: Lyle Stewart.

Leki, I. (1991–1992). Building expertise through sequenced writing assignments. *TESOL Journal, 1*(2), 19–23.

Leki, I. (1995). *Academic writing* (2nd ed.). New York: St. Martin's Press.

Leki, I., & Carson, J. G. (1994). Students' perceptions of EAP writing instruction and writing needs across the disciplines. *TESOL Quarterly, 28,* 81–101.

Leki, I., & Carson, J. G. (1997). "Completely different worlds": EAP and the writing experiences of ESL students in university courses. *TESOL Quarterly, 31,* 39–69.

Lemke, J. (1990). *Talking science: Language learning and values.* Norwood, NJ: Ablex.

Lewis, M. (1993). *The lexical approach.* Hove, England: Language Teaching Publications.

Littlejohn, A. (1991). *Writing 2.* Cambridge: Cambridge University Press.

Littlejohn, A. (1994). *Writing 4.* Cambridge: Cambridge University Press.

Long, M. (1983). Native speaker/non-native speaker conversation in the second language classroom. In M. Clarke & J. Handscombe (Eds.), *On TESOL '82: Pacific perspectives on language learning and teaching* (pp. 207–225). Washington, DC: TESOL.

Long, M., & Crookes, G. (1992). Three approaches to task-based syllabus design. *TESOL Quarterly, 26,* 27–56.

Lutz, W. (1995). With these words I can sell you anything. In G. Goshgarian (Ed.), *Exploring language* (7th ed.) (pp. 73–85). New York: HarperCollins.

MacGowan-Gilhooly, A. (1996a). *Achieving clarity in English.* Dubuque, IA: Kendall Hunt.

MacGowan-Gilhooly, A. (1996b). *Achieving fluency in English.* Dubuque, IA: Kendall Hunt.

Martin, J. R. (1989). *Factual writing: Exploring and challenging social reality.* Oxford: Oxford University Press.

Martin, J. R., & Veel, R. (Eds.). (1998). *Reading science: Critical and functional perspectives on discourses of science.* London: Routledge.

McCrum, R., Cran, W., & MacNeil, R. (1993). *The story of English* (rev. ed.). New York: Penguin.

McGowan, U. (1997). Metaphor and congruence in the media: Barriers for international students of economics and commerce. *Prospect: A Journal of Australian TESOL, 12*(1), 20–33.

McGowan, U., Seton, J., & Cargill, M. (1996). A collaborating colleague model for inducting international engineering students into the language and culture of a foreign research environment. *International Electronic Engineering Education: Transactions for Professional Communication, 39,* 117–121.

Mlynarczyk, R. (1991). Is there a difference between personal and academic writing? *TESOL Journal, 1*(1), 17–20.

Mohan, B. (1986). *Language and content.* Reading, MA: Addison Wesley.

Morgan, B. (1998). *The ESL classroom: Teaching, critical practice, and community development.* Toronto, Canada: University of Toronto Press.

Mutnick, D. (1996). *Writing in an alien world: Basic writing and the struggle for equality in higher education.* Portsmouth, NH: Heinemann/Boynton-Cook.

Namioka, L. (1996). The all-American slurp. In T. Smoke, *A writer's workbook* (3rd ed.) (pp. 120–126). New York: Cambridge University Press.

Nelson, G. (1999). Managing information for writing university exams in American history. In M. Pally (Ed.), *Using sustained content in ESL courses* (pp. 132–157). Boston: Houghton Mifflin.

New London Group. (1996). A pedagogy of multiliteracies: Designing social futures. *Harvard Educational Review, 66,* 60–92.

Nunan, D. (1988). *The learner-centred curriculum.* Cambridge: Cambridge University Press.

Nunan, D. (1992). *Research methods in language learning.* Cambridge: Cambridge University Press.

Paltridge, B. (1998). Systems of genre in the TESOL classroom. *TESOL in Context* (Journal of the Australian Council of TESOL Associations), *8*(1), 13–16.

Parenti, M. (1986). Methods of misrepresentation. In M. Parenti (Ed.), *Inventing reality* (pp. 213–227). New York: St. Martin's Press.

Parkinson, L., & O'Sullivan, K. (1990). Negotiating the learner-centered curriculum. In G. Brindley (Ed.), *The second language curriculum in action.* Sydney, Australia: National Centre for English Language Teaching and Research.

Parry, K. (1991). Building a vocabulary through academic reading. *TESOL Quarterly, 25,* 629–653.

Pennycook, A. (1997). Borrowing others' words: Text, ownership, memory, and plagiarism. *TESOL Quarterly, 30,* 201–230.

Pinker, S. (1994). *The language instinct.* New York: Harper Perennial.

Plato. (1960). *Phaedras* (Harold Fowler, Trans.) Boston: Harvard University Press.

Poulton, D. (1990). Concorde (Version 2.1) [Computer software]. Muscat, Oman: Sultan Qaboos University. (Available from MS-DOS Users' Group, CALL-IS, TESOL)

Powers, J. K. (1995). Rethinking writing center conferencing strategies for the ESL writer. In C. Murphy & S. Sherwood (Eds.), *The St. Martin's sourcebook for writing tutors* (pp. 96–103). New York: St. Martin's Press.

Quirk, R., Greenbaum, S., Leech, G., & Svartivik, J. (1985). *A comprehensive grammar of the English language.* London: Longman.

Roberts, M. B. V. (1986). *Biology: A functional approach* (4th ed.). Walton on Thames, England: Nelson.

Rodriguez, R. (1982). *Hunger of memory.* New York: Bantam Books.

Rose, M. (1989). *Lives on the boundary: The struggles and achievement of America's underprepared.* New York: Free Press.

Ross, S., Shortreed, I. M., & Robb, T. N. (1988). First language composition pedagogy in the second language classroom. *RELC Journal, 19,* 29–48.

Ryerson Polytechnic University. (1998). *Ryerson Polytechnic University* [University catalogue]. Toronto, Canada: Author.

Salzman, M. (1986). *Iron and silk.* New York: Random House.

Sasaki, M., & Hirose, K. (1996). Explanatory variables for EFL students' expository writing. *Language Learning, 46,* 137–174.

Savage, W., & Storer, G. (1992). An emergent language program framework: Actively involving learners in needs analysis. *System, 20*(2), 87–199.

Schenke, A. (1996). Not just a "social issue": Teaching feminism in ESL. *TESOL Quarterly, 30,* 155-159.

Shannon, P. (1995). *Text, lies, & videotape: Stories about life, literacy, & learning.* Portsmouth, NH: Heinemann.

Sharwar, Z. (1991, April). Adapting individualisation techniques for large classes. *English Teaching Forum,* 16–21.

Skehan, P. (1998). *A cognitive approach to language learning.* Oxford: Oxford University Press.

Smith, F. (1982). *Understanding reading: A psycholinguistic analysis of reading and learning to read* (3rd ed.). New York: Holt, Rinehart, & Winston.

Smith, F. (1988). *Joining the literacy club.* Princeton, NJ: Princeton University Press.

Smoke, T., & Haas, T. (1995). Ideas in practice: Linking classes to develop students' academic voices. *Journal of Developmental Education, 19,* 28–32.

Snow, M., & Brinton, D. (1988). *The adjunct model of language instruction: Integrating language and content at the university* (OERI Contract No. 400-85-1010). Los Angeles: University of California at Los Angeles, Center for Language Education and Research. (ERIC Document Reproduction Service No. 298 764)

Snow, M., & Kamhi-Stein, L. D. (Eds.). (1996). *Teaching academic literacy skills: Strategies for content faculty.* Los Angeles: California State University, Los Angeles/Fund for the Improvement of Postsecondary Education.

Spack, R. (1988). Initiating ESL students into the academic discourse community: How far should we go? *TESOL Quarterly, 22,* 29–52.

Stake, R. E. (1995). *The art of case study research.* Thousand Oaks, CA: Sage.

Stamford, J. (1996). *Connections: A multicultural reader for writers.* Mountain View, CA: Mayfield.

Swales, J. (1981). Aspects of article introductions [Aston ESP Research Reports No. 1]. Birmingham, England: Aston University, Language Studies Unit.

Swales, J. (1990). *Genre analysis: English in academic and research settings.* Cambridge: Cambridge University Press.

Swales, J., & Feak, C. (1994). *Academic writing for graduate students.* Ann Arbor, MI: University of Michigan Press.

Tan, A. (1990). Mother tongue. In T. Smoke, *Making a difference* (pp. 53–59). Boston: Houghton Mifflin.

Tang, G. M. (1992–1993). Teaching content knowledge and ESOL in the multicultural classroom. *TESOL Journal, 2*(2), 8–12.

Thonus, T. (1993). Tutors as teachers: Assisting ESL/EFL students in the writing center. *The Writing Center Journal, 13,* 13–26.

Tinto, V. (1987). *Leaving college: Rethinking the causes and cures of student attrition.* Chicago: University of Chicago Press.

Tinto, V. (1997). Classrooms as communities: Exploring the educational character of student persistence. *The Journal of Higher Education, 68*(6), 599–623.

Tinto, V., Goodsell Love, A., & Russo, P. (1993). Building community. *Liberal Education, 79*(4), 16–21.

Tinto, V., Goodsell Love, A. & Russo, P. (1994). *Building learning communities for new college students: A summary of research findings of the collaborative learning project.* Syracuse, NY: Syracuse University School of Education.

Tong, S. (1995). Bloody Sunday in Tiananmen Square. In S. Hirshberg (Ed.), *One world, many cultures* (pp. 407–415). Needham Heights, MA: Allyn & Bacon. (Original work published 1990)

Uzawa, K., & Cumming, A. (1989). Writing strategies in Japanese as a foreign language: Lowering or keeping up the standards. *The Canadian Modern Language Review, 46*, 178–194.

Ventola, E., & Mauranen, A. (Eds.). (1996). *Academic writing: Intercultural and textual issues.* Philadelphia: John Benjamins.

Verberg, C. (1997). *Making contact: Readings from home and abroad.* Boston, MA: Bedford.

Weigle, S. C., & Jensen, L. (1997). Assessment issues for content-based instruction. In M. A. Snow & D. Brinton (Eds.), *The content-based classroom: Perspectives on integrating language and content* (pp. 201–212). White Plains, NY: Addison Wesley Longman.

Weissberg, R., & Buker, S. (1990). *Writing up research. Experimental research report writing for students of English.* Englewood Cliffs, NJ: Prentice Hall Regents.

Williams, J., & Evans, J. (2000). *Getting there.* New York: Holt Rinehart.

Yezierska, A. (1975). *Bread givers.* New York: Persea Books.

Yin, R. K. (1994). *Case study research: Design and methods* (2nd ed.). Thousand Oaks, CA: Sage.

Yule, G. (1985). *The study of language.* Cambridge: Cambridge University Press.

Zimmerman, E. (1999). Grading San Diego high schools. *San Diego Magazine, 9*, 60–65.

Index

Also Available From TESOL

Action Research
Julian Edge, Editor

*American Quilt: A Reference Book
on American Culture*
Irina Zhukova and Maria Lebedko

Bilingual Education
Donna Christian and Fred Genesee, Editors

*CALL Environments:
Research, Practice, and Critical Issues*
Joy Egbert and Elizabeth Hanson-Smith, Editors

*Common Threads of Practice:
Teaching English to Children Around the World*
Katharine Davies Samway and Denise McKeon, Editors

*Implementing the ESL Standards for Pre-K–12 Students
Through Teacher Education*
Marguerite Ann Snow, Editor

Integrating the ESL Standards Into Classroom Practice: Grades Pre-K–2
Betty Ansin Smallwood, Editor

Integrating the ESL Standards Into Classroom Practice: Grades 3–5
Katharine Davies Samway, Editor

Integrating the ESL Standards Into Classroom Practice: Grades 6–8
Suzanne Irujo, Editor

Integrating the ESL Standards Into Classroom Practice: Grades 9–12
Barbara Agor, Editor

Internet for English Teaching
Mark Warschauer, Heidi Shetzer, and Christine Meloni

Managing ESL Programs in Rural and Small Urban Schools
Barney Bérubé

Reading and Writing in More Than One Language:
Lessons for Teachers
Elizabeth Franklin, Editor

Teacher Education
Karen E. Johnson, Editor

Teaching in Action: Case Studies From Second Language Classrooms
Jack C. Richards, Editor

Technology-Enhanced Learning Environments
Elizabeth Hanson-Smith, Editor

For more information, contact
Teachers of English to Speakers of Other Languages, Inc.
700 South Washington Street, Suite 200
Alexandria, Virginia 22314 USA
Tel 703-836-0774 • Fax 703-836-6447 • publications@tesol.org •
http://www.tesol.org/